THE ART OF
BEADWORK

HISTORIC INSPIRATION, CONTEMPORARY DESIGN

VALERIE HECTOR

FOREWORD BY LOIS SHERR DUBIN

Watson-Guptill Publications
NEW YORK

For my parents, Natalie F. and Louis G. Hector, Sr.,
who gave me beads to play with and books to read,
and for my brother, Joseph F. Hector (1962–2002),
an artist par excellence

SENIOR ACQUISITIONS EDITOR: *Joy Aquilino*
PROJECT EDITOR: *Andrea Curley*
DESIGNER: *Alexandra Maldonado*
PRODUCTION MANAGER: *Ellen Greene*

First published in 2005 by
WATSON-GUPTILL PUBLICATIONS,
a division of VNU Business Media, Inc.,
770 Broadway, New York, N.Y. 10003

www.wgpub.com

Library of Congress Cataloging-in-Publication Data
Hector, Valerie.
   The art of beadwork : historic inspiration, contemporary design /
Valerie Hector ; foreword by Lois Sherr Dubin.
      p. cm.
   Includes bibliographical references and index.
   ISBN 0-8230-0307-8
   1. Beadwork. 2. Beadwork—History. I. Title.
   TT860.H43 2005
   745.58'2--dc22

                              2004016469

Manufactured in China

First printing, 2005

2 3 4 5 6 7 8 9 / 13 12 11 10 09 08 07 06 05

PHOTO CREDITS: *Every effort has been made to ensure accuracy in this*
book and to acknowledge all copyright holders. We will be pleased to cor-
rect any inadvertent errors or omissions in future editions. Photographers'
names appear in capital letters at the end of individual credits. In the cap-
tions, dimensions are given either in metric units (mm and cm) or English
units (inches and feet), as established by customary usage or requested by
copyright holders.

OVERLEAF: *"Green" Necklace by Valerie Hector, 1998-2000, of glass beads,*
sterling silver, wood, and silk. 11¼" diameter x ¾" deep ■ *Collection of*
the artist ■ DON TUTTLE ■ FACING PAGE: *"Red Star" Brooch by Valerie*
Hector, 2002, of glass and metal beads peyote-stitched over a sterling
silver armature. 3¾" diameter x ½" high ■ *Collection of Kate Wall Ganz*
LARRY SANDERS

NOTE: *In the body of the text, the chronology of ancient Egyptian periods*
and dates follows Gifts of the Nile, edited by Florence Dunn Friedman,
p. 7; Chinese translations follow the pinyin system of Romanization.

ACKNOWLEDGMENTS

Many people have contributed their time and expertise to the development
of this book. I would like to give special thanks to:
   Joy Aquilino, for inviting me to do a book for Watson-Guptill
Publications.
   Project editor Andrea Curley, for superb editing, infinite patience, and
general good cheer. Without her, this would be a lesser book.
   Carrie Iverson, the gifted artist who with endless patience, grace, and effi-
ciency transformed my hand-drawn diagrams into digital works of art.
   The contemporary artists whose work appears in this book, for generously
sharing their talents and technical expertise.
   The anonymous artists of other times and cultures whose work provided
such compelling inspiration.
   Lois Sherr Dubin, for her insightful foreword and her encouragement
over the years.
   Larry Sanders, for spectacular images shot over a two-year period.
   Phumzile Dlamini, Henry John Drewal, Ph.D., Angela Fisher, Jonathan
Mark Kenoyer, Ph.D., Heidi Leigh-Theisen, Ph.D., Brian Lustig, and
Thomas Murray, for compelling field photographs.
   Colleagues who reviewed and commented upon various sections of the
manuscript: Margret Carey, Joyce Diamanti, Benson L. Lanford, Robert K.
Liu, Ph.D., Lindsay Obermeyer, Sidney Oliver, Alice Scherer, Stefany
Tomalin, Marian Vanhaeren, Ph.D., and Hilary Whittaker. Their suggestions
and corrections helped enormously. Any errors, inconsistencies, or misinter-
pretations that remain are my own.
   Colleagues and museum professionals who shared information about
beadwork techniques, traditions, collections, and bibliographic materials over
the years: Abrasha, Ani Afshar, Creina Alcock, Judith Anderson, Ellen
Benson, Bennet Bronson, Ph.D., Kenneth J. DeWoskin, Ph.D, Phumzile
Dlamini, Lois Sherr Dubin, Kevin Friedman, Fu Su Ping, Karen Hendrix,
Jesse Hendry, Hou Wei Liang, Marilyn Houlberg, Hu Jian Zhong, Frank
Jolles, Ph.D., Jonathan Kenoyer, Ph.D., Chap Kusimba, Ph.D., Benson L.
Lanford, Carole Lee, Vivian Mann, Ph.D., Lynn Meisch, Carole Morris,
Ph.D., Poppie Motshwene, Karen Muir, Thomas Murray, Lindsay
Obermeyer, David Pickler, Chief Irving Powless, Jr., He Qing, Alice Scherer,
Judith Schwab, Laura Shea, Alison Sheridan, Ph.D., Deborah Stokes, Peter
ter Keurs, Ph.D., Professor Yu, Marian Vanhaeren, Ph.D., Itie van Hout,
Ph.D., Gary van Wyk, Ph.D., and Michael and Jan Wong.
   Translators of Chinese, German, Russian, and "false" Arabic inscriptions,
letters, and texts: Bernice Ai, Joy Beckman, Licheng Gu, Ph.D., members of
the Department of Middle Eastern Languages and Literature at the
University of Chicago, Brent Newcomb, Kenneth J. DeWoskin, Ph.D., and
Albrecht Ragg, Ph.D.
   The artists who supplied sketches or diagrams of their techniques: JoAnn
Baumann, Robin Bergman, David Chatt, Sharon Donovan, Kathryn Harris,
NanC Meinhardt, Karen Paust, Don Pierce, Madelyn Ricks, Biba Schutz,
Laura Shea, and Mary Winters-Meyer.
   Collectors Ani Afshar, Flora Book, Luigi Cattelan, Karen Hendrix,
Marilyn Houlberg, Frank Jolles, Ph.D., Charon Kransen, Benson L.
Lanford, NanC Meinhardt, and Barbara Siciliano, for allowing their beauti-
ful pieces to be photographed and published.
   The Bead Society of Greater Washington and the Los Angeles Bead
Society, for grants that enabled me to research seventeenth-century English
beadwork.
   Kim Koet and Saing Yin Sith, my assistants for a combined total of
twenty-eight years, whose artful diligence allowed me to focus on writing
this book. I cannot thank them enough.
   Northwestern University, for allowing public access to their libraries,
where most of the research for this book was done.
   My colleagues at Beads-List, for promoting the lively exchange of ideas
and information.
   John Piwowarczyk, for many things.

"Imagination is more important than knowledge. Knowledge is limited. Imagination encircles the world."

ALBERT EINSTEIN

"You must enter the door to inventiveness. Be fearless."

JOYCE SCOTT

CONTENTS

Kenyah sun hat panel, ca. 1930 Borneo, of European glass beads and pineapple fiber 18" diameter ■ Private collection
DON TUTTLE

FOREWORD

Valerie Hector is a gifted scholar and an immensely talented artisan whose work I have long admired and always worn with pride. Her respect for the historical traditions of beadwork has brilliantly informed her contemporary creations, pushing this art form to yet another level of excellence. Now she generously reveals the secrets of the craft in this illuminating cross-cultural overview that synthesizes scholarship and "how-to" projects.

As I have discovered in my own research over the years, beadwork has played an important role in many peoples' daily and ceremonial lives for millennia. It is an art form that transcends the boundaries between art and craft, elitism and egalitarianism, past and present. *The Art of Beadwork* similarly crosses boundaries. We learn beadwork history as we meet master beaders, "kindred spirits in beadwork," who are actually separated in time and geography by hundreds of years and thousands of miles.

To place contemporary beadwork within a cultural continuum, Hector traces its roots from the earliest Paleolithic ivory beads to Egyptian faience and mass-produced wound and drawn glass seed beads in India, China, Europe, and Japan. The introduction of tiny, colorful, European-manufactured glass seed (micro) beads was particularly welcomed throughout the world during the late eighteenth and nineteenth centuries as a replacement for more labor-intensive adornment techniques. Tribal artisans were able to expand the range of decorative forms and colors on clothing and regalia by using glass beads rather than traditional shells, minerals, bones, or porcupine quills.

At the same time, ancient iconography was frequently retained while the artisans developed their own distinctive styles. From this process evolved a spectacular ethnographic art form that continues today, most impressively among Native North Americans, Africans, and Indonesians. And since the 1980s, Japanese "Delica" seed beads, as Hector writes, are "largely responsible for the current renaissance of contemporary [nonnative] beadwork."

For me, the beadwork that works best includes those items that are an intensification of their culture—they are an abstraction in miniature of larger concepts. And all of their components—the colors and patterns, the technical mastery, the purpose they served in their culture, how they tie back into their culture—seem to be unified into a whole. They belong to their time and place and have a patina. I am especially partial to older tribal beadwork, most having been created as items to be used, rarely as "art." Artistic expression was woven into the fabric of daily life. Each individual aspired to a standard of excellence that mirrored attitudes of respect for all life. There was an interconnectedness of the universe with the self, of an artifact with belief systems.

The author shares my passion for historic work created within context. Nonetheless, my conversations with Valerie over the years have also focused on the importance of maintaining content within contemporary beadwork. To bridge the historic/contemporary divide, Valerie invited several artists to each create an item of wearable beadwork that was inspired by an historic piece. Their descriptions of this fascinating process and their interviews add insight and help increase understanding of a remarkably adaptive art form.

The famed scientist Dr. Jonas Salk, who valued equally science and art, once noted that it was important to discover the magic; later, he said, one will discover the logic of the magic. Indeed beadwork, like any art, has to hit one in the gut physically—its beauty, form, materials, craftsmanship. Then, it has to stir the intellect.

That is what Valerie and her compatriots have done. But they have gone one step further. Through elegant photography and graphics blended with instructive diagrams, the reader is also encouraged to participate in the creative process.

Beadwork honors timeless concepts and traditions. Simultaneously, new ideas are incorporated, so that the art stays essential and alive. There are as many examples of cross-cultural fertilization today as in the past. Tribal artisans continue to influence one another. Native and nonnative artists still borrow from one another. In an era of increasing separateness, beadwork provides connections: The objects feel familiar, not arbitrary. Most astonishing are the high technical and design standards—the pride in attention to detail and craftsmanship—that still define today's finest beading. As *The Art of Beadwork* clearly illustrates, it is a craft that remains vital, with traditions reflecting both continuity and change.

LOIS SHERR DUBIN

In "Lips," a sculpture from 1992, Joyce Scott delivers a witty, Picasso-esque fragmentation of the human form that, with its emphasis on a single body part, questions our tendency to stereotype others on the basis of physical appearance.
10" wide x 16¼" high ■ Collection of the artist
JOHN DEAN PHOTO

Most of us experience at least one defining moment in our early years, a moment when something profound happens to us, something we will never forget. For me that moment came when I was eleven or twelve years old and my parents gave me a book by Betty J. Weber and Anne Duncan called *Simply Beads: An Introduction to the Art of Beading from North & Central America, Africa, & the Middle East*. It was a wisp of a book, just twenty-four pages long, with modest photographs and diagrams and a cover price of $1.50; but it meant the world to me. I turned the pages in excitement and disbelief to find an Arabic good luck amulet, a Maasai beaded collar, a Paiute headband, and a Zulu beaded doll. Here was a way of learning about people in cultures around the globe, their ways of living and thinking, their works of art. I was fascinated. I sat down and followed the diagrams until I understood how to do flower stitch, peyote stitch, chevron stitch, "Mexican lace," and "African mandala."

No one can predict what course a life will take, but as it happened I started collecting beadwork in 1981; and in January 1988, I became a full-time beadwork jeweler. This was only a few months after the publication of Lois Sherr Dubin's seminal book, *The History of Beads from 30,000 B.C. to the Present*, which sharpened my desire to learn more about beadwork from around the world and to make pieces of my own. And it was only a few years before the publication in 1992 of *The New Beadwork* by Kathlyn Moss and Alice Scherer, which documented the early years of the contemporary beadwork movement in the United States and, to a lesser extent, in Europe. Suddenly, a lowly stepchild of the textile arts had became a legitimate art form.

I have to confess that I have never been too interested in beads themselves. Always it is the things that get made with beads, and the people who make those things, that hold my attention. For me, "beadwork" implies a whole that is greater than the sum of its parts, whether the beads are connected with thread or wire or with wax, resin, glue, or cement. Even a simple strand of beads in a single color is an elementary kind of beadwork. And the techniques shown in this book, which represent the adaptations and inventions of many contemporary beadworkers, encompass more complex approaches involving netting, weaving, sewing, wirework, and inlay.

All artists need inspiration. Some, such as Joyce Scott, find it in human nature. Others, such as Natasha St. Michael, look to cellular formations, the tiny building blocks from which all creatures are made. Many, including Liza Lou and Tom Wegman, celebrate the everyday elements of American life. As for me, I have often found inspiration in the beadwork of other times and cultures. When I need a break from my work in the studio, I pull open the drawers of my small beadwork study collection. Revisiting these hundred-year-old pieces from India, China, Indonesia, and beyond inspires me. It doesn't matter whether they are humble or spectacular, whole or fragmentary, worth a little or a lot. They connect me to beadworkers whose names I will never know, who lived in cultures vastly different from my own. Each piece is an education with something important to teach, if I can just figure out what that is. Full of inspiration from colors, forms, patterns, and meanings, I return to the studio reenergized. I am not alone. Artists such as Marcus Amerman, Flora Book, Jacqueline Lillie, and Joyce Scott have long turned to historical pieces of beadwork for inspiration and for lessons in color, composition, and technique. History has much to offer, if we take the time to look.

"To inspire" means "to breathe into." In casual conversation, "inspiration" is something tangible or intangible, whether heard, seen, or felt. If it catches our interest, or triggers our desire to do, see, write, make, or be, it is inspiring. When I began writing *The Art of Beadwork*, I asked a number of artists to choose a piece of beadwork from another time or culture and let it inspire them to make a piece of their own. There were only two rules: There had to be some visual correspondence between the old piece and the new one; and the artist had to make something wearable.

Sometimes, I asked an artist to work with a specific piece. Usually, I sent from three to twelve color photocopies of old pieces and asked an artist to choose among them or to suggest a different piece altogether. Most artists made their choices this way, but there were a few exceptions. Marcus Amerman, Flora Book, and Jacqueline Lillie all contributed historically inspired pieces that they had made in years past. JoAnn Baumann worked not from an historical piece, but from a technique. And I chose the five pieces that I wanted to work from either based on my own interests or to assure a wide variety of techniques.

In the end, more artists chose to work with Asian and African pieces than with pieces from Europe or the Americas. Partly this reflects the artist's preferences and partly my own longtime interests in Asian and African beadwork. It does not mean that beadwork from Europe or the Americas is somehow less important or less influential than beadwork from Asia or Africa.

Most of the artists were willing to share their techniques, but Marcus Amerman, Mary Kanda, and Jacqueline Lillie declined. Instead, they shared their inspiration and personal stories. Sharon Donovan and NanC Meinhardt contributed projects that were later condensed into artist profiles due to space considerations, but their beautiful contributions remain. After all, this is a book that is only partly about technique. Of the twenty-four contributing artists, twenty-one are Anglo-Americans, one is African American, one North American Indian, and one European.

They are a diverse but by no means definitive group of artists. Like all of us, they love beadwork because it is portable, affordable, easily learned, and intriguing. Above all, they love beadwork because it is meditative. It restores an inner quiet that is most welcome in this hectic 24/7 digital age.

I hope you will be inspired by *The Art of Beadwork*, much as I was by *Simply Beads*. May the ideas of beadworkers past and present lead you to new discoveries of your own. Every voice is unique—not just the voice of an established artist. Now, it's your turn. If you get stuck, ponder these words from Liza Lou: "I am an artist, and I am going to bead the world." Liza spent five solitary years beading her 10-feet-by-10-feet "Kitchen," and went on to bead her 10-feet-by-20-feet "Backyard" with the help of dozens of volunteers. In 2003 she was awarded a MacArthur "genius" fellowship. "Anything is possible!" my mother always says. And she's right. Especially when it comes to beadwork.

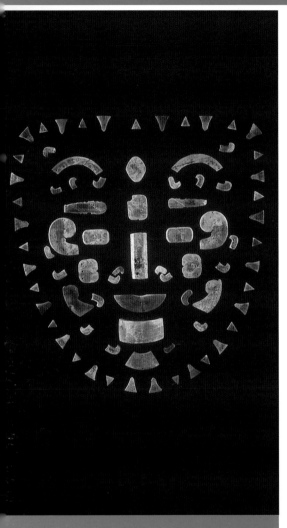

Rarely has the human face been so hauntingly depicted. Together with beads of agate or faience, these seventy-nine jade and hardstone plaques , some pierced, others unpierced, may have been stitched to a cloth face covering for the corpse of a high-ranking person in Shanxi Province, China, in the ninth-eighth centuries B.C.E.
Courtesy, Shanxi Provincial Institute of Archaeology, Taiyuan

While the early history of beads is increasingly well documented, little has been written about the early history of beadwork. Yet, if we are serious about beadwork as a medium, we will want to understand some of the major developments in its history. The paragraphs that follow are not comprehensive. They give only the faintest hint of the riches that were made in the past using beads. Although the history of beadwork is inseparable from the history of bead manufacture and trade, we will not be able to address those issues in any detail here.

DEFINING BEADWORK

What is beadwork? It can be defined in many ways, but for the purpose of this book, a broad definition is most productive. We will think of beadwork as a substance or form of embellishment created by the union, with or without thread, of a group of beads of any shape, size, or material. The essence of beadwork is union, and this union may take many guises, from a modest single-strand necklace to an opulent netted wall panel.

All beadwork techniques are either threadless or threaded. While there are relatively few ways of uniting beads without thread—with glue or tile grout, for instance—there are dozens, perhaps hundreds of approaches involving thread. There are so many, in fact, that it is fair to say that beadwork is primarily a textile art, which evolved long ago as beads were stitched to animal hides or worked into fishnets. With a few exceptions, most threaded beadwork techniques can be classified under the same general headings as textile techniques: sewing, netting, twining, plaiting, weaving, and so on.

EARLY EVIDENCE OF BEADS

The best introduction to early beadwork history is early bead history. Perhaps the only thing that all beads have in common is that they have holes. The first beads may have been naturally perforated objects that were readily strung, such as shells or stones, or manually perforated objects such as seeds or leaves. Eventually humans, or their hominid ancestors, began investing more effort in bead manufacture, intentionally adopting materials that were difficult to shape or pierce.

Archaeologists are still debating the timing of this development and its profound implications. "Long-range," or "high date," scholars argue that *Homo erectus* and *Homo sapiens neandertalensis*, the hominid species that preceded anatomically modern humans, *Homo sapiens sapiens*, were perforating wolves' teeth and other dense materials as early as 300,000-100,000 B.C.E. "Short-range," or "low date," scholars disagree, asserting that the earliest uncontroversial beads, made of ostrich eggshell disks found at Enkapune Ya Moto rock shelter in

EARLY EVIDENCE OF BEADWORK, CA. 26,000-23,000 B.C.E.

Before beadwork could evolve as an art form, threads had to be invented. Thread of animal sinew or other materials must have been invented early on, but no substantive evidence has survived. As Elizabeth Wayland Barber has shown, one of the greatest developments in human history was the invention of twisted vegetable fiber threads. With them, by 18,000 B.C.E. or before, in Europe at least, came string, rope, and the advent of the textile arts.

While beads may endure intact for thousands of years, threads of animal or vegetable fibers tend to disintegrate quickly. For this reason, there are relatively few intact or unreconstructed pieces of beadwork from before about 3000 B.C.E. Some of the earliest fragmentary evidence has been found at a Eurasian Ice Age burial site near the town of Sungir, some 130 miles northeast of Moscow in the modern Russian Republic. There, about 26,000-23,000 B.C.E., for reasons not well understood, two children were buried head to head, their bodies fully extended, in graves lined with red ochre, a powdered iron ore. The skeletons were covered with more than ten thousand mammoth ivory beads, a quantity that suggests the children were of high social or religious status. Assuming that each of these beads took an hour to make, then about 1,250 eight-hour days—more than three years—were invested in their manufacture. Archaeologists believe these and other beads found in the graves were originally stitched with thread of an unknown material to animal hide garments, boots, and caps—long since disintegrated—that the children were wearing when they

---

How old is the art of beadwork? If, as scientists believe, these reconstructed children's skeletons from an Ice Age archaeological site near present-day Moscow were originally covered with animal hide garments to which thousands of mammoth ivory beads were stitched, either singly or more likely in long strands, then a fair estimate would be at least 25,000 years old.

Vladimir-Suzdal Historical Museum, Vladimir, Russia. Photograph: Courtesy, National Geographic Image Collection., No. 721694 ■ KENNETH GARRETT

Kenya or marine shells found at Üçağizli Cave in Turkey, date to ca. 43,000-38,000 B.C.E., the era of *Homo sapiens sapiens*. Evidence of marine shell beads dating to ca. 75,000 B.C.E. has recently been found at Blombos Cave in South Africa, but this date is still in dispute. No beadwork has been found at these sites, only beads.

Why were early humans investing effort in beads, which, unlike stone tools, had no specific practical function? In the first place, then as now, beads were beautiful, tactile, intriguing, portable little objects, as expressive as they were evocative. They enhanced the body, perhaps making the wearer feel attractive. What's more, early humans may have attributed magical or talismanic powers to beads, and worn them in hopes of reaping tangible or intangible rewards, such as success in the hunt, recovery from illness, or spiritual fortitude. Somehow beads came to represent things, among them human hopes, fears, and memories. In short, the dawn of bead use and manufacture signals a monumental development in

human history: the beginning of symbolic expression, and the abstract thinking that goes with it. This is why the dates mentioned above are so hotly contested: These are the capacities, so fundamental to art and to creativity in general, that separate us from all other creatures.

Beads may have served other purposes as well. Scholars now hypothesize that early beads, whether made of organic materials adapted from living or formerly living creatures or of inorganic materials such as stone, may have formed part of a system of shared communication that instantly signaled important aspects of the wearer's social identity, such as group origin or marital status. Such communication could have facilitated social interactions and conferred other advantages at a time when parts of the world were becoming more heavily populated and there was more competition for resources. Whatever their underlying purpose, in time beads were destined to become "the most numerous of human artifacts." And that is no small achievement.

were interred. So it seems that the art, or if you prefer the craft, of beadwork was almost certainly under way by about 23,000 B.C.E., if not earlier.

FAIENCE BEADS AND EGYPTIAN BEADWORK, CA. 4000-323 B.C.E.

For several reasons, the Egyptian archaeological record is unusually rich when it comes to beadwork. This can be attributed to dry climatic conditions that favor artifact preservation, to the ancient Egyptians' love of beadwork, to their expertise in the textile arts, to their desire to outfit the dead for the afterlife, and to the numerous excavations that have been undertaken in Egypt. But most importantly, the Egyptians were able to mass-produce small, colorful beads of faience, a syn-

thetic, self-glazing nonclay ceramic that typically consists of a vitreous alkaline glaze over a core of crushed quartz or sand. Faience beads provided a new kind of raw material for beadwork, one that required less manual labor than beads of organic materials such as bone or inorganic materials such as stone. And faience was attractive and durable. Although they came in different shapes and sizes, the most numerous faience beads, and the ones most important for the development of beadwork as an art form, were the small disks that could produce dense and highly detailed geometric and pictorial compositions such as the ones shown below. Moreover, because its glazed surface was luminescent, faience evoked "the brilliance of eternity," something that greatly appealed to the ancient Egyptian concern for the afterlife.

Thanks in large part to these disk beads, the Egyptians developed one of the world's first significant beadworking traditions. While there is no question that faience beads and beadwork were being produced and traded in other parts of the ancient world—in Mesopotamia, Anatolia, the Indus Valley, and elsewhere—Egypt still provides the best vantage point from which to observe evidence of beadwork over a two-thousand-year period. Here we will mention just a few of those developments, which can be seen as watersheds of a sort in the history of beadwork as reconstructed from published Egyptian examples.

Stringing seems to have been the major technique in the Predynastic Period (5500-2920 B.C.E.), but there were several degrees of complexity. The more complex constructions featured multiple strands of beads

supported by periodic spacer beads. Both visually and technically, the spacer bead constructions of about 4000 B.C.E. seem to anticipate the netting techniques that would eventually appear in the Old Kingdom Period (2649-2134 B.C.E.), including ladder stitch, an open diamond-pattern netting stitch, and what might well be peyote stitch (see pages 70 and 71). Of course, we cannot be sure that the ancient Egyptians invented these bead-netting techniques. It is possible that they learned them by studying pieces imported from outside Egypt or by communicating with beadworkers from other regions. Nevertheless, a transition from simple techniques such as stringing to more complex techniques such as netting had occurred in Egypt by the Fourth Dynasty (2575-2465 B.C.E.), although stringing techniques never fell completely out of favor.

Beadwork continues to show further signs of aesthetic and technical development in the First Intermediate (2134-2040 B.C.E.), Middle Kingdom (2040-1640 B.C.E.), and Second

Intermediate Period (1640-1532 B.C.E.) both in Egypt and in the neighboring kingdoms of Nubia and Kush. By ca. 2000 B.C.E. Egyptian beadworkers were exploring three-dimensionality. Between about 2000 and 1500 B.C.E. in Kush, we have tentative evidence of beads inwoven on the weft threads—early beadweaving.

Pictorial beadwork was highly developed in Egypt by the New Kingdom (1550-1070 B.C.E.). For example, King Tutankhamun (reigned 1333-1323 B.C.E.) was buried with two of the earliest recorded depictions of the full human figure in beadwork (see page 76, bottom right), not to mention one of the first freestanding panels of curvilinear pictorial beadwork (see page 76, top right). While these pieces were probably made by craftspeople in the employ of the royal house, there is evidence that beadwork was also being imported into Egypt at this time. Pictorial beadwork continued to be produced in the ensuing centuries, when beaded mummy shrouds were fitted with haunting beaded faces, such as the one shown to the left, or beadwork panels containing symbolic motifs or hieroglyphs—some of the earliest writing ever rendered in beadwork.

By the time Egyptian beadwork petered out in the Late Period (712-332 B.C.E.), it had left an unparalleled legacy of artistic creativity and technical accomplishment, from which we continue to learn.

BEADWORK IN EARLY PICTORIAL RECORDS AND TEXTS

How else can we learn about beadwork history, apart from archaeological specimens? Well, we can look to the early pictorial record. In ancient Egypt alone, there are countless depictions of beadwork being made, displayed, or worn in paintings, relief scenes, sculptures, and other artifacts; and these can further expand our understanding of the ancient history of this medium. Many other depictions can be found in other early

cultures, and each has something to tell us about how ancient humans were relating to beadwork.

We can also examine references to beadwork in early texts, which sometimes discuss things that have not turned up in the archaeological record. As the examples that follow suggest, texts can provide invaluable evidence not only about what pieces were being made at a certain time, but how these pieces figured into the lives of people who lived with them and wrote about them.

Although there are references to beadwork and beadstringers in Egyptian hieroglyphic texts of the Old Kingdom, they do not reveal as much as we would like to know. Far more enlightening are references that Stephanie Dalley has found in ancient Near Eastern texts. Dalley has recently deciphered the probable meanings of the cognate words *taḥaš* in Hebrew and *duḫšu* in Akkadian, and related words in Sumerian, Hurrian, and Assyrian. In the past, these words had generally been translated as "leather," or "animal skin." As Dalley says, in Akkadian cuneiform texts from Mesopotamia from the early second millennium B.C.E., *duḫšu* embellishes the "sandals of a deity" and the "chariot seats of kings and gods." In the Hebrew Bible, *taḥaš* covers the tent that houses the tabernacle. In some parts of the ancient Near East, the craftsmen who worked in these materials enjoyed high social status.

Ancient Egyptian bead stringers and jewelry makers are depicted at work in this wall painting from the tomb of Sobkhotep in W. Thebes. 18th Dynasty, reign of Tuthmosis IV., 1401-1391 B.C.E. Copyright The Trustees of The British Museum, AES 920

After comparing textual references to *duḫšu* and *taḥaš* with beaded items actually found in the archaeological record in Egypt, Mesopotamia, Anatolia, and the Arabian Gulf, Dalley concludes that these words had a number of meanings, one of which was "multi-colored beadwork," probably made of glass or faience inlays or beads. Now, if the inlays did not have

The Chinese have long valued jade as a symbol of beauty, purity, nobility, and immortality. During the Western Han Dynasty (206 B.C.E.-24 C.E.), rulers were buried in jade shrouds, perhaps intended to prevent decomposition or fend off evil spirits. This famous example is from the tomb of Liu Sheng in Hebei Province. width at shoulders: 18⅛"; height: 74" Hebei Provincial Museum, Shijiazhuang, China. Photograph: Courtesy, National Gallery of Art, Washington, D.C.

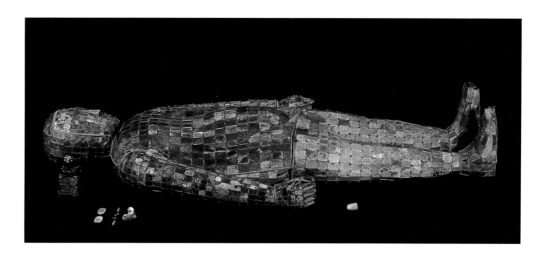

holes in them, what was made with them cannot be called beadwork. But some of these items were probably made of beads. *Duhšu* and *taḫaš* were not just decorative materials. Because they were sturdy, weighty, weather resistant, and yet flexible, they may have been put to practical use to fashion or reinforce shields, armor, and boat awnings. An example of this melding of decoration and function might be the beautiful beaded sandal of King Tutankhamun on page 76, which almost certainly could have withstood the weight of the human body.

First millennium B.C.E. texts from India and China also yield tantalizing references to beadwork. Indian writers of the eighth century B.C.E. tell of beads braided or woven into human hair and the tails of horses. By about 300 B.C.E., the *Vinaya Pitaka*, or book of rules for Indian Buddhist monks, warned against ornamenting shoes with beads and other materials. An early Chinese text, the *Xunzi*, compiled ca. 310-220 B.C.E., mentions "embroidery with added jade bead decoration." In later centuries, Chinese texts speak of a beaded net used as a bribe, a woven gold beaded Buddhist cassock, beaded curtains, and beaded lanterns.

GLASS "SEED" BEADS

The beads most often used in surviving pieces of beadwork around the world are small, from less than 1mm to 3 or 4mm in diameter. Many materials have been used, but glass has been a favored seed bead material for at least two thousand years. In English small glass beads are called "seed" beads, a term that may have derived from "seed pearl," which appeared in the *Oxford English Dictionary* in 1553. Other languages have other words for small glass beads, such as *charlotte* in French, *margarita* in Italian, and *mizhu* in Mandarin Chinese.

Glass seed beads are manufactured in two main ways: by drawing or winding molten glass. Drawn beads are formed as a hollow gather of

molten glass is then stretched or "drawn" out into a long, thin tube. The long tube is later cut into smaller tubes whose rough edges are softened or rounded by tumbling or reheating. Drawn beads are easily mass-produced in both seed and larger bead sizes. The earliest recorded examples of drawn glass beads date to the fourteenth century B.C.E. in Egypt. Wound beads, by contrast, are made one by one as a continuous thread of molten glass is "wound" once, twice, or many times around a coated mandrel of metal or bamboo. Wound beads, which also originated long ago, sometimes have conspicuous air bubbles or ridges that make them look as if they came from little springs or coils.

Great centers of glass seed bead manufacture and export arose in India, China, and Europe. Over the centuries, Indian, Chinese, and European glass seed beads were used locally and traded regionally and to other parts of the globe in successive and sometimes overlapping waves that we can only summarize here. As these irresistible beads, with their rich, gemlike colors, relatively uniform sizes, large holes, and

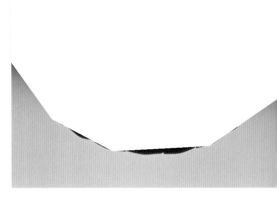

The "Poltalloch Spacer Plate" Necklace, made of Whitby jet and cannel coal beads and spacer plates, is one of fourteen such necklaces found in Bronze Age (ca. 2000 B.C.E.) burials in Scotland. Because jet gives off an electrostatic charge when rubbed, it may have been thought of as a magical or medicinal substance. 8½" diameter ■ Copyright The Trustees of the National Museums of Scotland. X.HPO.4

light-transmitting qualities circulated, they stimulated, even transformed, beadwork production in some areas. Not all beadworkers abandoned their traditional bead materials, which reflected traditional aesthetics, meanings, and procedures, in favor of the new, but some did.

In the first few centuries B.C.E., drawn glass beads less than 5mm in diameter were being made in southern India. In the centuries that followed, as Peter J. Francis, Jr. has shown, these "Indo-Pacific" beads were made in and traded to other parts of Asia and the world. Little evidence has survived, but Indo-Pacific beads, which were made in the millions, must have been strung into necklaces, bracelets, and more complex structures. Read Indian poet Nam Dev, writing in Sanskrit in the thirteenth or fourteenth century:

Everything is Govinda
Everything is Govinda
Just as there is one thread
And on it are woven breadthwise
    and lengthwise
Hundred of thousands of beads
So is everything woven unto the Lord.

A spherical beaded bead formed of Chinese wound glass beads united in spherical pentagon stitch adds texture and color to this silver and glass pei-jing, or pendant, that probably dates to the Qing Dynasty (1644-1911). 1¾" wide x 2¼" high ■ Courtesy, Artist Magazine, Taipei, Taiwan

The Kathi people of Gujarat State, India, still use "hundreds of thousands" of beads to this day to make their *pachhitpati* wall panels (see page 40). By the twelfth century C.E., the Indo-Pacific glass seed bead manufacturing industry had declined, although beads were still made in some areas. It is possible that Indian beadmakers were feeling the effects of competition from the Chinese, whose small wound coil beads were starting to be produced in large quantities at about this time. Although Chinese beadworkers must have used them, perhaps by the thirteenth century C.E. or before, coil beads were exported in huge quantities to other parts of the world. They can still be found in pieces of eighteenth- and nineteenth-century beadwork from Borneo, the Moluccas, and elsewhere.

The third significant wave of glass seed beads to travel the globe originated in Europe, largely in Venice, Italy, and in Bohemia and Moravia (in the modern Czech Republic) but also in other countries such as Holland and France. Glass beads of various sizes and shapes were made in many parts of Europe during the first millennium C.E. One of the earliest examples of European glass seed beadwork is a thirteenth-century German tablet-woven stole, embellished with small square panels of glass beads united in what looks like peyote stitch. But not until 1490, when the Venetians learned to make drawn glass beads, did the potential for mass production and export emerge. Before long, European explorers, merchants, missionaries, and settlers were carrying European drawn glass seed and larger beads to Asia, Africa, the Americas, and elsewhere, where they were used in trade with indigenous peoples.

By the later twentieth century, European glass seed beads had lost their dominance in world markets. Once again, another supplier was preparing to dominate the world seed bead trade. The Japanese had been making glass seed beads for many centuries. But in the early 1980s, Japanese manufacturers perfected a new process in which glass seed beads were extruded in computer-controlled furnaces. The most popular style is cylindrical in shape and about 1.5mm in diameter, with large holes that make it possible to pass through each bead multiple times, a necessity in certain techniques. Also, cylindrical seed beads come in an impressive range of colors and surface finishes. These beads, and their cousins the triangles, squares, and hex-cuts, met with instant success in the United States, Europe, Australia, and elsewhere. In fact, they are largely responsible for the current renaissance of contemporary (nonnative) beadwork.

When will this latest renaissance end? Probably not for a long time. As you will see, Japanese seed beads are now the beads of choice for some of the leading beadwork designers of the world, though some, such as Jacqueline Lillie, still prefer antique European glass beads (see pages 122-123).

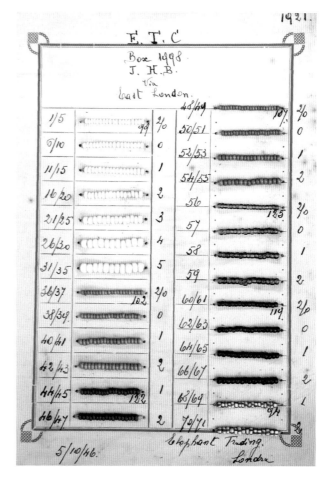

ABOVE, RIGHT A twentieth-century bead sample card shows Venetian drawn glass seed beads destined to be shipped from the South African port of East London (Cape Province) some 660 miles north to "J.H.B.," probably Johannesburg, for eventual use in "elephant trading."
Courtesy, Luigi Cattelan (formerly in the collection of the Società Veneziana Conterie)
VALERIE HECTOR

RIGHT Perfumed swatches of cloth or paper were secreted inside beaded scent bags made in China's late Qing Dynasty (1644-1911) of Chinese wound glass "coil" beads united in peyote or hexagon stitch. In the late Southern Song Dynasty (1127-1279), beaded net scent bags were attached to women's hair ornaments.
3½" wide x 8½" high ■ Private collection
DON TUTTLE

MATERIALS, TOOLS, AND TECHNIQUES

Shown here is an array of antique European and modern Japanese glass seed and bugle beads.
LARRY SANDERS

I n any creative endeavor, but especially in beadwork, experience is the best teacher, instinct the best guide, and an open mind the best ally. There are hundreds of beading materials, tools, and techniques on the market now. For a good assortment, visit a bead show or bead store. Here is a brief introduction with the basic information that beginners need to get started.

BEADS

GLASS BUGLE AND SEED BEADS

There are beadworkers who do amazing things with alternative bead materials such as lug nuts, cereal loops, bits of sponge, pencil erasers, or colorful foil platelets. But most would rather work with glass bugle or seed beads, especially now that there are so many colors on the market. "Bugle" beads are long and thin; they are made in Europe and Japan from plain, faceted, or twisted glass canes and come in many colors and surface finishes. They run from 2-99mm long and are usually 1-2mm wide.

There is no universally accepted definition of "seed" bead, but it generally means a bead of 4mm or less in diameter, although some would set the outer limit at 5mm. Most seed beads are currently made in Japan, the Czech Republic, France, and India. They come in many shapes—from oblate, round, cylindrical, and teardrop; to faceted 1-cut ("charlotte"), 2-cut, and 3-cut; to triangular, square, and hexagonal. They vary in size from $24°$, which is less than 1mm in diameter; to the popular sizes $11°$ and $12°$, which are about 2mm in diameter; to $8°$, which is about 3mm in diameter.

Different manufacturers use different sizing systems so that, for example, a Czech $11°$ might not equal a Japanese $11°$. The numbers determine how many "lines," or strands, of beads can be fit in an inch. For example, twelve "lines" of $12°$ beads will fit in a space that is 1 inch high, and 10 lines of $10°$ beads will fit in the same space.

Modern drawn glass seed and bugle beads get much of their appearance from the type of glass that is used and the surface treatment that is applied to it. Many combinations are possible. Beads may be transparent, translucent, or opaque; colored or uncolored; or lined.

Surface finishes may be permanent or "fugitive," which means "changeable." Finishes vary from iridescent (also known as "aurora borealis" or "AB," "iris," "oil slick," or "rainbow"), to luster (including "pearl" and "Ceylon" finishes), matte, semi-matte, matte iridescent, matte metallic, metallic (including "galvanized"), metallic iridescent, painted, and dyed.

Dyed, painted, color lined, galvanized, and other noniridescent metallic finishes are the ones most likely to be fugitive. To test for permanence, dip a few beads in chlorine bleach, alcohol, or acetone and see what happens. Or file away at the sur-

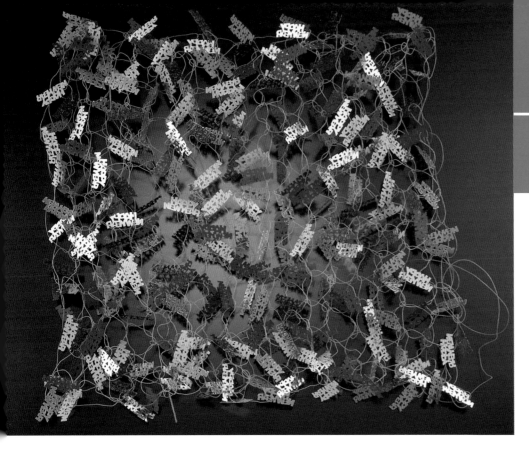

Unconventional materials and techniques can produce fascinating effects. Foil "Happy New Year" platelets connected by nearly invisible loops of iron wire drift like confetti in this innovative panel made by Verena Sieber-Fuchs of Zurich, Switzerland, in 2000 to commemorate the new millennium. 12" wide x 12" high ■ Courtesy, Charon Kransen Arts, New York City ■ LARRY SANDERS

face. Coating fugitive colors may help them last longer. Try a little clear nail polish or a commercial fixative spray.

Color names vary from manufacturer to manufacturer, and bead numbers change over time. In the projects that follow, I have used the most accurate color names possible. When in doubt, trust your color instincts and use the color you like best.

When choosing beads, an important issue is the size of the holes with respect to the size of the beads. If holes are too small, they make work difficult. Large holes are best, especially for netting or weaving, because they can accommodate multiple passes of the needle.

METAL SEED BEADS

Metal seed beads are also available from some suppliers. My favorites are the Japanese 1.4mm-diameter hex-cuts that come in electroplated gold, silver, bright nickel, black nickel, rhodium, or copper finishes. Although electroplated finishes are long lasting, they may rub off over

time. They are called for in the project beginning on page 72.

Seed and bugle beads are also available in sterling silver, karat golds, and other metals. For the widest variety, consult bead supply or jewelry findings catalogs.

STONE BEADS

Very few artists are making complex structures in stone beads, because their holes tend to be small and sometimes irregular. But they are worth the extra effort, as you will see in the project beginning on page 48.

A collage of curious motifs including scissors, a book, a pear, a flower pot, and two flamingos float across the black ground of this fragmentary panel from eighteenth-century Spain. 17" wide x 10½" high ■ The Metropolitan Museum of Art, Gift of Mrs. Henry J. Bernheim, 1959. (59.13.1). Photograph: Copyright, 2001 The Metropolitan Museum of Art

Shown are some of the many threads, needles, and thread-waxing compounds on the market.
LARRY SANDERS

THREADS

Many beading threads are available. The two brands used most often by the artists in this book are Nymo and Silamide threads, which are available in many colors. Nymo is an unwaxed nylon thread made of several parallel strands of monofilament. Silamide is a prewaxed nylon thread made of two twisted strands. While Silamide comes in only one weight, A, Nymo comes in several: from OOO, OO, and O, which are light; to A and B, which are medium; to D, E, F, and G, which are heavy.

Other threads and wires used by the beadworkers in this book include silk, prewaxed nylon fishing line, plastic-coated steel cable, colored wire, and my own favorite, cotton/polyester hand-quilting thread. Each of these materials has its own characteristics, best learned through experimentation.

CHOOSING THE RIGHT THREAD WEIGHT

One of the first lessons a beadworker learns is to adapt the thickness of the thread to the project. If bead holes are large, or if you are working on a sculpture, use thicker threads, double a thin thread, or make extra passes through bead holes to add strength. If bead holes are small, use a thinner thread, but not so thin that it breaks. Thread colors will also affect the outcome of a piece, especially if the beads are transparent. In the projects that follow, thread colors are not always specified. You can choose the thread color that best matches the bead color. When in doubt, use a neutral color such as medium beige or medium gray.

MAINTAINING TENSION

Once you have selected your thread and wax, you must maintain the same even thread tension in every stitch. This will produce a uniform appearance in the finished piece. Maintain a too-tight tension and your piece may kink or ripple. With a too-loose tension, it may not hold its shape at all. Some techniques, such as peyote stitch, will accommodate inconsistencies in thread tension, but others, such as tubular polygon stitch, will not. Of course, in some cases, you may want to manipulate thread tension to produce a desired effect. Once you understand the basic principles, you can do this easily.

KNOTS

There are four knots that I use most often. I like the overhand knot (Figure 1) for tying around the first bead, often called a "stop," or "stopper," bead, because an overhand knot can be undone later. In some cases, the "stop" bead becomes part of the piece; in other cases it is only temporary.

For more permanent knots, I use either the double overhand knot (Figure 2), the square knot (Figure 3), or the surgeon's knot (Figure 4).

When possible, I avoid knots altogether, because they can block bead holes and often show. Once you learn peyote stitch, for example, you do not need to make a knot around the first bead. You can just start beading and secure the first row of beads by weaving the tail thread back into the beads.

TYING OFF AND ADDING ON

You can tie off an old thread or add on a new one using one or more knots. But you can often eliminate the need for knots altogether if you use the following approach; this works for almost every stringing, netting, and weaving technique where it is possible to insert the needle back through beads already added. When tying off, or what I call anchoring, an old thread, work it back through the body of the piece for 2-3 inches, taking a zigzag path, and snip. (See Figure 5.) If the thread is still not secure, knot it.

When adding a new thread, do the same in reverse. (See Figure 6.) It may help to tie a stop bead near the end of the new thread. Starting 2-4 inches away from where you stopped

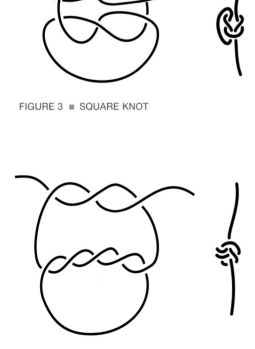

FIGURE 1 ■ OVERHAND KNOT

FIGURE 2 ■ DOUBLE OVERHAND KNOT

FIGURE 3 ■ SQUARE KNOT

FIGURE 4 ■ SURGEON'S KNOT

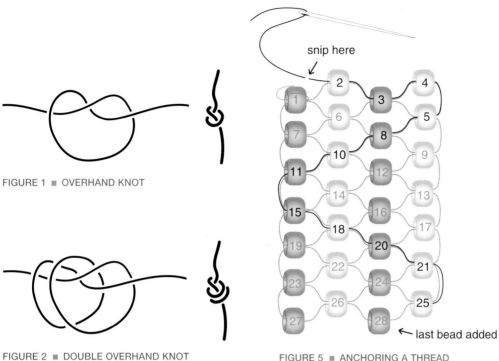

snip here

last bead added

FIGURE 5 ■ ANCHORING A THREAD

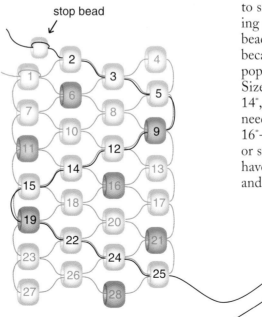

stop bead

FIGURE 6 ■ ADDING ON A THREAD

working, pass through the beads in a zigzag path until you arrive at your destination bead. Pull the thread so that the stop bead sits tightly against the work. Later, you can snip away the stop bead.

WAX

Except for Silamide, most threads come unwaxed. Waxing threads is not necessary, but it helps to smooth and strengthen them, and to prevent kinks and knots. Beeswax is my favorite, but other beadworkers prefer microcrystalline waxes for their softness and stickiness.

NEEDLES

No needles are needed for wirework projects, because the wire acts as its own needle and the tip can be snipped off if it kinks. But most other beading projects call for steel beading needles, which come in various lengths and thicknesses. Short, inflexible "sharps," only 1 inch long, rarely break and make it easy to work in tight spaces. The most common steel beading needles are 2 inches long and flexible. They range in thickness from size 10 to size 16, with the thickness decreasing as the numbers get larger. Many beadworkers prefer size 12 needles, because they work well with the most popular seed bead sizes, 11° and 12°. Size 13 and 14 needles work with 13°, 14°, and 15° beads; and the thinnest needles, size 16, work with bead sizes 16°-18°. Needles made of twisted brass or steel wire are also available. These have large eyes that you can twist open and closed.

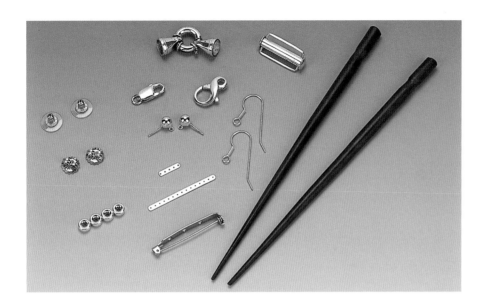

FINDINGS

Findings are the metal elements that make earrings, bracelets, necklaces, pins, and hair ornaments wearable. From my point of view, commercial findings are as much a blessing as a curse. Although they offer an easy solution to a difficult problem, they tempt us to settle for a less-than-ideal solution. If you are not planning to sell beaded jewelry professionally, commercial findings are fine. But if you want to go professional, you should learn the basic metalsmithing techniques needed to make your own findings. There is no liberation quite like it.

TOOLS

Only a small number of tools are needed to do beadwork. For some projects, a needle, small sharp scissors, a bright adjustable light, and a few small dishes or trays to hold beads will be enough. Tweezers will also come in handy, as will a short measuring stick that shows both inches and millimeters. If you are planning to work with stone bead chips, which tend to have small holes, you may want to purchase a diamond-encrusted bead reamer.

Beadworking tools include scissors, various types of pliers, and (from left to right) a thread-burning tool, a diamond-plated bead reamer, tweezers with a bead scoop at one end, a beading awl, and a measuring stick.
LARRY SANDERS

By rotating the reamer inside a bead of glass, stone, pearl, metal, or ceramic, you can enlarge its hole. To work with wire and some metal findings, you will need cutting pliers, round-nose pliers, and a jeweler's file. Flat- or chain-nose pliers will be helpful, both for wirework and for grasping a stuck needle. With its pointy tip, a beading awl will help you make knots or pick them apart. For crochet, knitting, or tambour-work, additional tools are needed. To minimize the appearance of cut thread ends in the surface of a piece, many beadworkers now burn them away with the same kind of battery-operated "zapping" tool that fishermen use to cut fishing line. A cigarette lighter also works for this purpose.

Some of the artists in this book use graph paper to generate patterns, either plain graph paper or the kind that is specifically designed for a particular stitch. Others design on the computer, using software programs formatted for beadworkers. I have always designed the old-fashioned way, with a pen, some paper, a ruler—and a good bit of trial and error.

BEADWORK TECHNIQUES

There are a few stringing projects in this book, but most of the projects teach what are called "off-loom" techniques. We often call these techniques "weaves" because, as we sit there stitching, it feels as if we are "weaving" beads using a needle and thread—thus the term "needle-weaving."

There is nothing wrong with these terms in everyday conversation, but I favor the more specific terms textile scholars use. As you will see, I call "off-loom" stitches "nets," or "netting techniques." Nets may be made with one thread that typically moves right-left-left-right, as in peyote stitch, or with multiple threads that act in unison, usually moving vertically or diagonally. (Biba Schutz used a multiple-thread net to make the earrings on page 48.) True weaves are different from nets in that they involve a single, active thread called a "weft" and a number of passive threads called "warps" (see Figure 1 on page 137). As long as you understand this basic difference beween nets and weaves, you can use any term you wish!

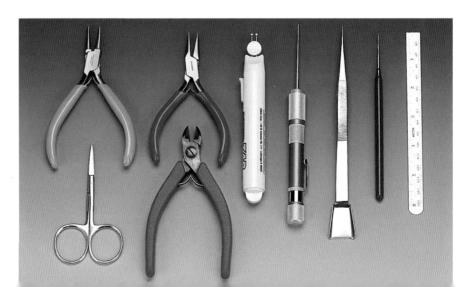

DESIGN OPTIONS

Many artists rely on instinct, intuition, experience, and personal preference to guide them through the choices required to create a new piece. Artists make some choices consciously, others unconsciously. When these choices are consistent, they tend to result in a personal style. As a beadwork artist, you will make better choices if you know what some of your options are.

Twelve sets of design options, derived from the artists who contributed to this book, are listed below, just to get you started. As you explore them in your own work, try to maintain a sense of play. Refuse to take mishaps and mistakes seriously. They will only make you a better beadworker.

ABSTRACTION Abstraction has great design potential. For our purposes, to abstract is to adapt a motif, color scheme, structure, technique, or theme from its original source.

BEAD MATERIALS Step away from seed beads and try bugles, plastic alphabet, or fishing lure beads; semiprecious stone chips, sterling silver tubes, or foil platelets. Make your own beaded beads.

Turn unusual things such as pistachio shells or sponges into beads.

COLOR Color is a powerful communicator of emotional and psychological states. Spend a little time studying color theory if you can. For a start, learn to distinguish monochrome from polychrome and warm from cool color combinations.

CROSS-FERTILIZATION Adapt ideas from architecture, biology, botany, computer graphics programs, consumer goods, geometry, or photography, to name a few possibilities.

DIMENSIONALITY Three-dimensionalize a flat shape or technique, attach one flat shape to another, convert horizontal to vertical, mix flat and three-dimensional in a single piece, tie knots in tubes, or bead on top of a beaded form, as described in "Texture."

LIGHT Some beads reflect light, others absorb it. Learn about light effects by experimenting. Try using just metallics or matte opaques or iridescents. Then create mixtures.

LINE AND SHAPE Make a straight line zigzag, turn an arc into a spiral, invert or intersect shapes.

MOVEMENT Introduce one or more moving elements, such as tassels or abacuslike elements. Be aware of the sound they make. The more senses you engage, the better.

NEGATIVE SPACE Negative space is empty space on the outside or inside of a shape or object, which can seem like part of the object. Negative space takes many forms; sometimes it equals positive space in importance.

SYMMETRY Symmetry involves balance of structure, color, shape, motif, or texture. Asymmetry involves imbalance. A piece may be totally symmetrical or totally asymmetrical, or have some symmetrical and some asymmetrical elements.

TECHNIQUE Take a technique and double-layer it, lengthen it, or build three-dimensional structures, whether asymmetrical or symmetrical, with it. Combine multiple techniques in one piece.

TEXTURE Bead on top of a beaded surface, insert a fringe or some tassels, use faceted or textured beads. Incorporate metal or other materials for contrast.

ASIAN INSPIRATIONS

Imperial craftsmen spent the years 1761-1764 devising this breathtaking twelve-piece suit of armor for the Chinese emperor Qianlong. It depicts sixteen golden dragons, symbolic of imperial authority, emerging from a silvery background of clouds.
upper garment: 28 ¾"; lower garment: 24" ■ Courtesy, Palace Museum, Beijing ■ HU CHUI

The splendors of Asian beadwork are many and varied. Beautiful necklaces, belts, and bracelets were made in what is now Pakistan and western India during the Harappan Phase of the Indus Valley Civilization (about 2600-1900 B.C.E.). The rare double-spiral brooch shown on the facing page, which must have been magnificent in its day, attests to the elegance of beadwork from this era and the sophistication of early bead-mosaic techniques.

Turning to China, we find occasional references to sumptuous pearl- or bead-encrusted garments in texts compiled during the first millennium B.C.E. Although these garments probably disintegrated long ago, other evidence survives. A fragmentary face covering from this era, shown on page 10, suggests how imaginative early Chinese beadwork could be. Many centuries later, to make the suit of armor shown here for Emperor Qianlong (reigned 1736-1798), Chinese craftsmen manufactured an estimated 600,000 steel platelets measuring 1mm deep by 1.5mm wide by 4mm long. These platelets were pierced at one end and hammered round at the other, then colored with gold, silver, or copper leaf or black lacquer, and finally stitched to a padded cotton ground in complex imperial motifs. The resulting fabric is so fine that it is nearly impossible to tell that it is, in effect, a kind of beadwork; it looks more like a delicate metallic brocade.

Other Asian peoples worked in equally large formats using beads of Chinese or European glass. The enormous beaded hanging from the Lampung region of southern Sumatra shown on the facing page features strands of beads couched to a plaited rattan mat in curving parallel rows reminiscent of brushstrokes. The beads depict two monumental ships on either side of a patchwork mountain or tree of life, motifs whose exact meaning is not fully understood.

These impressive pieces notwithstanding, much of the history of beadwork in Asia can be told only by humbler pieces worked in age-old organic materials such as shell, bone, or seed, and techniques such as twining or plaiting. Captain James Cook (1728-1779) brought back to Europe many such pieces from his three voyages to the Pacific in the eighteenth century. The basket from Tonga shown on the facing page is but one example, with beads used sparingly to outline the perimeters of archaic triangle motifs.

ABOVE Gold-capped steatite (a form of soapstone) beads were inlaid in a curving gold frame to create this refined double-spiral brooch from the Indus Valley Civilization.
2⅝" wide ■ Courtesy, Department of Archaeology and Museums, Ministry of Culture, Government of Pakistan ■ JONATHAN MARK KENOYER

RIGHT This basket, of twined coconut fibers studded with marine shell disk beads, was collected on the island of Tonga during Captain Cook's second voyage to the Pacific from 1772-1775.
20⅞" wide x 14½" high ■ Copyright, The National Museum of Ethnography, Stockholm, Sweden. 1799.2.33

BELOW Measuring more than 13 feet wide by 4 feet tall and weighing more than 150 pounds, this spectacular old ceremonial hanging from the Lampung region of southern Sumatra is made of glass beads stitched to a cloth-covered rattan mat.
162" wide x 48½" high ■ Courtesy of The Metropolitan Museum of Art, Gift of Anita E. Spertus and Robert J. Holmgren, in honor of Douglas Newton, 1990. (1990.335.28). Photograph: Copyright, 1995 The Metropolitan Museum of Art

INSPIRATIONAL PIECE
Chinese bamboo bead jacket

ARTIST
Kathryn Harris

TECHNIQUES
Three-Dimensional Triangle Stitch and Three-Dimensional Right Angle Weave

BEADWORK PROJECT
"Ka-Ching" Necklace elements

Full Coin: 2⅛" diameter x ⅝" deep

A seventeenth-century Chinese short story entitled "The Pearl-Sewn Shirt" tells of the disasters that befall a young housewife who parts with her most precious family heirloom, a pearl-sewn shirt, under compromising circumstances. Nowhere is the shirt described in detail, so we can only imagine what it looked like. But it could not have been more elegant than the jacket shown below, which was made of bamboo, a far humbler material, at the end of the nineteenth century. Such a jacket was not decorative, but functional. Worn beneath several layers of embroidered outer garments, it kept the wearer cool by providing ventilation, while it shielded the costly outer garments from perspiration. Here is a brilliant example of form following function: A knotted bead-netting technique is combined with a lightweight bead material to encourage maximum air circulation. The entire garment weighs just a few ounces.

Only wealthy Chinese could afford to own such labor-intensive garments, composed of thousands of bamboo beads knotted two at a time with thread so fine it hardly shows. Only a skilled artisan could have rendered the delicate coin motifs that circle the waist in complex variations of the basic netting technique, as shown in the detail below. These auspicious symbols testify as much to the owner's current prosperity as to his hope for more wealth.

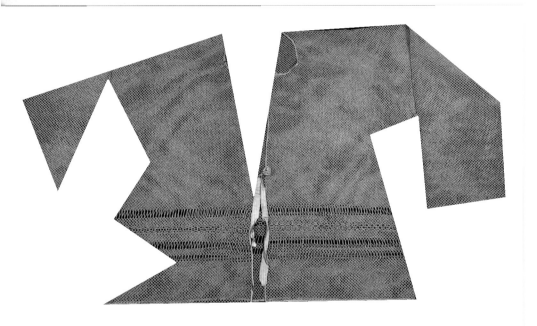

ABOVE The Chinese admire bamboo for its flexibility; it bends in the wind but never breaks. Bamboo stems are easily hollowed out to make durable, lightweight beads. Shown here is a bamboo bead jacket edged in silk from late nineteenth-century China. 44½" wide by 26¼" high ■ *Private collection*
MAGGIE NIMKIN

RIGHT Coin motifs, emblematic of prosperity in Chinese culture, break up the otherwise plain net of this unusually large jacket, which is worked in an estimated 141,000 bamboo beads measuring 1/16 inch wide by ⅛ inch long. Private collection ■ TOM VAN EYNDE

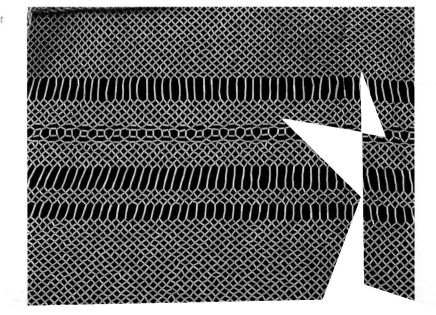

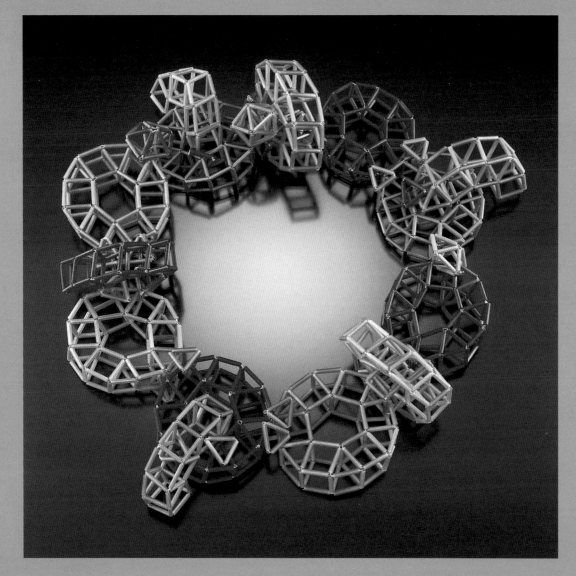

Formed of glass bugle beads that seem to mimic steel girders, Kathryn Harris's "Ka-Ching" Necklace, made in 2002, follows an asymmetrical logic of its own. 2⅛" wide x 2⅛" deep x 23" long
■ Collection of the artist
LARRY SANDERS

KATHRYN HARRIS FOUND MUCH TO WORK with in the bamboo bead jacket. In her "Ka-Ching" Necklace pictured above, she retains the netted feeling of the garment and the tubular shape of its beads, but transforms the coin motifs from two to three dimensions and intersects them with other geometric structures she thinks of as pyramids and cubes. In contrast to the symmetrical layout of the jacket with its careful patterning, she experiments with asymmetry and the absence of pattern. The result is a playful architectural structure. "My desire," she explains, "was to activate the geometric forms, lift them off the body, and create a rich, whirling shoulder full of coins."

The main elements in the necklace are 11 Full and 3 Half Coins, connected by 14 Single Pyramids, 11 Double Pyramids, 2 Double Pentagons, and 1 Double Cube. The Toggle Clasp, which fits through the center of a Full Coin, consists of a pointed oval, attached to the body of the necklace by a chain of 4 more interlocking Single Pyramids. The techniques include three-dimensional interpretations of right angle weave and triangle stitch. Following are instructions for making the main elements of the "Ka-Ching" Necklace.

Rather than duplicate her necklace exactly, Kathryn encourages you to create one of your own. Or you can make individual elements into earrings, pendants, or bracelets.

Kathryn Harris of San Diego, California, worked at the Costume Institute of the Metropolitan Museum of Art in New York under Diana Vreeland before studying jewelry design with Helen Shirk and Arline Fisch in San Diego. She is currently moving away from jewelry and toward vessel forms.

"KA-CHING" NECKLACE ELEMENTS

MATERIALS

12mm glass bugle beads with holes close to 2mm in diameter (*Note* The number of grams you need depends upon the elements you decide to make. Gram weights needed for each element are provided below.)

1 or more spools .012" diameter Acculon brand wire (*Note* Each spool contains 30' of wire. The number of yards you need depends upon the elements you decide to make. Approximate lengths needed for each element are provided below.)

small scissors or wire cutters

To simplify the instructions, I have used these abbreviations.

    a = add
    gt = go through
    gbt = go back through

MAKING THE 6-BEAD SINGLE PYRAMID (*.5 gram of beads; 22" of wire*)

1 Cut 22" of wire. Only one end of the wire will be active. a 3 beads. Slide them down to within 6" of the end of the wire. This forms the tail, which you will hold on to as you work. gt bead 1. (See Figure 1.)

2 a beads 4 and 5, and gbt bead 1 until a double triangle takes shape. (See Figure 2.) Pull gently but firmly after this and every step. Take the tail end of the wire and knot it around the wire between beads 1 and 3.

3 Next, insert the working end of the wire through bead 2. a bead 6, and gt bead 4 until a Pyramid takes shape. (See Figure 3.) Anchor the wire by going through beads 1, 3, 6, and 5. If the wire does not seem secure, knot it.

4 Anchor the tail end of the wire. Snip both wires.

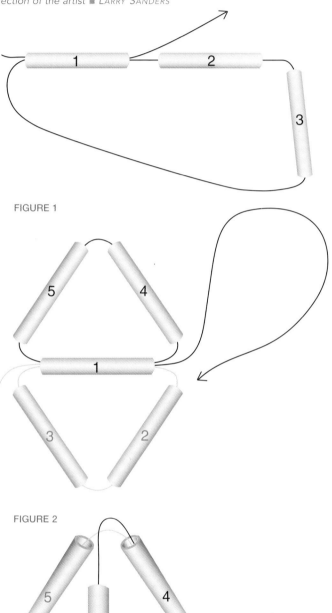

FIGURE 1

FIGURE 2

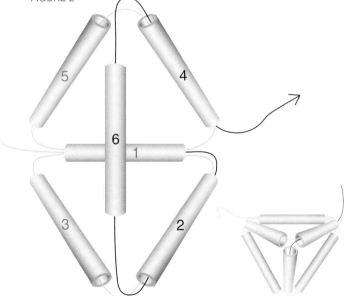

FIGURE 3

THE 6-BEAD SINGLE PYRAMID

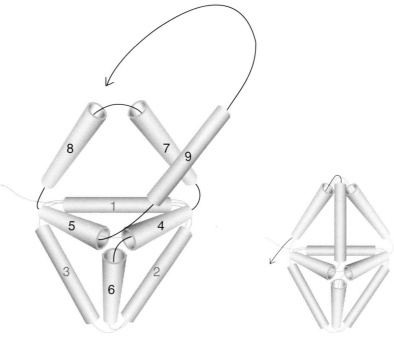

FIGURE 4

THE DOUBLE PYRAMID

MAKING THE 9-BEAD DOUBLE PYRAMID *(.7 gram of beads; 26" of wire)*

1 Cut 26" of wire. Only one end of the wire will be active. Following Figures 1, 2, and 3, build a Single Pyramid. Take the tail end of the wire, and knot it around the wire between beads 1 and 3. (Do not anchor the working end of the wire that is coming out of bead 4.)

2 Following Figure 4, a beads 7 and 8, and gt bead 5. Pull tightly after this and the next steps. a bead 9, and gt beads 8, 5, and 9. Anchor and snip both wires.

MAKING THE 12-BEAD SINGLE CUBE *(1 gram of beads; 24" of wire)*

1 Cut 24" of wire. Both ends of the wire will be active. String bead 1, and slide it down to the center of the wire. a bead 2 to the left wire and beads 3 and 4 to the right wire.

2 Insert the wire bearing bead 2 through bead 4 to form a square. (See Figure 5.) Pull tightly after this and every step.

3 Following Figure 6, begin building a right angle weave ladder by adding bead 5 on the left, and beads 6 and 7 on the right. Insert the wire bearing bead 5 through bead 7 to form the second square. Continue adding beads 8–12 in the same way. Do not add a bead 13.

4 Now form the Cube by inserting the wires bearing beads 11 and 12 in opposite directions through bead 1. Anchor and snip both wires.

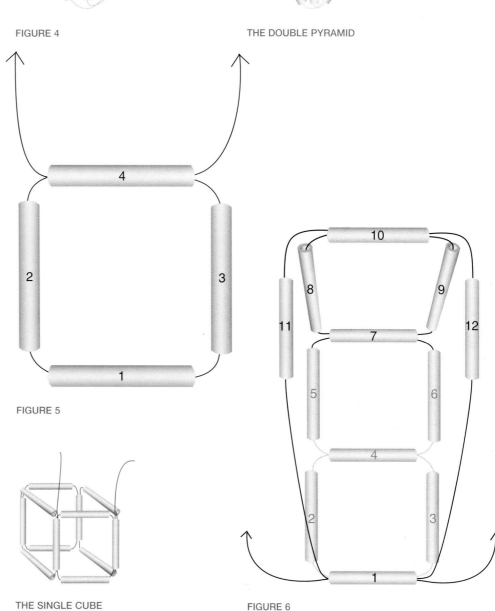

FIGURE 5

THE SINGLE CUBE

FIGURE 6

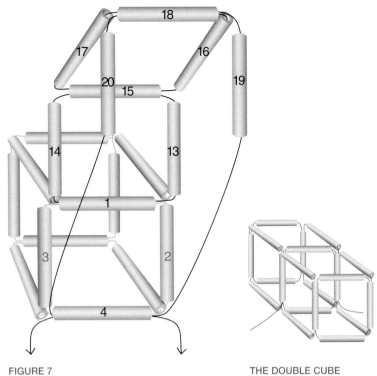

FIGURE 7

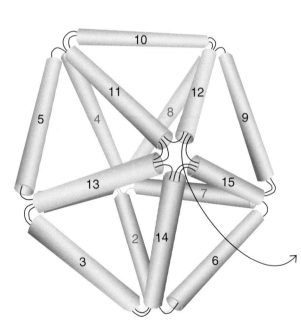

THE DOUBLE CUBE

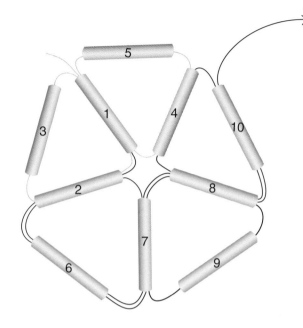

FIGURE 8

FIGURE 9

FIGURE 10 ■ THE DOUBLE PENTAGON

MAKING THE 20-BEAD DOUBLE CUBE *(1.7 grams of beads; 38" of wire)*

1 Cut 38" inches of wire. Both ends of the wire will be active. Following Figures 5 and 6, make a Single Cube. Do not anchor the ends of the wire.

2 Following Figure 7, position the Single Cube so that bead 1 is at the top and facing you. Build another right angle weave ladder on top of the Single Cube by adding beads 13-20.

3 Next, complete the Double Cube by inserting the wires bearing beads 19 and 20 in opposite directions through bead 4. Pull tightly. Anchor and snip both wires.

MAKING THE 15-BEAD DOUBLE PENTAGON *(1.2 grams of beads; 44" of wire)*

1 Cut 44" of wire. Only one end of the wire will be active. a 3 beads and slide them down to within 6" of the end of the wire. This forms the tail, which you will hold on to as you work. Following Figures 1 and 2, build a double triangle so that the working end of the wire is coming out of bead 1. Take the tail end of the wire and knot it around the wire between beads 1 and 3.

2 Following Figure 8, insert the wire coming out of the right side of bead 1 through bead 2. a beads 6 and 7, and gt beads 2, 6, and 7. a beads 8 and 9, and gbt

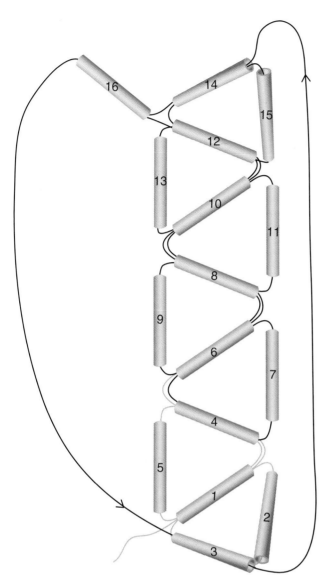

THE TUBULAR TRIANGLE
STITCH LADDER

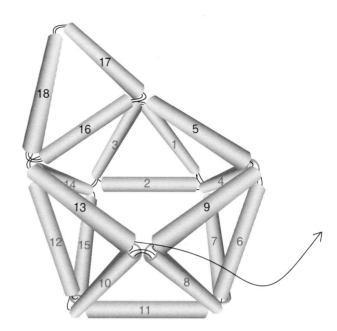

FIGURE 12

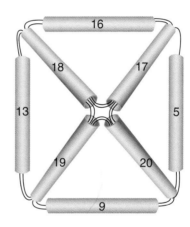

FIGURE 13

THE FIRST POINTED END CAP
IN PLACE

FIGURE 11 ■ THE TRIANGLE STITCH LADDER

beads 7 and 8. Pull tightly after this and every step. a bead 10 and gt beads 4, 8, and 10, pulling until the beads take on a domed shape. Now the first half of the Pentagon is complete.

3 Following Figure 9, begin the other half of the Pentagon with bead 10 on top and facing away from you, with the wire coming out of its left side. a beads 11 and 12, and gbt beads 10 and 11.

4 Following Figure 10, a bead 13, and gt beads 5, 11, 13, and 3. a bead 14, and gt beads 13, 3, and 14. a bead 15, and gt beads 6, 14, 15, 9, 12, 15, 9, and 12. If the wire is not

firmly anchored by now, anchor or knot, and snip.

MAKING THE 24-BEAD POINTED OVAL (*2.1 grams, not including 4-Pyramid chain; 74" of wire*)

First, you will form the center by making a Tubular Triangle Stitch Ladder, then you will add 2 Pointed End Caps. (To turn a Pointed Oval into a Toggle Clasp, see below.)

MAKING THE TUBULAR TRIANGLE STITCH LADDER

1 Cut 74" of wire. Only one end of the wire will be active. Following Figures 1 and 2, build a double triangle so that the working end of the wire is coming out of the right side of

bead 1. Take the tail end of the wire and knot it around the wire between beads 1 and 3. Insert the working end of the wire through bead 4.

2 Following Figure 11, begin building a Triangle Stitch Ladder by adding beads 6 and 7 and going through beads 4 and 6. Pull tightly after this and every step. a beads 8 and 9, and gt beads 6 and 8. a beads 10 and 11, and gt beads 8 and 10. a beads 12 and 13, and gt beads 10 and 12. a beads 14 and 15, and gt bead 12. a bead 16.

3 Close the tube by going through the left side of bead 3 and pulling slowly

until the two ends meet. Then gt beads 14, 16, 3, 14, and 16. Leave the wire intact.

MAKING THE POINTED END CAPS

1 Following Figure 12, form the first End Cap by adding beads 17 and 18, and going through beads 16, 17, 18, and 13.

2 Following Figure 13, a bead 19, and gt beads 18, 13, and 19. a bead 20, and gt beads 9, 19, 20, 5, 17, 20, and 5.

3 Now work the wire down to the bottom edge of the Tubular Stitch Ladder so that it is coming out of bead 2, 7, 11, or 15, and form the other Pointed End Cap in the same manner. Anchor and snip both wires.

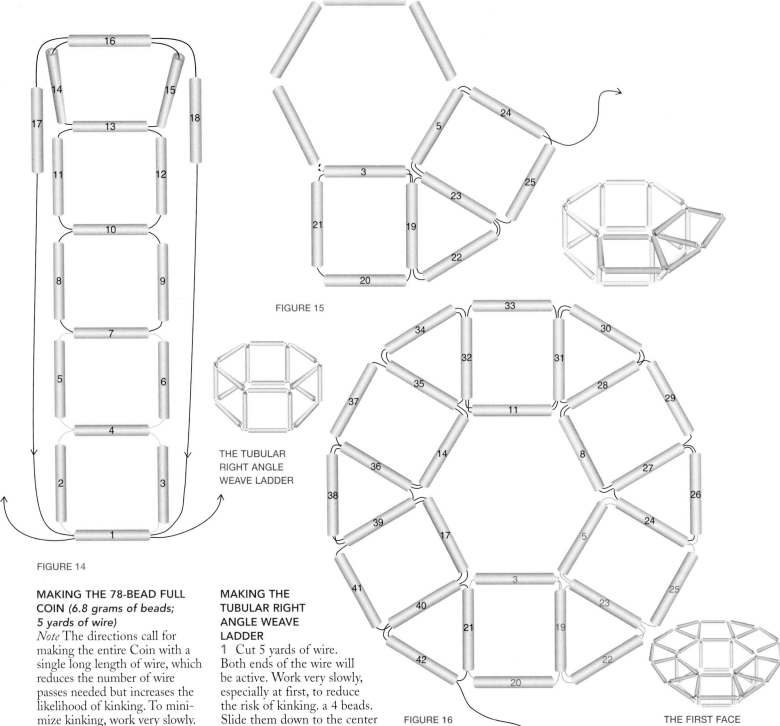

FIGURE 14

FIGURE 15

THE TUBULAR
RIGHT ANGLE
WEAVE LADDER

FIGURE 16

THE FIRST FACE
OF THE FULL COIN

MAKING THE 78-BEAD FULL COIN (6.8 grams of beads; 5 yards of wire)

Note The directions call for making the entire Coin with a single long length of wire, which reduces the number of wire passes needed but increases the likelihood of kinking. To minimize kinking, work very slowly. You can also make the Coin with shorter lengths of wire and connect the pieces later, but this increases the number of wire passes needed. You may then find it impossible to go through certain beads that already have too much wire in them.

You will form the center of the Full Coin first by making a Tubular Right Angle Weave Ladder, then work outward from the tube to create the first and second faces of the Coin. Finally, you will add the vertical rungs that join the two faces.

MAKING THE TUBULAR RIGHT ANGLE WEAVE LADDER

1 Cut 5 yards of wire. Both ends of the wire will be active. Work very slowly, especially at first, to reduce the risk of kinking. a 4 beads. Slide them down to the center of the wire. Following Figure 5, form a square.

2 Following Figure 14, build an 18-Bead Ladder. Insert the wires bearing beads 17 and 18 in opposite directions through bead 1 to form a tube. Pull gently but firmly after this and every step.

3 Knot the left wire around the wire between beads 1 and 2, and then gt bead 2. Knot the right wire around the wire between beads 1 and 3 and then gt bead 3. Leave both wires intact.

MAKING THE FIRST AND SECOND FACES OF THE COIN

The wire coming out of bead 3 will be used to create the first face of the Coin, and the wire coming out of bead 2 will create the second face. Each face consists of 6 squares, separated by 6 triangles.

1 Following Figure 15, work slowly to form the first square of the first face by adding beads 19, 20, and 21 to the wire coming out of bead 3. gbt beads 3

and 19. Pull gently but firmly after this and every step.

2 Form the first triangle by adding beads 22 and 23. gt beads 19, 22, 23, and 5.

3 Form the second square by adding beads 24 and 25, and going through beads 23, 5, and 24. If the end of the wire kinks, snip it off. You will have plenty of wire left.

4 Following Figure 16, continue building the squares and triangles in the first face of the

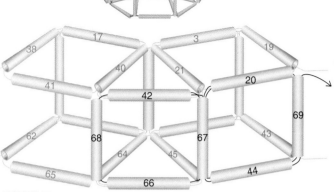

THE FULL COIN

Coin in this way until you have added bead 42, the final bead. gt beads 21 and 40. Make a knot around the wire between beads 40 and 42, and gt bead 42 again. The first face of the Coin is now complete.

5 Turn the Coin over and begin making the second face in the same way, using the wire coming out of bead 2 to add beads 43-66.

6 When the second face is complete, anchor the wire so that it emerges from the final bead, bead 66.

MAKING THE COIN'S 12 OUTER CONNECTING RUNGS

1 Following Figure 17, take the wire coming out of bead 66 and a bead 67. gt bead 42, and a bead 68. gt beads 66, 67, and 20. a bead 69, and gt beads 44, 67, 20, and 69.

2 Continue building rungs in this way, by moving in a counterclockwise direction around the Coin. If the wire gets too short, anchor and snip it, and begin working in the opposite direction using the remaining wire coming out of bead 42.

3 When all the rungs are in place, anchor both ends.

MAKING THE 51-BEAD HALF COIN
(4.5 grams of beads;
3½ yards of wire)

1 Cut 3½ yards of wire. Both ends of the wire will be active. Starting with a square of 4 beads at the center of the wire, make a 13-Bead Right Angle Weave Ladder. Do not turn it into a tube. It will form the curving inside of the Half Coin.

2 Working as you did to build the first face of the Full Coin, begin forming the first face of the Half Coin. Form a square first, then a triangle. Continue working until there are 4 squares separated by 3 triangles.

3 Next, form the second face. Add vertical rungs to join both faces of the Half Coin just as you did to join the faces of the Full Coin. Anchor and snip both wires.

CONNECTING ELEMENTS TO ASSEMBLE THE NECKLACE

As mentioned in the "Tips", there are two ways to connect elements to form a necklace. The first method is simple, and allows you to complete all needed elements first. The second method is complex, and requires you to complete the Full Coins and Half Coins first. Then, you form the

smaller elements by interlocking them with the Coins. These are the connections Kathryn used in the "Ka-Ching" Necklace.

Assembling the Necklace with Simple Connections

1 Complete a number of elements of your choice, until you have enough for a full necklace. You will probably want at least 6-8 Full Coins, 2-4 Half Coins, 6-8 Single Pyramids, 2-4 Double Pyramids, 2-4 Single Cubes, 2-4 Double Cubes, and 1-2 Double Pentagons, in addition to at least 1 Pointed Oval for the Toggle Clasp.

2 Lay out the elements in a circle and use safety pins or wire to attach them temporarily.

3 Next, connect the elements with small rings formed of size 11 or 12 seed beads strung on wire. (See Figure 18.) Lay out the elements in a circle and use safety pins or wire to attach them temporarily. Remember to situate a Full Coin at one end and a Pointed Oval Clasp (see Figure 20) at the other.

Assembling the Necklace with Complex Connections

1 Make 8-12 Full Coins and 2-4 Half Coins, and position them into a rough circle. *Do not complete any Pyramids, Cubes, or Double Pentagons in advance of assembling the necklace. Because all of these elements interlock with the Coins, they must be made partially, then situated between two Coins and then finished.*

2 Many types of connections are possible. For example, you can connect two Full or Half Coins with a Single Pyramid. (See Figure 19.) *Note* As you lay out your necklace, remember to situate a Full Coin at one end of the necklace and a Toggle Clasp at the other end.

FORMING THE TOGGLE CLASP

1 Take one Pointed Oval and attach a chain of 4 Single Pyramids to any one of these beads in the Pointed Oval: 1, 3, 4, 6, 8, 10, 12, or 14. (See Figure 20.)

2 Finish the necklace so that the Toggle Clasp is attached to one end and a Full Coin is attached to the other end.

3 To close the necklace, insert the Toggle Clasp through the opening of the Full Coin.

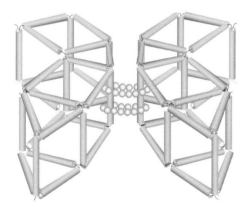

FIGURE 17

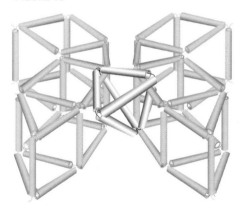

FIGURE 18

FIGURE 19

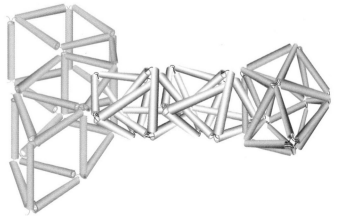

FIGURE 20

ARTIST
Laura Shea

TECHNIQUES
Spherical Pentagon Stitch and Spherical Hexagon Stitch

BEADWORK PROJECT
Beaded polyhedrons: Plato Bead, Archimedes Bead, and Eureka Bead

Plato Bead: ⁵⁄₁₆" diameter; Archimedes Bead: ½" diameter; Eureka Bead: 1" diameter

Sometimes, a single beaded bead makes all the difference. Imagine the *pei-jing* shown on page 14, for example, without the spherical beaded bead that completes it so elegantly. The Chinese have been making these beaded beads and using them in jewelry since at least the Qing Dynasty (1644-1911).

Beadworking techniques tend to get passed on through the generations, so perhaps it is no surprise that young pearlweavers in Beijing's bustling Hong Qiao pearl market still make similar beaded beads today in several configurations known collectively as *mei*, or "plum blossoms," after the flowers they are thought to resemble. Some of these plum blossoms are sold locally, while others are exported to the farthest corners of the globe, like silent messengers from a glorious but largely undocumented beadworking tradition that originated centuries ago.

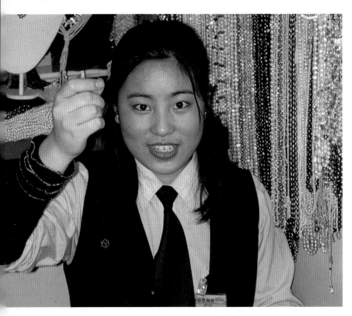

Jing Lingfei spends her days stringing and selling pearls at Beijing's Hong Qiao Pearl Market, home to dozens of small shops specializing in pearls and semiprecious stone beads that attract an international clientele. Shown here in 2000, she holds a newly finished mei, or "plum blossom."

VALERIE HECTOR

These "plum blossoms" were made in Beijing in 2000 of glass, coral, pearl, hematite, and malachite beads united with a single thread in cubic and spherical right angle weave and spherical pentagon stitch.
plum blossom at lower right: ¾" diameter ■ Private collection ■ LARRY SANDERS

A SINGLE BEADED BEAD can alter the course of a life, too. Laura Shea knew nothing about Chinese beaded plum blossoms when, in 1997, she began to combine her love of beadwork with her interest in the three-dimensional geometric structures known as polyhedrons. By 1998 she had formed her first hollow beaded polyhedron, which replicated the pattern of a dodecahedron, with thirty beads forming twelve faces and thirty sides. Since the dodecahedron once served as the ancient Platonic symbol for the universe, Laura named her discovery the "Plato Bead." It was only after this that Laura saw a Chinese plum blossom for the first time at a gem show. She was surprised and delighted to realize that her fascination with bead polyhedrons was shared by beadworkers she had never met, who lived half a world away. When shown the *pei-jing* on page 14, she immediately identified its plum blossom as a dodecahedron.

Not surprisingly, Laura also feels a sense of kinship with Kathryn Harris. Shown the polyhedrons in Kathryn's "Ka-Ching" Necklace (see page 25), Laura quickly identified the Single Pyramid as a tetrahedron and the Double Pyramid as an octahedron. However, while Kathryn beads intuitively, discovering structures through experimentation, Laura beads analytically, by translating the principles of geometry into beadwork.

Laura eventually taught herself to make other bead polyhedrons, including the truncated icosahedron, which has thirty-two faces and ninety sides. Modern Chinese pearlweavers apparently do not use this structure, but it was

Laura Shea's "Rainbow Lei" Necklace, made in 2002, features twenty-five of her signature "Eureka Beads" and an ingenious toggle clasp made of "Plato" Beads.
1" wide x 29" long ■ Collection of the artist ■ LARRY SANDERS

known to the ancient Greek philosopher Archimedes. Thus, Laura calls this her "Archimedes Bead." Now a leading authority, she continues to innovate. By combining 1 Archimedes Bead with 12 Plato Beads, she creates the larger Eureka Beads that form the body of her "Rainbow Lei" Necklace shown here. To create this necklace, she used 25 Eureka Beads, 6 Archimedes Beads, and 12 Plato Beads. The Toggle Clasp elements in the necklace are made of interconnected Plato Beads: 4 for the T-bar and 10 for the ring.

Laura is undoubtedly the first person ever to bead these ingenious structures or to invent a toggle clasp made of dodecahedrons. Following, she shares her secrets for making the Plato, Archimedes, and Eureka Beads. It's a good idea to learn the Plato first, then the Archimedes, and the more demanding Eureka last.

Laura Shea of Denver, Colorado, is an artist, teacher, and bead supplier. She is fascinated by geometry and geometric structures, and has developed innovative ways of rendering these structures in beads. She is currently at work on a book. For more information, see www.adancingrainbow.com.

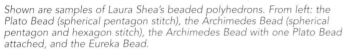

Shown are samples of Laura Shea's beaded polyhedrons. From left: the Plato Bead (spherical pentagon stitch), the Archimedes Bead (spherical pentagon and hexagon stitch), the Archimedes Bead with one Plato Bead attached, and the Eureka Bead.
Collection of the artist ■ LARRY SANDERS

PLATO BEAD

The Plato Bead consists of 30 beads forming 12 interconnected pentagons. In the diagrams, these pentagons resemble circles of 5 beads each. The color pattern Laura provides creates one 5-pointed star at either end of the Bead and a line of the same color around the equator. In 11° Japanese round seed beads, the Bead will measure about ³/₈" in diameter.

MATERIALS

11° Japanese round seed beads, presorted for uniformity

   20 Color A

   10 Color B

2 yards Nymo D thread

1 size 12 beading needle

wax

Note To simplify the instructions, I have used these abbreviations.

   a = add

   gt = go through

ROW 1

1 Cut 2 yards of Nymo D thread and wax it. Thread the needle, and slide it down to the center of the thread to create a 1-yard doubled length. a beads 1, 2, 3, 4, and 5 in Color A. Slide them down to within 6" of the end of the thread. Do not form a knot. The beads will lock themselves in place as you continue to work.

2 Holding on to this 6" tail as you work, gt bead 1 to form a circle. (If you form a teardrop, try again.) (See Figure 1.) Pull tightly after this and all following steps, being sure not to leave extra thread kinked inside any bead.

ROW 2

1 a beads 6, 7, 8, and 9 in Colors BAAB. gt beads 1 and 2. (See Figure 1.)

2 Following Figure 2, a beads 10, 11, and 12 in Colors BAA. gt beads 6, 2, and 3. a beads 13, 14, and 15 in Colors BAA. gt beads 10, 3, and 4. a beads 16, 17, and 18 in Colors BAA. gt beads 13, 4, 5, and 9. a beads

19 and 20 in Colors AA. gt beads 16, 5, and 9 and 8. Now you have reached the end of the second row of beads and your partially completed Plato Bead should have a 5-pointed shape.

ROW 3

1 Following Figure 3, a beads 21, 22, and 23 in Colors BAB. gt beads 19, 8, 7, and 12. a beads 24 and 25 in Colors BA. gt beads 21, 7, 12, 11, and 15. a beads 26 and 27 in Colors BA. gt beads 24, 11, 15, 14, and 18. a beads 28 and 29 in Colors BA. gt beads 26, 14, 18, 17, 20, and 23. a bead 30 in Color A. gt beads 28, 17, 20, and 23.

ROW 4

All of the beads for the Plato Bead are now in place. But 5 of the beads still need to be connected. Row 4 is created by connecting these beads, which are all in Color A.

1 Following the dotted lines of Figure 3, gt beads 22, 25, 27, 29, 30, and then gt bead 22 again to complete the circle. Anchor and snip.

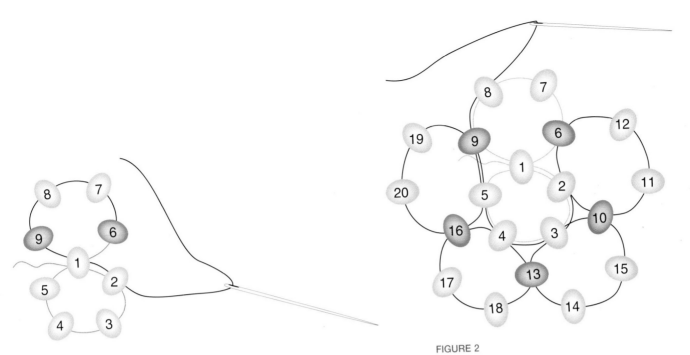

FIGURE 1

FIGURE 2

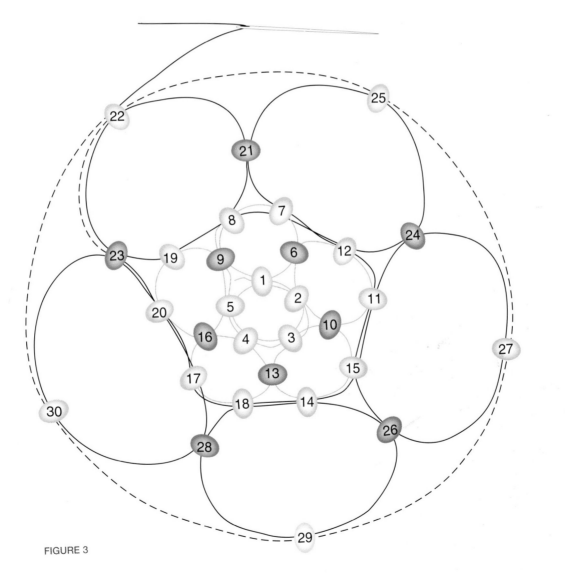

FIGURE 3

ARCHIMEDES BEAD

The Archimedes Bead is made of 90 beads forming 12 pentagons and 20 hexagons. In the diagrams, these polygons resemble circles of 5 or 6 beads respectively. The color pattern Laura provides reproduces that of a traditional soccer ball. In 11° Japanese round seed beads, the Archimedes Bead will measure about ¹/₂" in diameter.

MATERIALS

11° Japanese round seed beads, presorted for uniformity

> 60 Color A
> 30 Color B

3-4 yards Nymo D thread

1 size 12 beading needle

wax

ROW 1

1 Cut 3-4 yards of Nymo D thread and wax it. Thread the needle, and slide it down to the center of the thread. Then double the thread to create a 1¹/₂-2 yard length. a beads 1, 2, 3, 4, and 5 in Color A. Slide them down to within 6" of the end of the thread. Do not form a knot. The beads will lock themselves in place as you continue to work.

2 Holding on to this 6" tail as you work, form a circle by inserting the needle through bead 1. (If you form a teardrop, try again.) (See Figure 4.) Pull tightly after this and all following steps, being sure not to leave extra thread kinked inside any bead.

ROW 2

1 a beads 6, 7, 8, 9, and 10 in Colors BABABB. gt beads 1 and 2. (See Figure 4.)

2 Following Figure 5, a beads 11, 12, 13, and 14 in Colors BABA. gt beads 6, 2, and 3. a beads 15, 16, 17, and 18 in Colors BABA. gt beads 11, 3, and 4. a beads 19, 20, 21, and 22 in Colors BABA. gt beads 15, 4, 5, and 10. a beads 23, 24, and 25 in Colors ABA. gt beads 19, 5, 10, and 9.

ROW 3

1 Following Figure 6, a beads 26, 27, and 28 in Color A. gt beads 23, 9, and 8. a beads 29,

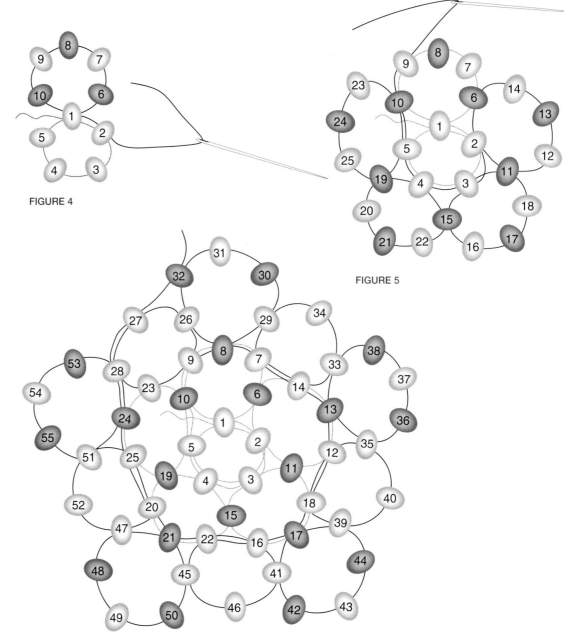

FIGURE 4

FIGURE 5

FIGURE 6

30, 31, and 32 in Colors ABAB. gt beads 26, 8, 7, and 14. a beads 33 and 34 in Color A. gt beads 29, 7, 14, and 13. a beads 35, 36, 37, and 38 in Colors ABAB. gt beads 33, 13, 12, and 18. a beads 39 and 40 in Color A. gt beads 35, 12, 18, and 17. a beads 41, 42, 43, and 44 in Colors ABAB. gt beads 39, 17, 16, and 22. a beads 45 and 46 in Color A. gt beads 41, 16, 22, and 21. a beads 47, 48, 49, and 50 in Colors ABAB. gt beads 45, 21, 20, and 25. a beads 51 and 52 in Color A. gt beads 47, 20, 25, 24, and 28. a beads 53,

54, and 55 in Colors BAB. gt beads 51, 24, 28, 27, and 32.

ROW 4

1 Following Figure 7, a beads 56, 57, and 58 in Colors ABA. gt beads 53, 27, 32, and 31. a beads 59, 60, and 61 in Color A. gt beads 56, 31, 30, 34, and 38. a beads 62 and 63 in Colors AB. gt beads 59, 30, 34, 38, and 37. a beads 64, 65, and 66 in Color A. gt beads 62, 37, 36, 40, and 44. a beads 67 and 68 in Colors AB. gt beads 64, 36, 40, 44, and 43. a beads 69, 70, and 71 in Color A. gt beads 67, 43, 42, 46, and 50. a beads 72 and 73 in

Colors AB. gt beads 69, 42, 46, 50, and 49. a beads 74, 75, and 76 in Color A. gt beads 72, 49, 48, 52, and 55. a beads 77 and 78 in Colors AB. gt beads 74, 48, 52, 55, 54, and 58. a beads 79 and 80 in Color A. gt beads 77, 54, 58, 57, and 61. Now the Archimedes Bead looks like a bell with 5 circles (or pentagons) sticking up on the edge.

ROW 5

1 Following Figure 7, a beads 81, 82, and 83 in Colors BAB. gt beads 79, 57, 61, 60, 63, and 66. a beads 84 and 85 in Colors BA. gt beads 81, 60,

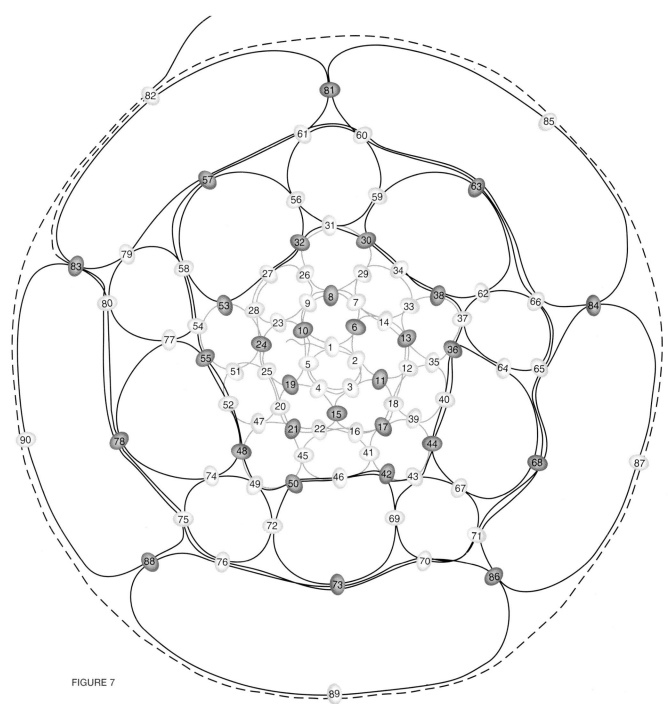

FIGURE 7

63, 66, 65, 68, and 71. a beads 86 and 87 in Colors BA. gt beads 84, 65, 68, 71, 70, 73, and 76. a beads 88 and 89 in Colors BA. gt beads 86, 70, 73, 76, 75, 78, 80, and 83. a bead 90 in Color A. gt beads 88, 75, 78, 80, and 83.

ROW 6

1 All 90 beads have now been added, but 5 remain to be connected. Row 6 is created by connecting these beads, which are all in Color A. Following the dotted lines in Figure 7, gt beads 82, 85, 87, 89, and 90, and then gt bead 82 again to complete the circle. Anchor and snip.

EUREKA BEAD

This Bead consists of 1 Archimedes Bead supporting 12 Plato Beads. In 11° round Japanese seed beads, this Bead will measure about 1" in diameter.

1 Begin by making 1 Archimedes Bead using 2-3 yards of waxed Nymo D. Worked with a single thread, this Archimedes Bead will start out being very limp and will not stiffen up until the addition of the tenth or eleventh Plato Bead. (Resist the temptation to use a double thread, which would fill the bead holes too quickly, before the entire Archimedes Bead has been covered with Plato Beads.)

2 As you complete the Archimedes Bead, do not anchor the thread coming out of bead 82. Instead, start a Plato Bead using beads 82, 85, 87, 89, and 90 to form beads 1-5 of the first row of the Plato Bead. Simply pretend that you are beginning at Row 2 of the Plato Bead.

3 Complete this Plato Bead, and then go down through various beads so as to return to the Archimedes Bead. Be careful to move only through adjacent, not opposite, beads.

4 Continue through the beads of the Archimedes Bead until your thread is coming out of another one of the circles of 5 beads of Color A.

5 Begin once again at Row 2, Step 1 of the Plato Bead to create the second Plato Bead.

6 Continue making Plato Beads until you have completed all 12. Anchor the thread, and snip.

INSPIRATIONAL PIECE	ARTIST	TECHNIQUE
Eleventh-century Japanese lantern	*Sharon Donovan*	*Framed Parallel Stringing*

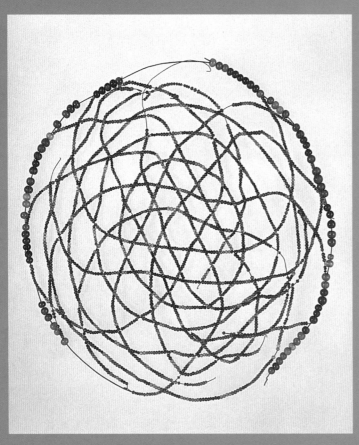

Nearly nine thousand ancient artifacts from Japan, China, India, and else-where are preserved in the Shōsō-in Repository, which was built around 756 C.E. in Nara, the capital of Japan from 710 to 784 C.E.. This 1,200-year-old Japanese basket made of glass beads and silver wire is an impressive example.

9" diameter ■ Shōsō-in Repository, Nara, Japan ■ BENRIDO CO., LTD.

Kasuga-taisha, a Shinto shrine founded in 710 C.E. in Nara, is famous for its lanterns of stone and bronze. Once a year, during the Mantoro, or Lantern, Festival, worshippers light these lanterns to guide the spirits of deceased ancestors back to Earth for a brief visit. This beaded lantern dates to around 1038 C.E.

13⅜" wide x 16½" high ■ Courtesy, Kasuga-taisha Treasure House, Nara, Japan. Photograph: Kasuga-taisha Treasure House, Nara, Japan

Judging by the few pieces that survive, the ancient Japanese must have been brilliant beadworkers. Fortunately for us, they did at least some of their beading on wire, which resists the disintegration so common to animal or vegetable fiber threads.

One of the most intriguing pieces is the circular basket shown above. It was made in the mid-eighth century of multi-color glass beads connected with silver wire. Part of a pair, this basket may have been used to hold blossoms during flower-scattering ceremonies at Todai-Ji, a major Buddhist temple complex in Nara, Japan. At first glance, we see only the net-work of beaded wires that gives the basket its circular structure. At second glance, the network almost looks like a flower with many petals. Was this flowerlike pattern an accidental by-prod-uct of the beading technique or a purposeful aligning of the basket's form with its intended function?

Early Japanese beadworkers also knew how to use simple beading techniques to great effect when more complex tech-niques would have seemed out of place. Shown above is a rare beaded lantern, given in 1038 C.E. to Kasuga-taisha, the shrine of the powerful Fujiwara family. It features beaded panels made of strings of translucent blue Japanese glass beads, interlaced at intervals to keep them in place. It is hard to imagine a simpler technique, but it is perfect in this context. Neither the long verti-cal strings that form the lantern's large panels nor the short horizontal strings in the small panels above compete for atten-tion with the lantern's hexagonal wooden framework, its inverted lotus-shaped roof, or its graceful bronze brackets. In fact, the tiny spaces between the bead strings almost invite us to peer inside, where a small candle would have been placed, illuminat-ing the shrine with a soft blue glow. Of the many lanterns at Kasuga-taisha, this is the only beaded one.

Sharon Donovan's "Treasure House" Bracelet, which she fashioned in 2002 of sterling silver, 14-karat gold, and glass beads, translates the panes of the ancient Japanese lantern into a modern, wearable format. 1⅞" high x 7 ⅝" long ■ Collection of the artist ■ LARRY SANDERS

Pearls, emeralds, and glass beads are attached to delicate 14-karat gold frames in Sharon Donovan's "Baroda" Necklace, made in 2002. It was inspired by the famous beaded "Baroda Carpet" made in India in 1865. ⅜" deep x 1⅞" high x 20" long ■ Collection of the artist ■ LARRY SANDERS

As a jeweler known for situating seed beads and pearls inside metal frames of her own design, Sharon Donovan feels a strong sense of solidarity with the beaded lantern's designer of a thousand years ago.

Her "Treasure House" Bracelet, shown above, leaves out all but the most essential features of the lantern: the blue beaded panels and the frames that support them. Quoting directly from the lantern, Sharon alternates the directions of the strings according to the size of the niche that supports them, running some strings vertically and others horizontally. Of the many shades of beads that she could have chosen, she opts for translucent matte cobalt blue beads with an aurora borealis finish that hints of green, yellow, and pink—color variations that suggest the flickering of candlelight. Light touches of 14-karat gold in the bracelet's hinge pins and clasp quietly echo the lantern's bronze plates and suspension ring.

Sharon Donovan of Ann Arbor, Michigan, is a

social-worker-turned-jeweler who began her second career after taking a workshop with celebrated artist Arline Fisch. Equal parts beadworker and metalsmith, Sharon is constantly working on new ways to blend the two media. She exhibits her innovative designs at juried art fairs around the country.

INSPIRATIONAL PIECE
*Sakhia, or vertical door panel,
from ca. 1900 Gujarat State, India*

ARTIST
Rachel Weiss

TECHNIQUES
*Ladder Stitch, Brick Stitch,
Tubular Peyote Stitch, and
Single-Thread Vertical Netting*

BEADWORK PROJECT
"Mahalakshmi" Pin

4⅛" wide x 4¼" high

Few Asian peoples have loved beadwork more than the Kathi peoples of western India's Gujarat State in the late nineteenth and early twentieth centuries. During festival season from November to March, these wealthy members of Gujarat's Hindu landowning class decorated the living rooms of their rural mud-brick homes with wall panels, door surrounds, window decorations, pillows, and hanging ornaments made entirely of the Venetian glass seed beads that were flowing into nearby ports such as Bombay, Veraval, and Bhuj. A dozen or more smaller pieces, including fans, gaming boards, and ink pots, might complete the display, effectively creating a fully beaded interior. The Kathi may have commissioned professional craftsmen to make some of these pieces, but the majority were made by the women of the family.

LEFT Hindu gods and goddesses are often depicted in Kathi beadwork, both to thank them for the earthly blessings they have bestowed and to invoke further blessings in the future. The blue face of the central figure in this vignette from the pachhitpati shown below suggests that it is Krishna, the cowherd god, who is often shown with Radha, his favorite milkmaid.
Private collection ■ DON TUTTLE

BELOW This pachhitpati from the late nineteenth-century unrolls to nearly 19 feet long. It contains an estimated 265,000 Venetian glass beads, worked in a three-bead, single-layer scallop stitch at a rate of 186 beads per square inch.
6⅜" wide x 18' ¾" long
Private collection ■ DON TUTTLE

Some of the Kathis' largest pieces took the form of long narrow scrolls called *pachhitpati*, which were hung horizontally across the living room walls just under the ceiling. Dozens of colorful motifs, worked against a stark white ground, stretch from one end to the other. Scenes that celebrate everyday life, such as children swinging in cradles or domestic animals at play, are placed at random alongside vignettes showing Hindu deities or characters from local legends.

Other large panels called *sakhia* were hung vertically in pairs on either side of a door as signs of welcome. Like *pachhitpati*, *sakhia* depict a benevolent universe, teeming with life and positive energy.

This detail of a sakhia, or vertical door panel, from the late nineteenth century shows Maha Lakshmi, goddess of wealth and destiny, sitting on her pedestal above two figures churning curd into butter—a common domestic scene.
14½" wide x 74" high ■ Private collection ■ Tom van Eynde

IN HER "MAHALAKSHMI" NECKLACE, pictured to the right, Rachel Weiss abstracts motifs from the *pachhitpati* and the *sakhia* and reconfigures them to fit into triangular or diamond-shaped panels. By varying the size of these panels as well as their shape, she creates a compelling, rhythmic structure that carries the eye across the outer corners of the necklace. In contrast to the white background of the Kathi pieces, Rachel chose sparkling grays and shining golds, colors we associate with precious metals. For the remainder of her color palette, she drew on her "visual images of India, heavy on saffron and spices and punctuated with bright hibiscus, teals, and deep pinks." Instead of working with the three-bead, single-layer scallop stitch that her Kathi counterparts preferred (for an 8-bead version of this technique, see page 96), Rachel works in single-bead brick stitch. The essence of the original motifs is preserved, but now they compete for attention with a dense, radiant, highly structured background. The result is a necklace fit for a goddess.

Her elegant "Mahalakshmi" Pin, pictured on page 42, follows a similar approach in a smaller format. You will learn how to make the pin, which depicts the goddess in its central panel. Although it may look difficult, the pin is actually fairly easy to make and allows you to practice combining several techniques in a single piece.

Rachel Weiss of Charleston, South Carolina, is a beadworker and jewelry artist who credits her design ideas to her background in art and anthropology. Her pieces often reflect her own tendency to look at a single issue or event from as many vantage points as possible. Rachel exhibits her work at juried art fairs around the country.

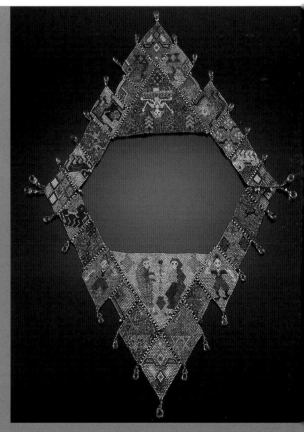

Rachel Weiss's "Mahalakshmi" Necklace, created in 2002, beaded with the help of Holly Polizzi-Hogan, places the goddess in one large triangular niche and two curd-churning maidens in the other.
11½" wide x 18¾" high ■ Collection of the artist
Larry Sanders

"MAHALAKSHMI" PIN

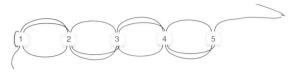

Shown is Rachel Weiss's "Mahalakshmi" Pin, of glass and sterling silver beads and crystals. Collection of the artist ■ LARRY SANDERS

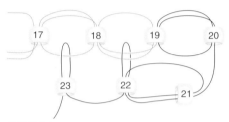

FIGURE 1

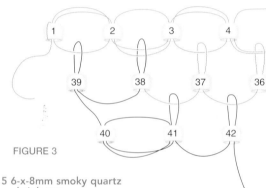

FIGURE 2

FIGURE 3

MATERIALS

Cylinder seed beads

  8 silver-lined crystal

  12 crystal aurora borealis

  16 galvanized silver

  80 Ceylon beige

  115 taupe silk satin

  6 matte opaque yellow

  2.25 grams galvanized yellow gold

  88 24 karat gold iris (24KG for short)

  15 matte transparent amber

  14 lined dark topaz aurora borealis

  1 matte opaque orange

  12 matte metallic dark maroon

  6 transparent wine red aurora borealis

  14 opaque old rose luster

  8 matte rose

  8 lined lilac

  14 galvanized purple

  44 metallic midnight purple

  4 grams faceted metallic purple/gold iris (FMP for short)

  15 silver-lined teal

  60 galvanized dark aqua

  22 matte opaque light sapphire

  15 matte metallic sapphire

  30 opaque chartreuse

  16 translucent green aurora borealis

  22 matte transparent pine green

  10 metallic gunmetal

  9 faceted black

Other beads

  1 5mm biconical crystal, bronze color

  7 4mm biconical crystals, bronze color

  5 3mm oval fire polish glass, silver color

  5 6-x-8mm smoky quartz briolettes

  2 6mm Indonesian sterling silver rondelles

  2 5mm 14/20 gold-filled saucers

  44 2.5mm faceted 12/20 gold-filled beads (FGF for short)

1 bobbin Nymo B thread, tan

size 12 beading needles

wax

2" base metal pin stem with holes for stitching

MAKING THE BRICK STITCH PANELS

First, make the three brick stitch panels using cylinder seed beads. Each of the panels begins with a row of ladder stitch and continues with a series of brick stitch rows that decrease in width until the bottom tip of the panel is reached. The two triangular panels are worked from the top down. The diamond-shaped panel is worked from the center down, then turned upside down and worked from the center down once again. (This ensures that you are only decreasing rows, which most beaders find easier than increasing.)

1 To begin the first row in the triangular panel at the top left of the pin as shown in Figure 4, thread a needle a few inches down a 72" length of waxed thread. The first row is worked in ladder stitch. Add bead 1 in faceted metallic purple/gold iris (FMP), and slide it down to about 6" from the end of the thread. Make an overhand knot around this bead to keep it in place. You will undo this knot later.

2 Following Figure 1, add bead 2 in the same color, then go back up through bead 1 and down through bead 2. Pull tightly so that the sides of the beads press against each other. Add bead 3 in the same color, and go down through bead 2 and up through bead 3. Make sure there is no excess thread

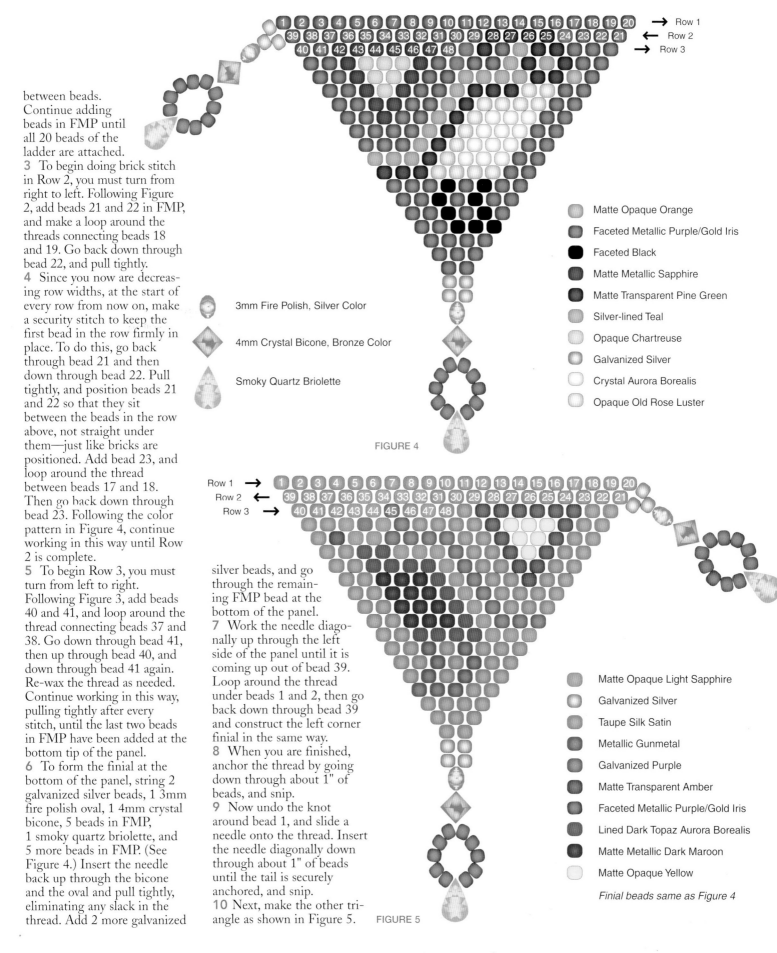

between beads. Continue adding beads in FMP until all 20 beads of the ladder are attached.

3 To begin doing brick stitch in Row 2, you must turn from right to left. Following Figure 2, add beads 21 and 22 in FMP, and make a loop around the threads connecting beads 18 and 19. Go back down through bead 22, and pull tightly.

4 Since you now are decreasing row widths, at the start of every row from now on, make a security stitch to keep the first bead in the row firmly in place. To do this, go back through bead 21 and then down through bead 22. Pull tightly, and position beads 21 and 22 so that they sit between the beads in the row above, not straight under them—just like bricks are positioned. Add bead 23, and loop around the thread between beads 17 and 18. Then go back down through bead 23. Following the color pattern in Figure 4, continue working in this way until Row 2 is complete.

5 To begin Row 3, you must turn from left to right. Following Figure 3, add beads 40 and 41, and loop around the thread connecting beads 37 and 38. Go down through bead 41, then up through bead 40, and down through bead 41 again. Re-wax the thread as needed. Continue working in this way, pulling tightly after every stitch, until the last two beads in FMP have been added at the bottom tip of the panel.

6 To form the finial at the bottom of the panel, string 2 galvanized silver beads, 1 3mm fire polish oval, 1 4mm crystal bicone, 5 beads in FMP, 1 smoky quartz briolette, and 5 more beads in FMP. (See Figure 4.) Insert the needle back up through the bicone and the oval and pull tightly, eliminating any slack in the thread. Add 2 more galvanized silver beads, and go through the remaining FMP bead at the bottom of the panel.

7 Work the needle diagonally up through the left side of the panel until it is coming up out of bead 39. Loop around the thread under beads 1 and 2, then go back down through bead 39 and construct the left corner finial in the same way.

8 When you are finished, anchor the thread by going down through about 1" of beads, and snip.

9 Now undo the knot around bead 1, and slide a needle onto the thread. Insert the needle diagonally down through about 1" of beads until the tail is securely anchored, and snip.

10 Next, make the other triangle as shown in Figure 5.

3mm Fire Polish, Silver Color

4mm Crystal Bicone, Bronze Color

Smoky Quartz Briolette

FIGURE 4

Matte Opaque Orange
Faceted Metallic Purple/Gold Iris
Faceted Black
Matte Metallic Sapphire
Matte Transparent Pine Green
Silver-lined Teal
Opaque Chartreuse
Galvanized Silver
Crystal Aurora Borealis
Opaque Old Rose Luster

FIGURE 5

Matte Opaque Light Sapphire
Galvanized Silver
Taupe Silk Satin
Metallic Gunmetal
Galvanized Purple
Matte Transparent Amber
Faceted Metallic Purple/Gold Iris
Lined Dark Topaz Aurora Borealis
Matte Metallic Dark Maroon
Matte Opaque Yellow

Finial beads same as Figure 4

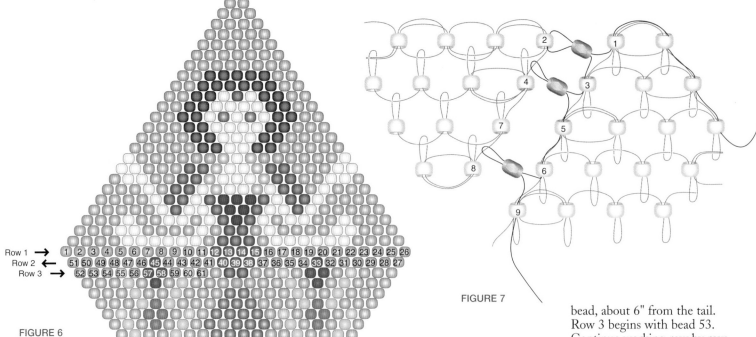

FIGURE 6

Row 1 → 1 2 3 4 5 6 7 8 9 10 11 12 13 14 15 16 17 18 19 20 21 22 23 24 25 26
Row 2 ← 51 50 49 48 47 46 45 44 43 42 41 40 39 38 37 36 35 34 33 32 31 30 29 28 27
Row 3 → 52 53 54 55 56 57 58 59 60 61

FIGURE 7

Legend:
- ○ Ceylon Beige
- ○ Silver-lined Crystal
- ● Galvanized Silver
- ○ Matte Rose
- ● Lined Lilac
- ● Transparent Wine Red Aurora Borealis
- ● Faceted Metallic Purple/Gold Iris
- ○ Galvanized Yellow Gold
- ○ Opaque Chartreuse
- ● Translucent Green Aurora Borealis
- ● Galvanized Dark Aqua
- ● Metallic Midnight Purple

Finial beads same as Figure 4

11 To make the diamond, use a 96" length of waxed thread. Start with the center row of the diamond first, using ladder stitch to add beads 1–26 in the color pattern shown in Figure 6. Work slowly as you add all remaining rows in brick stitch, rewaxing the thread as necessary.

12 Construct the finial at the bottom. Once the finial is in place, anchor the thread by going diagonally up through 1¹/₂" of beads, and snip. Thread a needle onto the tail thread, go down through about 1" of beads, and snip.

13 Cut a 94" length of thread to work the second half of the diamond, and run the thread up diagonally through beads along either the right or the left edge of the panel until the needle is coming out of either bead 1 or bead 26. Leave a 6" tail.

14 Turn both the panel and Figure 6 over and add the remaining rows in the color pattern shown until the diamond is complete.

CONNECTING THE PANELS

The three panels are connected with two sets of 11 2.5mm faceted gold-filled beads (FGF) worked in brick stitch.

1 To begin, place the left triangle to the left of the

diamond as shown in Figure 7. Thread a needle onto an 18" length of waxed thread. Following Figure 7, insert the needle up through about 1" of beads along the right edge of the diamond, leaving a 6" tail. Go down through bead 1, and add a FGF bead. Go through bead 2, back through the FGF bead, and down through bead 3. Add the second FGF bead, and loop around the thread, connecting beads 2 and 4. Go back through the FGF bead, then down through beads 5 and 6. Add the third FGF bead, loop around the thread between beads 7 and 8, go back through the FGF bead, and down through bead 9. Continue working in this way,

skipping 2 beads on each edge, until you have used all 11 FGF beads.

2 Join the right triangle to the diamond in the same way.

MAKING THE PEYOTE STITCH TUBE AND FINIALS

1 The panels are suspended from a peyote stitch tube 3" long by ¹/₄" in diameter, worked entirely in FMP beads. (See Figure 8.) To make the tube, follow the peyote stitch tube instructions on pages 72–73, which show you how to form a flat rectangle of peyote stitch first and then roll it into a tube. To start the rectangle, thread a needle onto a 98" length of waxed thread, then string 52 beads. Tie an overhand knot around the first

bead, about 6" from the tail. Row 3 begins with bead 53. Continue working row by row until the rectangle is ten vertical beads (counting straight down from bead 1, which has a knot around it), or twenty bead rows high on either side. Keep the tension a little slack so that the tube will not become too rigid, because you will have to stitch into it to attach the brick stitch panels.

2 When the rectangle is complete, roll it into a tube and stitch across the seam twice. When you come to the edge of the tube, add a finial by going through one of the beads at the edge of the tube, stringing 2 FMP beads, 1 gold saucer, 1 silver rondelle, 1 4mm crystal bicone, and 1 FMP bead. Go back down through the bicone, the rondelle, and the saucer, and add 2 more FMP beads. Pull tightly. Go down through an edge bead 2 beads to the right of where you placed the first two FMP beads and then up through a bead two beads to the right of that. Pull tightly. Work the needle through the saucer, rondelle, bicone, and FMP bead once again. Go back down through the bicone, rondelle, and saucer, and add 2 more FMP beads. Continue working until you have 5 2-bead spokes of FMP beads in place and the finial is firmly connected. Anchor the thread, and snip.

3 Add a second finial at the other end of the tube, using an 18" length of thread that you have inserted into the tube, starting about 1" away from the

FIGURE 8

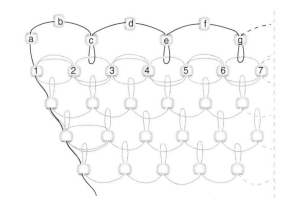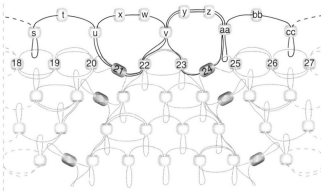

FIGURE 9

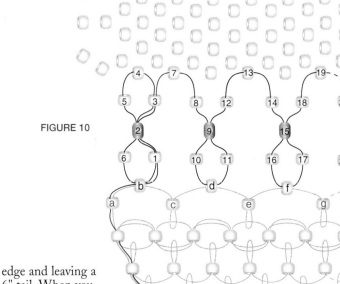

FIGURE 10

edge and leaving a
6" tail. When you
are finished adding
the finial, anchor both
threads, and snip.

ATTACHING THE BRICK STITCH PANELS TO THE PEYOTE TUBE

Rachel attached the brick stitch panels to the peyote tube in two steps, working left to right each time. First, she added a brick stitch edging across the upper edges of the panels. Then she connected this edging to the tube, using a vertical netting technique.

1 To begin the edging, which is worked entirely in 24-karat gold iris (24KG) beads, thread a needle onto a 24" length of thread, and wax it. Following Figure 9, insert the needle up through the left edge of the left triangle, leaving a 6" tail. Go through bead 1, add beads a–c in 24KG, and loop around the thread between beads 2 and 3. Continue working in this way until you come to bead u. Go through beads 21 and 22, add beads v–x, and go through beads u, 21, 22, and v. Add beads y, z, and aa, and go through beads 24, 23, v, y, z, and aa. Loop around the thread that connects beads 24 and 25, and go back up through aa. Add beads bb and cc, and continue working across the top of the right triangle. Anchor, and snip.

2 The vertical netting that connects the edging beads to the peyote tube is worked in a combination of 24KG beads and FGF beads. To begin, thread a needle onto a 28" length of waxed thread. Following Figure 10, insert the needle up through about 1" of the beads that run along the left side of the left triangle, leaving a 6" tail. Go through beads a and b, and add bead 1 in 24KG, bead 2 in FGF, and bead 3 in 24KG. Go through bead 4 of the peyote tube, and add bead 5 in 24KG. Go down through bead 2, and add bead 6 in 24KG. Go through beads b, 1, 2, and 3.

Go through bead 7 of the peyote tube, and add bead 8 in 24KG, bead 9 in FGF, and bead 10 in 24KG. Go through bead d of the edging. Continue the netting in this way, following Figure 10, until all connections are complete. Bead 68 is a 5mm crystal bicone, which sits just below the peyote tube to act as a focal point for the connecting areas. Anchor the threads, and snip.

ADDING THE PIN STEM

1 Using a 30" length of waxed thread doubled to 15", stitch the pin stem in place at the back center of the peyote tube.

SA'DAN TORAJA BEADWORK, SULAWESI, INDONESIA

INSPIRATIONAL PIECE
Kandaure, or conical beaded ornament, from the Sa'dan Toraja peoples of Sulawesi, Indonesia

ARTIST
Biba Schutz

TECHNIQUES
Multiple Vertical-Thread Netting and Tasseling

BEADWORK PROJECT
"Time Revisited" Earrings

1⅜" wide x 3⅛" high
(including wires)

(basic metalsmithing skills are required)

Kandaure are draped over the shoulders of women dancers in Buntoloko, near Rantepao, Sulawesi, during a ceremony inaugurating a newly built tongkonan, or traditional house, in 1976.
HEIDE LEIGH-THEISEN

Rarely does a single piece of beadwork act as an architectural ornament at certain times and as a body ornament at others. Among the Sa'dan Toraja peoples of the island of Sulawesi in Indonesia, a fascinating beaded object called a *kandaure* does just that. *Kandaure* are large, cone-shaped structures, not unlike half-open umbrellas, formed over removable rattan frameworks from old trade beads of European or Asian glass or metal. Every high-ranking family owns one or more *kandaure*, which they regard as precious, sacred heirlooms, equal in price to one or more buffalos. Some *kandaure* are given proper names. Others are believed to possess supernatural powers. Although no two *kandaure* look exactly alike, all follow a similar design format established in generations past, with small anthropomorphic figures appearing in white beads at the narrow end of the cone, a set of hooked diamond motifs in the middle, and long flowing tassels attached to the cone's wide end.

The Toraja display their *kandaure* only during important ceremonies such as funerals, weddings, or house blessings. Almost as if they are alive, *kandaure* can change dimensionality according to the requirements of a specific occasion. During certain ceremonies, with their rattan frameworks in place, *kandaure* may be suspended, umbrella-like, from poles or platforms in front of a family's ancestral house. During other ceremonies, with their frameworks removed, they can be folded in half and draped over the backs of women dancers. Yet, throughout these changes of dimensionality and context, the essential significance of the *kandaure* stays more or less the same. With multiple tassels flowing from a single, narrow point of origin, a *kandaure* is a sign of abundance, one that symbolically re-creates the relationship of a family's few founding ancestors to its many flourishing descendants. A *kandaure* also represents abundance in that it is composed of many valuable beads that were typically assembled over several decades—even generations—at great expense. For helping them achieve abundance in all of its manifestations, the Toraja repeatedly honor their ancestors in ceremonies large and small.

LEFT *Sa'dan Toraja boys in a village near Rantepao, Sulawesi, are seen in 1994 making* kandaure *by uniting glass beads in a multiple-thread net over a conical rattan framework. In Toraja culture, the making of a* kandaure, *like the making of jewelry, is classified as a male task.*
THOMAS MURRAY

ABOVE *Several* kandaure *hang from the canopied roof of a temporary platform erected alongside a* tongkonan *featured in a funeral ceremony that took place in a village near Rantepao in 1994.*
THOMAS MURRAY

BIBA SCHUTZ IS A GIFTED METALSMITH with a strong appreciation for fiber art. She had never worked seriously in beads before completing the spectacular pendant shown here, which preserves both the basic shape of the *kandaure* and the multiple-thread beadnetting technique used to make it. Not finding any glass or metal beads that seemed right, Biba selected small chips of semiprecious stones such as carnelian, garnet, amethyst, and peridot, as much for their luminosity as for their texture. The irregularity of the chips makes them less-than-ideal candidates for beadwork, but Biba skillfully graduates them between the metal framing elements at top and bottom. To offset the chip density in the body of the pendant, she lightens the tassel elements by leaving a random length of thread between each chip.

In designing the matching earrings for the project in this book, Biba used many of the same strategies but opted for a simpler rectangular shape. Like the pendant, the earrings are made in four sections, consisting of an upper framing bar, a knotted net, a lower framing wire, and a series of tassels. Biba darkened her sterling silver elements by oxidizing them, but you can leave them bright silver if you prefer. Either way, they are nearly hidden by the stone chips that surround them.

Biba Schutz evokes the shape of a kandaure *in her "Time Revisited" Pendant, created in 2002, and substitutes semiprecious stone chips and a framework of sterling silver and copper for the* kandaure's *glass beads and rattan.*
1⅞" diameter x 6" high (excluding chain)
Collection of the artist ■ LARRY SANDERS

Biba Schutz of New York City is an oft-published jewelry designer and sculptor who is recognized for her textilelike use of sterling silver wire. More a metal artist than a beadworker per se, Biba nevertheless admires beads and enjoys incorporating them into her work from time to time. She sells her work at juried art fairs and through galleries nationwide.

"TIME REVISITED" EARRINGS

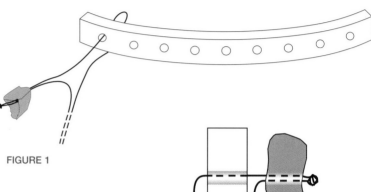

Shown are Biba Schutz's "Time Revisited" Earrings, of sterling silver and semiprecious stone chips.
Collection of the artist ■ *LARRY SANDERS*

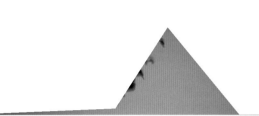

FIGURE 1

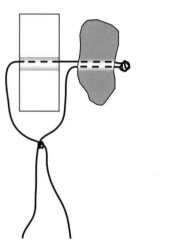

FIGURE 2

MATERIALS

approximately 314 semiprecious stone chips in 4 colors, presorted for uniformity (*Note* Dimensions are approximate.)

   67 garnet chips, $\frac{1}{8}$" x $\frac{1}{8}$"
   156 peridot chips, $\frac{1}{8}$" x $\frac{3}{16}$"
   61 amethyst chips, $\frac{1}{8}$" x $\frac{3}{16}$"
   30 carnelian chips, $\frac{3}{16}$" x $\frac{3}{16}$"

11 yards 14-lb. test Fire Line brand fishing line, smoke color, cut into 18 20" lengths and 4 9" lengths (you can also use waxed lengths of Nymo D thread, but the fishing line works better because of its stiffness)

3" 18 gauge, $\frac{1}{8}$"-wide sterling silver bezel wire

$3\frac{1}{2}$" 18 gauge sterling silver round wire

5" 22 gauge sterling silver round wire

jeweler's electric drill or Dremel Moto-Tool and several size 62 drill bits with matching collets

7" medium-cut jeweler's flat or half-round hand file

7" fine-cut jeweler's flat or half-round hand file

small piece 150-grit or finer sandpaper

diamond bead reamer tool

permanent fine-point marker

jeweler's saw frame, medium-duty saw blade, and blade-lubricating compound, or wire cutters capable of cutting 18 gauge sterling silver bezel wire

round-nose pliers

wire-cutting pliers

chain-nose pliers

12" high x 10" wide x $\frac{1}{2}$" deep foam board

2 small finishing nails or T-pins

(optional) liquid chemical compound for oxidizing sterling silver (available at jewelry supply houses) (*Note* Follow all of the instructions provided with the oxidizer. Use with adequate ventilation.)

(optional) jeweler's polishing wheel and polishing compound

PREPARING THE UPPER FRAMING BAR

Note These instructions assume you will be attaching garnet chips measuring approximately $\frac{1}{8}$" x $\frac{1}{8}$" to the upper framing bar. If you are using larger chips, you will have to accommodate them by using longer pieces of 18 gauge bezel wire for the upper framing bars and longer pieces of 18 gauge round wire for the lower framing wires.

1 Using a jeweler's saw, cut the 18 gauge bezel wire into 2 pieces measuring $1\frac{5}{16}$" each. (You can also cut the bezel wire using sturdy wire cutters, but the cuts will not be as accurate and you will have to leave extra room for filing the rough edges. If using wire cutters, cut the bezel wire into 2 pieces $1\frac{1}{2}$" long each.)
2 File the ends of both pieces first with the medium-cut file and then with the fine-cut file until they are smooth and measure about $1\frac{1}{4}$" or slightly longer. (If you have polishing equipment, polish the ends.)
3 Next, find the exact center of one piece of bezel wire and make a small dot there using a permanent marker. Make 2 more dots, one $\frac{1}{8}$" away from the right edge of the bezel and one $\frac{1}{8}$" away from the left edge.
4 Next, make 3 more dots, $\frac{1}{8}$" apart, between the center dot and the dot at the right

edge. Do the same on the other side until all 9 dots are present. (See Figure 1.)
5 Next, check the positioning of the dots by placing a garnet chip on top of each dot. If you are not happy with the positioning of the chips, try substituting other chips, but do not reposition the dots. Mark the other piece of bezel wire in the same way.
6 Using a size 62 drill bit, drill holes where the dots are on both pieces of bezel wire. (If one bit breaks, use another.) Enlarge the center hole of each bar by drilling through it several times. This will make it easier to accommodate the earring wires later.
7 With your fingers, gently bend each bezel wire until it takes on a slight curve. Lightly sand all areas of the bezel wires, front, back, and sides, to smooth the holes and to leave a matte finish on the metal. (Optional: Oxidize the bezel.)

ATTACHING THE FIRST ROW OF CHIPS TO THE UPPER FRAMING BAR

1 Take a 20" length of fishing line and make a knot in the center that is just large enough to stop up the hole of a garnet chip. Fold the thread in half to double it. String 1 garnet chip, and push it down to the knot. Following Figure 1, insert one of the threads through the far left hole of the bezel wire, and pull tightly so that the stone chip sits firmly against the bar.

2 Following Figure 2, bring the other thread down under the bar and knot it to the first thread using a square knot.

3 Continue adding garnet chips in this way until all 9 are in place on each framing bar. (See Figure 3.) Remember to attach a garnet chip with an extra-large hole through the center hole of each bar. The hole of this center chip will eventually have to accommodate a 22 gauge earring wire.

SECURING THE UPPER FRAMING BARS TO THE WORK SURFACE

It will be easier to bead the upper framing bars if they are secured to a stable surface so that they cannot move around too much. Securing the bars will also help you achieve even thread tension as you work. You can prepare a stable surface by pushing two nails or T-pins, spaced about 6" apart, into a piece of $^1/_2$" thick foam board.

1 Following Figure 4, take 2 9" lengths of fishing line and loop one around the left side of an upper framing bar and one around the right side. Knot the ends of the fishing line to the nails or T-pins. Do the same with the other framing bar. Leave 2-3" of fishing line between the nails or pins and the upper framing bars so that the framing bars can move somewhat as you work with them. (If you don't have

foam board, you can attach the bars to your worktable using duct tape, but the board is better because it allows you to tilt the work toward you.)

BEGINNING THE KNOTTED NET

Between the framing bars, form a knotted net of 76 chips in 8 horizontal rows. Odd-numbered rows will have 10 stone chips and even-numbered rows will have 9 chips. Chips at the left and right edges of odd-numbered rows will have only one thread running through them. All other chips will have two threads running through them, one each from two adjacent pairs of threads.

1 To begin Row 1, string a peridot chip onto Thread 1. Push it up to within $^1/_{16}$" of the upper framing bar, and form an overhand knot under the chip. (See Figure 4.) String another peridot chip onto Threads 2 and 3, and push it up to within $^1/_{16}$" of the upper framing bar. Form a square knot under this chip. Continue adding peridot chips in this way until the first row is complete.

COMPLETING THE KNOTTED NET

1 Begin Row 2 by stringing a peridot chip onto Threads 1 and 2. Push it up the thread so that it sits $^1/_{16}$" below the chips in Row 1. Form a square knot under the chip.

2 String the next peridot chip onto Threads 3 and 4, push it up to within $^1/_{16}$" of the chips in Row 1, and form a square knot under it. (See Figure 5.) Continue finishing Rows 2 and 3 by adding peridot chips in this way.

3 Rows 4-8 contain combinations of peridot, amethyst, carnelian, and garnet chips that create a triangular pattern in the net. To add Rows 4-8, follow the color pattern shown in Figure 7 on page 50.

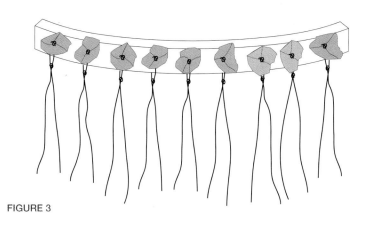

FIGURE 3

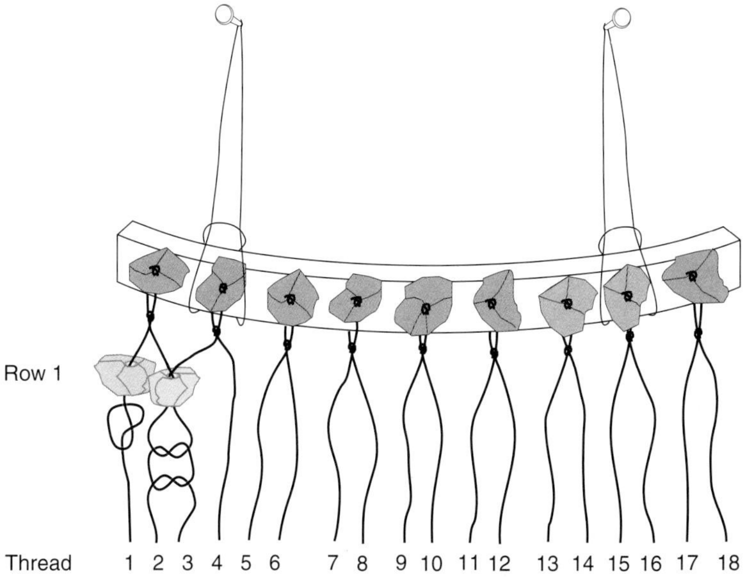

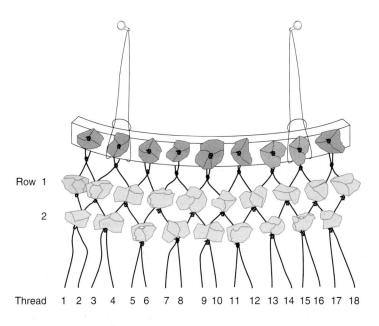

Row 1

Thread 1 2 3 4 5 6   7 8   9 10 11 12   13 14 15 16 17 18

FIGURE 4

Row 1

2

Thread 1 2 3 4   5 6   7 8   9 10 11 12   13 14 15 16 17 18

FIGURE 5

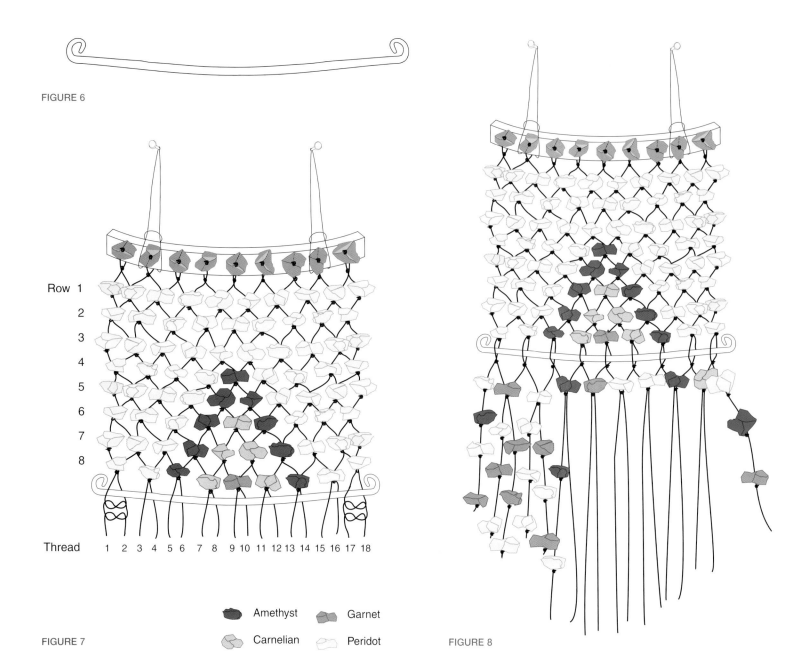

FIGURE 6

Row 1
2
3
4
5
6
7
8

Thread   1 2 3 4 5 6 7 8 9 10 11 12 13 14 15 16 17 18

FIGURE 7

Amethyst   Garnet
Carnelian   Peridot

FIGURE 8

USING 18 GAUGE ROUND WIRE TO FORM THE LOWER FRAMING WIRES

1 Next, prepare the lower framing wires that stabilize the knotted net and support the tassels. With wire cutters, cut the 18 gauge round wire into 2 pieces about $1^3/4$" long each. File the ends first with the medium-cut file and then with the fine-cut file until they are smooth and the wires measure about $1^5/8$" long each. (Optional: Polish the ends.)

2 With round-nose pliers, form one small, nearly closed loop at each end of the wire. (See Figure 6.) Reduce or enlarge the loops until each wire measures $1^1/4$" or slightly longer. With your fingers, curve each wire to the same extent that you curved the upper framing bars. (Optional: Oxidize the wires.)

ATTACHING THE LOWER FRAMING WIRES TO THE KNOTTED NET

1 Position one wire under the final row of chips in one

earring. Adjust the length of the wire if necessary so that it can comfortably accommodate all threads. Following Figure 7, place Thread 1 in front of the wire and Thread 2 in back. Push the framing wire up to within $1/16$" of Row 8 and knot Threads 1 and 2 together under the wire using a square knot. Then do the same at the right edge of the wire using Threads 17 and 18. Form the remaining knots under the wire until it is securely in place.

2 Repeat for the other earring.

ADDING THE KNOTTED TASSELS

The tassel section begins with a ninth horizontal row of stone chips knotted directly under the lower supporting wire.

1 For this row, follow the thread paths and color patterns shown in Figure 8. Chips in this row should sit about $1/16$" under the lower framing wire. The chips at the far left and right will have only one thread running through them. The other chips in this row will have two threads running

FIGURE 9

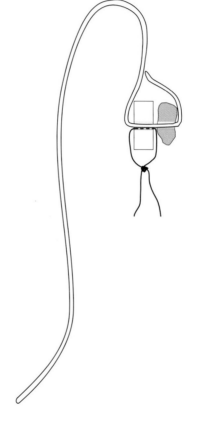

FIGURE 10

through them. After this row, all remaining chips in the tassel section will have only one thread running through them. These chips will be knotted at random intervals from $1/16$" to $1/4$" apart. (See Figure 8.)

2 Following Figure 9, knot the remaining chips in the tassel section. Graduate the tassels so that the longest ones, measuring about $1^1/2$", sit in the center of the earring and the shortest, measuring about $5/8$", near the edges. (Biba used a total of approxi-

mately 72 chips in the tassel section of each earring, but you can use more or less as you wish.)

SHAPING AND ATTACHING THE 22 GAUGE EARRING WIRES

1 Using wire cutters, cut the 22 gauge sterling silver round wire into 2 pieces measuring $2^1/2$" each. File the ends with the fine-cut file until they are smooth. (Optional: Polish the ends.) With your fingers, form a U-shape in one of the wires about $3/4$" from one end.

2 Following Figure 10, gently bend the longest section of the wire so that it takes on a graceful curve. (Optional: Oxidize the wires.) Make another wire to match.

3 Next, insert the shorter section of one wire through the back of one of the upper framing bars so that it comes out through the garnet chip in the center of the bar. The wire should extend out slightly more than $1/4$" in front of the chip. With chain-nose pliers, gently form a loop around the garnet

chip and upper framing bar. If you have too much wire left over, snip it, smooth it, and continue forming until the wire is securely attached to the bar. (The center garnet chip may shift its position slightly upward so that it sits higher than the other chips on the bar, but this will not be noticeable when the earrings are worn.)

4 Finish the pair of earrings by attaching the other wire to the other framing bar.

STRAITS CHINESE BEADWORK, PENANG, MALAYSIA

INSPIRATIONAL PIECE
Straits Chinese wedding bed panel from late nineteenth-century Penang, Malaysia

ARTIST
Valerie Hector

TECHNIQUE
Tasseling

BEADWORK PROJECT
Tasseled earrings

¾" wide x 2½" high (including wires)

Over the centuries, beadwork has decorated countless wedding celebrations across the world. One hundred years ago, in peninsular Malaysia and Indonesia, women of the "Straits," or *Peranakan* (locally born), Chinese communities spent many months preparing beaded decorations for the bridal chamber, which was the focus of the twelve-day-long wedding ceremony. A typical set of decorations might include a pair of mirror covers, a pair of pillowcases, a table mat or flower vase, and several long bed tassels. Members of the wedding party might also wear beaded slippers, belts, and headdresses such as the one shown on the facing page.

The most impressive piece of all, however, was the 6-foot-long horizontal panel that stretched across the upper rim of the canopied wedding bed, or sometimes across the mattress. This sumptuous piece of beadwork would delight all who entered the chamber and bear witness to the bride's needleworking skills and the family's wealth and social position. Some of these panels depict elaborate wedding processions in progress, but the one shown below, from the island of Penang, is subtler. It presents an earthly paradise, far from the cares of everyday life, full of vibrant colors. The paired phoenixes and peonies that alternate across the upper half of the panel quietly underscore the major themes of the wedding day: the bringing together of complementary opposites and the joys of being a couple.

The Straits Chinese were consummate beadworkers, committed to perfection in every stitch. They loved the small European glass one-cut seed beads, or "charlottes," that made every inch shimmer with irregular facets of

ABOVE *This detail of the wedding bed panel pictured below shows the vibrant color combinations characteristic of Straits Chinese beadwork.*
Private collection ■ TOM VAN EYNDE

BELOW *This late nineteenth-century Straits Chinese wedding bed panel from the island of Penang is made of European glass beads and cotton. It would have been accompanied by a matching pair of beaded mirror covers.*
9¾" high x 6' 5" long ■ *Private collection* ■ TOM VAN EYNDE

reflected light. Almost without exception, the Straits Chinese also liked to apply beads as densely as possible. The upper half of the wedding bed panel shown here, contains about 360 size 14° beads per square inch, or a total of about 176,000 beads, united in a demanding netting technique requiring dozens of diagonally moving threads. With its elegant three-dimensional tassel elements, the bottom half of the panel is no less impressive. All things considered, this panel is a visual and technical masterpiece—an example of Straits Chinese beadwork at its finest.

Two three-dimensional phoenix birds alight on this early twentieth-century headdress worn by a penyapit, or page girl, during a wedding ceremony. Formed of stitched and netted European glass beads and cotton, it was probably used by Straits Chinese living in Sumatra.
6" diameter x 7½" high ■ Private collection ■ DON TUTTLE

ALTHOUGH I ADMIRE the upper half of the wedding bed panel, the lower half interests me more. I have used tassels many times. I like the simplicity of the stringing technique; the slow, repetitive building up of layers of solid, movable color; and the soft, brushlike texture. I designed the tasseled pieces shown on page 54 to incorporate the color intensity and bead density of the wedding bed panel. I wanted to keep the metal supporting components as simple as possible. In most of the pieces, I used simple strung tassels, but for the green spherical earrings I used hundreds of looped tassels sewn to a sterling silver bead studded with tiny holes. While I used antique size 18°-22° Venetian glass seed beads, the instructions for making the tasseled earrings, which follow, call for 15° seed beads, because they work perfectly in this context.

The element I most enjoyed making for my "Green" Necklace was the tasseled one, because the work took on a meditative quality. The tassels are attached to a silk-wrapped armature of sterling silver.
11¼" diameter x ¾" deep ■ Collection of the artist
DON TUTTLE

TASSELED EARRINGS

Shown are Valerie Hector's tasseled bracelet, brooch, and earrings, in sterling silver, 18-karat gold, and antique Venetian glass seed beads. The project earrings are shown at right.

Collection of the artist and private collection ■ *LARRY SANDERS*

MATERIALS

13¼" 20 gauge sterling silver round wire, cut into:

    2 5⅛" pieces

    2 1½" pieces

15" Japanese round seed beads

    11 grams Color A

    72 Color B

2 10mm round black glass or onyx beads

16 yards Silamide A thread, cut into 36 16" lengths

1 size 12 beading needle

7" fine-cut jeweler's flat or half-round hand file

small piece 150 grit or finer sandpaper

wire cutters

round-nose pliers

chain-nose pliers

(optional) jeweler's polishing wheel and polishing compound

PREPARING THE WIRES

1 Take one 5⅛" piece of sterling silver round wire and file both ends until they are smooth and about 5" long. (If you have polishing equipment, polish the ends.) With round-nose pliers, bend one end around the pliers to form a small ring with a hole about ⅛" in outer diameter. With chain-nose pliers, squeeze the ring closed. (See Figure 1.)

2 Next, thread a 10mm bead onto this wire, and slide it down to the ring. Prepare the coil that keeps this bead in place by taking one 1½" long piece of 20 gauge round wire and filing or sanding one end until it is smooth. (Optional: Polish this end.)

3 Press the smooth end of the wire up against the longer wire just above the bead. Use the chain-nose pliers and your fingers to coil the shorter wire tightly around the longer wire. (See Figure 2.)

4 Continue coiling 4-5 times to form a tight, even spiral. Trim the excess wire to within ¹⁄₁₆" of the coil, and file or sand the end to remove rough spots. (Optional: Polish the end of the wire.) Use the chain-nose pliers to finish the coil by pressing the end into place. Then squeeze the coil firmly with the chain-nose pliers so that the coil does not move and the bead is firmly in place. (The coil will flatten somewhat as you squeeze it.)

5 Make another wire for the second earring.

ADDING TASSELS

1 Take a 16" piece of thread and insert one end through the ring of one earring. Pull until both sides of the thread are equal in length. Following Figure 3, secure the thread to the ring using a square knot. The knot should sit tightly against the ring.

2 Thread a needle onto one of the threads. Add 1½" inches of beads (about 35 15° beads) in Color A and 1 bead in Color B. With your fingers, push the beads up to the ring so that there is no air space between them. Carefully make an overhand knot around the Color B bead so that it becomes part of the knot. Check again to see that the beads sit tightly against the ring. If they do not, insert your needle into the Color B bead and gently move it upward.

3 Next, make a second overhand knot around this bead. Following Figure 4, anchor the thread by inserting the needle through 22-30 Color A beads. Pull tightly, and snip the excess thread.

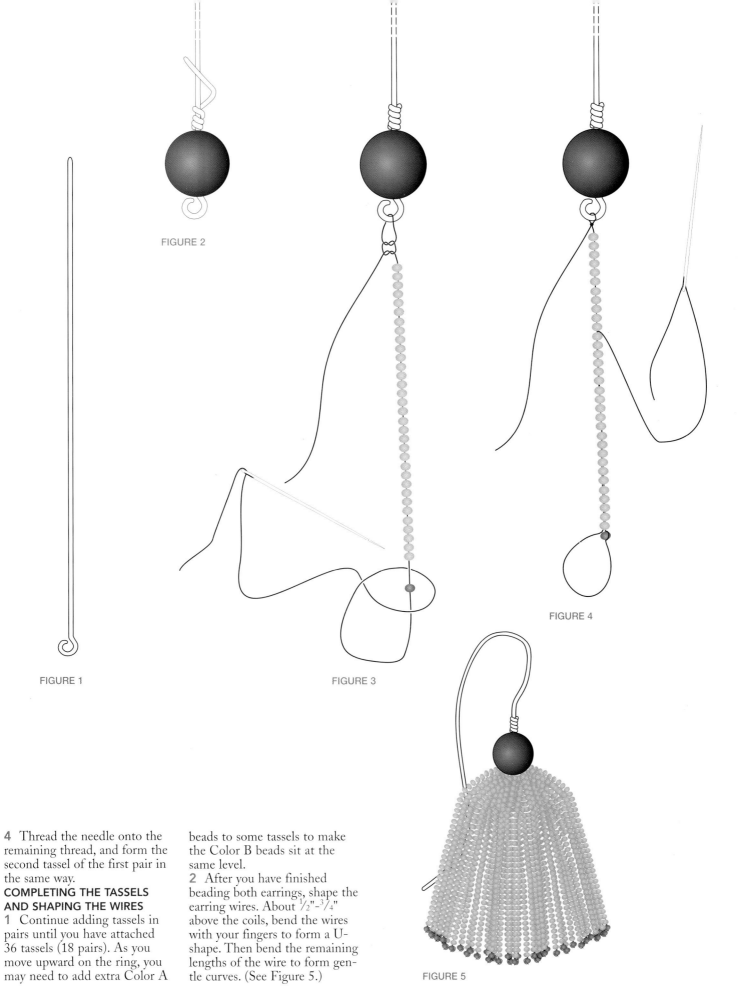

FIGURE 2

FIGURE 1

FIGURE 3

FIGURE 4

FIGURE 5

4 Thread the needle onto the remaining thread, and form the second tassel of the first pair in the same way.

COMPLETING THE TASSELS AND SHAPING THE WIRES

1 Continue adding tassels in pairs until you have attached 36 tassels (18 pairs). As you move upward on the ring, you may need to add extra Color A beads to some tassels to make the Color B beads sit at the same level.

2 After you have finished beading both earrings, shape the earring wires. About $\frac{1}{2}$"–$\frac{3}{4}$" above the coils, bend the wires with your fingers to form a U-shape. Then bend the remaining lengths of the wire to form gentle curves. (See Figure 5.)

KENYAH BEADWORK, INDONESIAN/MALAYSIAN BORNEO

INSPIRATIONAL PIECE
Baby carrier panel with dragon-dog motifs from the Kenyah Dayak peoples of Borneo, ca. 1930

ARTIST
Carol Perrenoud

TECHNIQUES
Ladder Stitch, Tubular Ndebele Herringbone Stitch, and Fringing

BEADWORK PROJECT
Tasseled hair sticks

¾" wide x 6¾" high

ABOVE *An elderly, bespectacled Kenyah woman photographed in central Borneo in the early 1930s displays her wooden beading board. A paper template is attached to the board, guiding her as she shapes the motifs.*
Courtesy, Rijksmuseum voor Volkenkunde, Leiden. Neg. No. Till n-122
H. F. TILLEMA

RIGHT *Eight* kalétau *encircle this fragmentary Kenyah sun hat panel from ca. 1930 made of European glass beads united in a complex, multiple-thread diagonal net. Only high-ranking Kenyah aristocrats were allowed to render* kalétau *and other full-bodied anthropomorphs.*
18" diameter ■ Private collection ■ DON TUTTLE

Today, if we want to generate a pattern, we can turn to a computer program or to special beadwork graph paper. Beadworkers of other cultures have fashioned patterns in other ways, using simple but highly effective methods. Some of the native Dayak peoples of Borneo, such as the Kenyah, developed superior pattern-making abilities by following an approach similar to the one that Western children learn to make valentine hearts or paper dolls. A Kenyah artist hired specifically for this purpose would take a piece of bark cloth or newspaper, fold it in half or in quarters, sketch a design on the uppermost face, and then carefully cut out the designs. Once unfolded, the template would reveal a design composed of two halves or four quarters forming perfect mirror images of one another. After attaching the template to a wooden board, a woman would bead over it, using colors appropriate to the motifs being shown. She might insert a few minor motifs not called for in the template—small dots, dashes, or zigzags, for example. But in general, like the woman in the photograph shown here, she probably followed the template rather closely, trying hard to render smooth lines while manipulating multiple threads.

These intricate panels were not mere exercises in graphic design or beadwork technique, but attempts to harness spiritual power. Traditionally, the Dayak believed that their rainforest environment was full of unseen spirit forces, both positive and negative, that might help or harm. Humans could try to influence these spirits by making small offerings or by wearing talismans of metal, wood, stone, hornbill ivory, or beadwork intended to ward off negative spirits and attract positive ones who would help the rice plants thrive, the hunters bring home their prey, and the children grow to adulthood.

Often, these talismans bore the likeness of the spirits whose protection was sought. One such spirit is the *aso'*, a mythological underwater being, part dragon and part dog, typically shown in profile, sometimes with multiple heads extending from a single body. Four *aso'* motifs with enlarged, penetrating eyes are seen in profile on the panel on the facing page. It would have been stitched to the back of a rattan baby carrier to act as a kind of spiritual shield for the baby's body and soul. Another kind of protective motif is the *kalétau*, or humanlike figure (see the image to the right). It is typically shown squatting, with splayed arms and legs. It is not known whether *kalétau* represent ancestors, other beings from the spirit realm, or perhaps burden-bearing slaves, but the Dayak believe them to be beneficent and powerful.

SHOWN A DOZEN OR SO IMAGES OF Dayak bead-work, Carol Perrenoud and her business partner, Virginia Blakelock, quickly selected the panels with *aso'* and *kalétau* motifs, because of the intricacy of the work and the symbolic significance of the iconography. Next, they set about designing suitably complex pieces of their own, relying upon tracing paper, graph paper, colored pencils, and their own artistic sensibilities to map out and then modify the Dayak motifs.

Virginia selected one of the figures in the hat panel shown on the previous page, adding an elaborate neckpiece to the chest area, flamelike tendrils to the torso and legs, and a cheerful smile. She makes this figure the focal point of the small bag shown below, worked in 20° antique Venetian glass seed beads netted horizontally with a single thread.

Carol began by doing some research into the *aso'* motif. She wanted to see as many versions of it as she could before she started designing. Looking through Bernard Sellato's book *Hornbill and Dragon*, she found an *aso'* she admired. But what to make with it? Having seen an image of

For the Dayak, the aso' motif represents a mythological feminine underwater spirit being that will protect humankind if properly invoked. Here, four aso' with enlarged eyes and entwined limbs stand guard on a baby carrier panel to repel negative spirits. 10½" wide x 9½" high ■ Private collection ■ DON TUTTLE

a Dayak hair ornament, she decided to make the four-piece set of hair ornaments in shades of yellow and violet shown on page 58. The largest piece in the set, which is meant to be suspended from a beaded comb worn at the back of the head above a bun of hair, displays what appears to be a single large *aso'* composed of two smaller *aso'* joined at their heads. Carol beaded this piece in a traditional Dayak beadweaving technique, which requires warp and weft threads that orient beads in a herringbone configuration. Finally, she made two matching hair sticks, which show only the most powerful part of the *aso'*: the face. Wanting a faster, easier technique, she opted for Ndebele herringbone, a stitch from South Africa first documented by Virginia in the late 1980s, which requires only a single thread yet produces an appearance very much like its woven counterpart. Even the Dayak might have appreciated Ndebele herringbone stitch had they known it. Following, you will learn how to make these appealing tasseled hair sticks.

Carol Perrenoud of Wilsonville, Oregon, remembers playing with her grandmother's beads, which were organized by color in old candy boxes. She is now a leading bead artist, with several instructional videos to her credit. Along with Virginia Blakelock, another gifted beadworker with an international reputation, Carol runs Bead Cats, a beadwork supply company, and teaches workshops around the country. For more information on either artist, see www.beadcats.com.

In her "Celebratory Spirit" Bag, made in 2002 with an Ultrasuede-covered plastic bottle, Virginia Blakelock uses tiny 20° beads in a single-thread net to render a full-bodied Kenyah spirit figure whose torso, limbs, and head seem to sprout plantlike tendrils. 3¾" wide x 5" high (bag only) Collection of the artist ■ LARRY SANDERS

TASSELED HAIR STICKS

Carol Perrenoud's "Watch My Back" set of four hair ornaments, worked in loomweaving, warp/weft herringbone stitch, and Ndebele herringbone stitch. The project hair sticks are shown at the right.
Collection of the artist ■ LARRY SANDERS

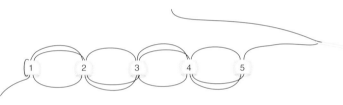

FIGURE 1

MATERIALS

(to make a pair of hair sticks)

2 wooden hair sticks, ¾" wide x 6 ¾" high

2 pieces white or cream-colored Ultrasuede Lite or other padding material, 1¼" long x ¹³/₁₆" wide

1 bobbin Nymo B thread, tan

wax

14° Japanese seed beads

    56 crystal aurora borealis

    2 grams transparent topaz aurora borealis

    2 grams transparent light amber luster

    2 grams transparent white-lined amber

    22 beads magenta-lined clear luster

    2 grams opaque royal purple luster

    1 gram opaque bright olive green aurora borealis

    8 beads transparent teal aurora borealis

MAKING THE CENTRAL HERRINGBONE PANEL

Before beginning the panel, pad the hair stick so that the beads don't slide across its surface. To do this, wrap an Ultrasuede panel lengthwise around a hair stick until the edges meet. Stitch across the edges tightly several times to hold the panel in place.

1 The first step is to form a 16-bead ladder, just like Rachel Weiss used to begin her brick stitch panels. (See Figure 1, page 42.) All of the beads in this first row will be in transparent white-lined amber. (See Figure 4 on page 60.) To begin, thread a needle onto a 68" length of waxed thread. Following Figure 1, add bead 1, and make an overhand knot around it, leaving a 6" tail. Add bead 2, and go back up through bead 1 and down through bead 2. Pull tightly so that the sides

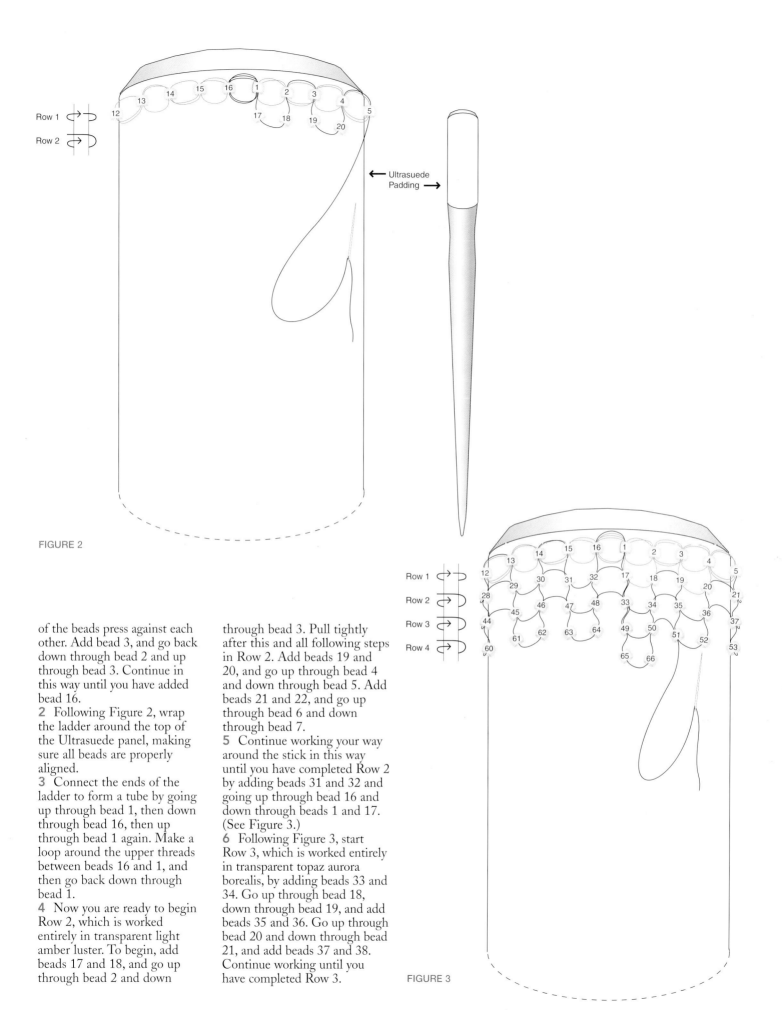

FIGURE 2

FIGURE 3

← Ultrasuede Padding →

Row 1
Row 2

Row 1
Row 2
Row 3
Row 4

of the beads press against each other. Add bead 3, and go back down through bead 2 and up through bead 3. Continue in this way until you have added bead 16.

2 Following Figure 2, wrap the ladder around the top of the Ultrasuede panel, making sure all beads are properly aligned.

3 Connect the ends of the ladder to form a tube by going up through bead 1, then down through bead 16, then up through bead 1 again. Make a loop around the upper threads between beads 16 and 1, and then go back down through bead 1.

4 Now you are ready to begin Row 2, which is worked entirely in transparent light amber luster. To begin, add beads 17 and 18, and go up through bead 2 and down

through bead 3. Pull tightly after this and all following steps in Row 2. Add beads 19 and 20, and go up through bead 4 and down through bead 5. Add beads 21 and 22, and go up through bead 6 and down through bead 7.

5 Continue working your way around the stick in this way until you have completed Row 2 by adding beads 31 and 32 and going up through bead 16 and down through beads 1 and 17. (See Figure 3.)

6 Following Figure 3, start Row 3, which is worked entirely in transparent topaz aurora borealis, by adding beads 33 and 34. Go up through bead 18, down through bead 19, and add beads 35 and 36. Go up through bead 20 and down through bead 21, and add beads 37 and 38. Continue working until you have completed Row 3.

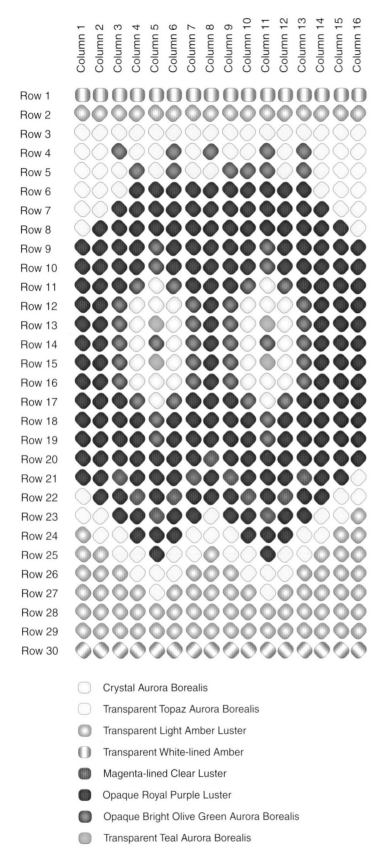

Column 1 Column 2 Column 3 Column 4 Column 5 Column 6 Column 7 Column 8 Column 9 Column 10 Column 11 Column 12 Column 13 Column 14 Column 15 Column 16

Row 1
Row 2
Row 3
Row 4
Row 5
Row 6
Row 7
Row 8
Row 9
Row 10
Row 11
Row 12
Row 13
Row 14
Row 15
Row 16
Row 17
Row 18
Row 19
Row 20
Row 21
Row 22
Row 23
Row 24
Row 25
Row 26
Row 27
Row 28
Row 29
Row 30

○ Crystal Aurora Borealis

○ Transparent Topaz Aurora Borealis

◐ Transparent Light Amber Luster

◑ Transparent White-lined Amber

◉ Magenta-lined Clear Luster

● Opaque Royal Purple Luster

◉ Opaque Bright Olive Green Aurora Borealis

◐ Transparent Teal Aurora Borealis

FIGURE 4

THE ART OF BEADWORK | 60

7 Follow the color pattern in Figure 4 to add Rows 4-30. Finish the panel by undoing the knot around bead 1 and adding a needle to the end of the thread. Work the needle back down through about 1" of the beads in the center panel. Anchor and snip.

MAKING THE HERRINGBONE TASSELS

The herringbone tassels are as fast and easy to make as the center panel. All even-numbered beads are worked in transparent white-lined amber; odd beads are worked in transparent light amber luster. The two beads at the tip of each tassel are in opaque bright olive green aurora borealis.

1 To begin, thread a needle onto a 48" length of waxed thread. Insert the needle into a bead located about 1" above bead 449 in Figure 5, and work downward until the needle is emerging from bead 465. Leave a 6" tail. Add beads 1 and 2, and go up through bead 466 and down through beads 465 and 1. Pull tightly after this and all following steps. Add beads 3 and 4, and go up through bead 2 and down through beads 1 and 3. Continue working in this way until you have added beads 31 and 32 in bright olive green aurora borealis. Next, go back up through bead 30 and all even-numbered beads above it until the needle is coming out of bead 466.

2 Start the second tassel by going down through bead 467 and adding beads 33 and 34. Go up through bead 468, down through beads 467 and 33, and add beads 35 and 36.

3 Continue in this way until all 8 tassels have been added. Anchor and snip.

ADDING THE OUTER TASSELS AT THE TOP OF THE HAIR STICK

The top of the hair stick is completely covered with 32 6-bead tassels. The first 2 beads in each tassel are worked in transparent light amber luster, and the second 3 are in transparent topaz aurora borealis. The final bead is worked in opaque bright olive green aurora borealis. It is best to start forming tassels around the outer perimeter of the hair stick first, working upward from each of the beads in the Row 1 ladder. After that, you can fill in the remaining tassels.

1 To start, thread a needle onto a 48" length of waxed thread. Following Figure 6, insert the needle up through about 1" of the central herringbone panel until it comes out of bead a of the ladder. Leave a 6" tail. Add beads 1-6 in the colors noted above, and go back down through beads 5-1 and bead a. Be sure the tassel sits tightly against the ladder. Go up through bead b, add beads 7-12, go back down through beads 11-7 and bead b. Pull tightly.

2 Continue working your way around the ladder until you have added 16 tassels.

FILLING THE INNER TASSELS

Now add tassels to the inside center top of the hair stick. First, you must create a baseline to attach these tassels to.

1 You have just added Tassel 16 to the ladder. Put your needle down through bead p of the ladder. Go back through Tassel 16 to reinforce it. Come up through bead p. Following Figure 7, add 6 beads in transparent light amber luster, or enough beads to span the distance from one side of the hair stick to the other, and loop your thread around the thread that connects beads h and g in the far side of the ladder. Go back through beads 6 and 5.

2 Form Tassel 17 by adding beads 7-12 and going back through beads 11-7. Go through bead 4, and add Tassel 18. Go through beads 3 and 2, and add Tassel 19.

3 Go through bead 1, and loop twice around the thread that connects beads p and a. Start a second baseline by adding beads 25-30 and looping around the thread that connects beads g and f.

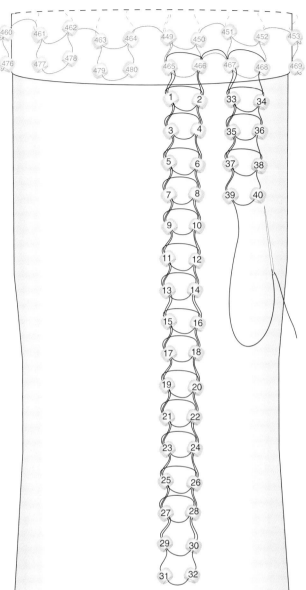

FIGURE 5

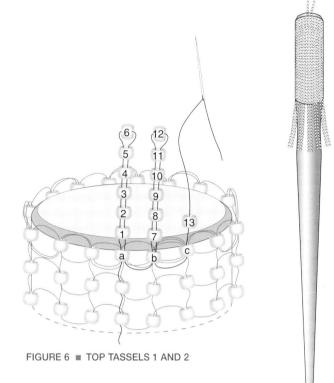

FIGURE 6 ■ TOP TASSELS 1 AND 2

4 Continue adding tassels and baselines where possible until the hair stick is full. Note that some tassels will point straight up and others will tilt somewhat.

MAKING THE SECOND HAIR STICK

1 Make the second hair stick in the same way, varying the formation of the tassels at top and bottom if you wish. (Carol used a set of scalloped tassels at the bottom of the second hair stick and twisted fringe embellished with bugle beads at the top. For instructions on making twisted fringe, see Figure 7 on page 142.)

FIGURE 7 ■ TOP TASSELS 17-19

AMBAI ISLAND BEADWORK, PAPUA, INDONESIAN NEW GUINEA

INSPIRATIONAL PIECE
Apron from Ambai Island in northwest Papua, Indonesian New Guinea

ARTIST
Mary Winters-Meyer

TECHNIQUES
Flat and Double-Layer Right Angle Weave

BEADWORK PROJECT
Sample diamond from Mary's "Elementary" Shawl shown on page 63

3⅞" wide x 3⅞" high

Red has never been more effectively used. In this early twentieth-century sireu, *it not only breaks the symmetry of the black scroll motifs, but it also injects a dash of vibrant color into an otherwise stark composition.*
15" wide x 18" high (not including drawstrings)
Private collection ■ TOM VAN EYNDE

For the most part, we know where our seed beads come from: the Czech Republic, perhaps, or Japan. We can buy them from any number of outlets: a local bead store, a regional bead show, a catalog merchant, or an internet site. They may be beautiful, but they are rarely mysterious. In remote parts of the world, where beads can be obtained only in small quantities at certain times of the year from itinerant foreign merchants, internet access is rare, and formal schooling is limited, there is more room for the imagination.

For example, natives of Ambai Island in the Cenderawasih Bay region of Papua, the Indonesian part of the island of New Guinea, believe that older European glass beads are seeds from a tree that grows in nearby coastal areas. Natives of the Humboldt Bay and Lake Sentani regions of Papua also envisioned magical bead trees, brought to the region long ago by ancestors who came from the east.

In reality, colorful glass beads from Europe and Asia have been filtering into remote Papua for centuries along ancient Chinese and Indian maritime trading routes. For the natives of northwest Papua, who make their living by fishing, hunting, and harvesting sago, taro, and other foodstuffs, these special beads from abroad have often commanded more attention, and carried more value, than locally made beads of shell, bone, seed, or wood.

Traditionally, without some of these special beads, a man from coastal northwest Papua could not hope to marry, for he was required to give his future wife several gifts: a necklace of large yellow glass beads, a shell bracelet, and an apron, called a *sireu*, made of European glass seed beads. His wife would wear this apron only during ceremonies or on other important occasions.

Of all the wedding gifts, the *sireu* was the most valuable. If a man could not inherit one from a female relative, he would have to purchase one at great expense or commission one from the natives of Ambai Island, where *sireu* were made by women skilled in the required multiple vertical thread technique, which orients beads at right angles.

Structurally, all *sireu* are alike. But stylistically, each *sireu* is different. Some reveal careful planning, and a preference for symmetry, as in the *sireu* shown on the facing page. Others are wildly asymmetrical, suggesting a looser, design-as-you-bead approach, as in the one shown to the left. Most make bold use of diamond and scroll motifs, combined in countless original ways that express a wealth of design ideas perfectly suited to the rectilinear nature of the beading technique. Once in a while, an abstract reptilelike figure appears in the center of an apron, perhaps to suggest a clan symbol. Otherwise, scholars are not sure how to interpret the motifs that appear on most *sireu*.

ABOVE The crisp geometrics of Ambai beadwork are instantly recognizable. But the meaning of the motifs, if any, is not known. A set of concentric diamonds, enlivened by small white or red dots, becomes the focal point of this sireu from ca. 1925.
22" wide x 26" high ■ Private collection ■ MAGGIE NIMKIN

LEFT Pictured here is an Ambai woman completing a sireu, ca. 1950. Photograph: Courtesy, Koninklijk Instituut voor de Tropen, Photodepartment No. (951):677.77: 666.27 N. 15.

AT FIRST, MARY WINTERS-MEYER WAS not inspired by the apron shown above. But soon, after scanning its image into her computer, she began playing with specific pattern elements until she had developed more than thirty variations of six basic patterns for small, diamond-shaped panels to be worked in single-needle right angle weave. To offset the complexity of these patterns, she limited the color palette to three colors: white, black, and red. Wanting to link the panels together to form a larger structure, she decided to make a triangular shawl with a scalloped upper edge. To give the shawl some texture, she situated the panels within three-dimensional borders formed of two intersecting layers of right angle weave rectangles. She had invented this clever double-layer approach several years earlier.

Eight months and thousands of stitches later, she finished her magnificent "Elementary" Shawl, shown to the right, which captures the design sensibility of the Papua apron while articulating an aesthetic of its own. With 136 small and 6 large diamonds, the shawl weighs nearly 10 pounds. Here, Mary shares her methods for making one of the small bordered diamonds. If you don't want to make a shawl, consider making a long, narrow scarf. Or back a single diamond with fabric and wear it as a pin or pendant.

For some beading projects, the will to finish is as important as the ability to conceive the design. Here, Mary Winters-Meyer's "Elementary" Shawl, beaded in 2002, more than repaid her eight months of effort.
64" wide x 37" high ■ Collection of the artist
RALPH GABRINER

Mary Winters-Meyer of Champaign, Ilinois, began beading in 1996. She quickly mastered the major techniques and went on to create new variations of her own. She teaches widely and is the author of *Linked Chain Stitch Basics*. For more information, see www.beadingbanshee.com.

SAMPLE OF "ELEMENTARY" SHAWL

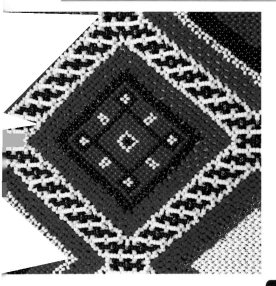

Here is a detail of the "Elementary" Shawl, showing a small diamond.
Collection of the artist
RALPH GABRINER

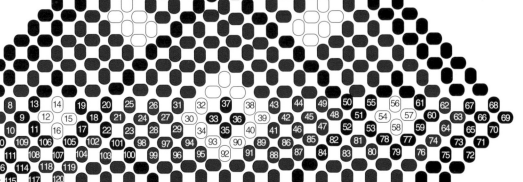

→ Row 1
← Row 2
→ Row 3

FIGURE 1

MATERIALS

(for one small bordered diamond, 3⁷⁄₈" wide by 3⁷⁄₈" high, in the "Elementary" Shawl)

15° Japanese seed beads

  4 grams red (for the patterned diamond and the connecting area)

  5 grams black (for the patterned diamond and the upper layer of the border)

  4.25 grams white (for the patterned diamond and the lower layer of the border)

24′ Silamide thread, black (optional: Use red for the red beads and white for the white beads.)

size 12 beading needles

MAKING THE PATTERNED DIAMOND

Mary believes that the patterned diamonds in the "Elementary" Shawl should be worked as diamonds, not as squares. Working them as squares will leave too many threads along their outer perimeters, which makes it harder to attach connecting rows later. Of the thirty or so patterns in the shawl, we focus on the one shown above, which is diagrammed in Figure 1. Mary advises beaders to make the bottom half of this diamond first, beginning with the center row, then turn it over and work on the top half. In this way you are always decreasing rows, which is easier than increasing. Each unit in this patterned diamond has 1 bead per side. In the center row and at the beginning of each row, add 3 beads per stitch. In the middle of each row, add 2 beads per stitch.

1 To begin, thread a needle about ¹⁄₃ of the way down a 5′ length of thread. Following Figure 2, string 4 black beads and make a square knot between beads 1 and 4, leaving a 4" tail. Go through beads 1, 2, and 3, and add beads 5 in black, 6 in red, and 7 in black. Go through beads 3, 5, and 6, and add beads 8 in red, 9 in black, and 10 in red. Pull tightly after every stitch. Continue working across Row 1, following Figure 1 for bead colors, until you have added beads 68, 69, and 70 and gone through beads 66, 68, 69, and 70.

2 To begin Row 2, first anchor Row 2 to Row 1, and at the same time position the needle to turn from right to left by going through beads 66, 67, 63, and 65. (See Figure 3.) Add beads 71–73, and go through beads 65, 71–73, and 64. Add beads 74 and 75, and go through beads 73, 64, and 74.

3 Continue in this way until you have added beads 112 and 113 and gone through bead 5. (See Figure 4.) To anchor Row 2 to Row 1 and to position the needle to turn from left to right, go through beads 6, 7, 3, 5, 110, and 111.

4 At this point, you can either continue with a little more anchoring by going through beads 109, 10, 110, and 111 and then starting Row 3, or you can start Row 3 immediately by adding beads 114, 115, and 116 and going through beads 111 and 114. To continue Row 3, add beads

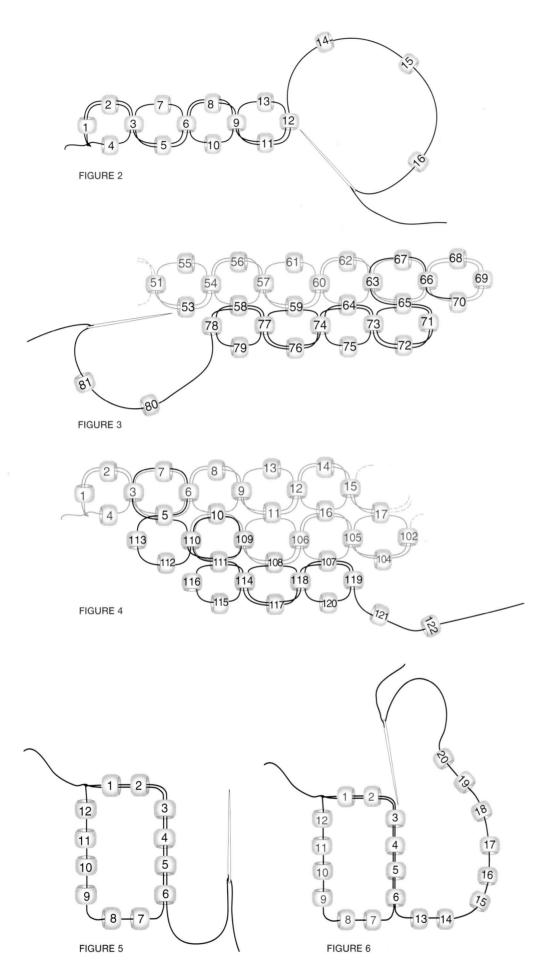

FIGURE 2

FIGURE 3

FIGURE 4

FIGURE 5

FIGURE 6

117 and 118 and go through beads 108, 114, 117, 118, and 107.

5 Continue adding rows in this way until you have reached the bottom tip of the patterned diamond. Anchor the thread by working the needle through nearby beads until it comes out of the left side of the red bead closest to the bottom. Then go through $1^{1}/_{2}$" to 2" of the red beads that run diagonally up to the left. Snip the thread. Anchor the tail thread between beads 1 and 4 by working it through nearby beads until it is secure, and snip.

6 To work the top half of the patterned diamond, you will need to add on a new length of thread. Thread a needle $^{1}/_{3}$ of the way down a 5′ length of thread. Anchor this thread by inserting it into the left side of the red bead nearest the bottom of the diamond, leaving a 2" tail. Then go through all of the red beads that run diagonally up to the right, until you come out of bead 63. Pull tightly on the 2" tail, and snip. Go through bead 67, and turn the patterned diamond upside down so that the beaded point faces upward. Turn Figure 1 upside down and follow it to bead the second half of the diamond just as you did the first.

MAKING THE DOUBLE-LAYER BORDER

The border consists of 2 intersecting layers of right angle weave rectangles. Each rectangle has 2 beads on the horizontal sides and 4 beads on the vertical sides, for a total of 12 beads per unit. You will make the lower layer first as a separate element, in the stepped-diamond pattern shown in Figure 10 on page 66. Then you will make the upper layer, intersecting it rectangle by rectangle with the lower layer. The result will be a piece of double-layer beadwork where both upper and lower layers show on either side of the piece.

MAKING THE LOWER LAYER OF THE BORDER *(white beads)*

1 Thread a needle $^{1}/_{3}$ of the way down a 9′ length of thread. Following Figure 5, begin the first row by stringing 12 beads and making a square knot between beads 1 and 12, leaving a 6" tail. Go through beads 1-6. Pull tightly after every stitch.

2 Following Figure 6, add beads 13-20.

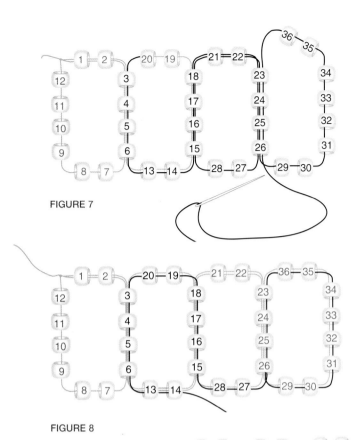

FIGURE 7

FIGURE 8

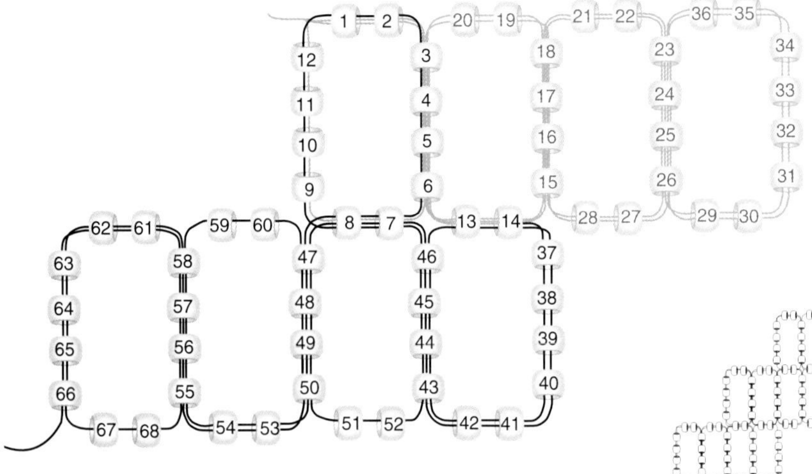

FIGURE 9

7 Follow Figure 10 to complete the rest of the lower layer. (You have already completed 3 rows in the upper left quadrant.) Anchor the thread by going through several rectangles until it is secure, and snip. Anchor the 6" tail thread in the same way, and snip.

MAKING THE UPPER LAYER OF THE BORDER (black beads)
The upper layer is worked in the same way as the lower layer, but it demands much closer attention. As you form the rectangles of the upper layer, you must cross them over and under the rectangles of the lower layer. Study Figure 11 carefully before you begin work so that you understand which beads in the upper layer sit above and which sit below, the beads in the lower layer.

1 Begin the upper layer by threading a needle $\frac{1}{3}$ of the way down a 9' length of thread. String 12 black beads and move them down to within 6" of the end of the thread. Holding the tail so the beads do not slip off, insert the needle down through the first rectangle of white beads at the left of Row 1 of the lower layer. Bring the needle up into the rectangle of white beads just below. Form a square knot between beads 1 and 12, pulling tightly. Beads 1-2, 7-8, and 9-12 will sit above the lower layer. Beads 3-6 will sit below it. (See Figure 11.)
2 Following Figure 12, continue working until you have finished intersecting the upper and lower layers. Pull tightly after every stitch. Anchor the threads in the upper layer, and snip.

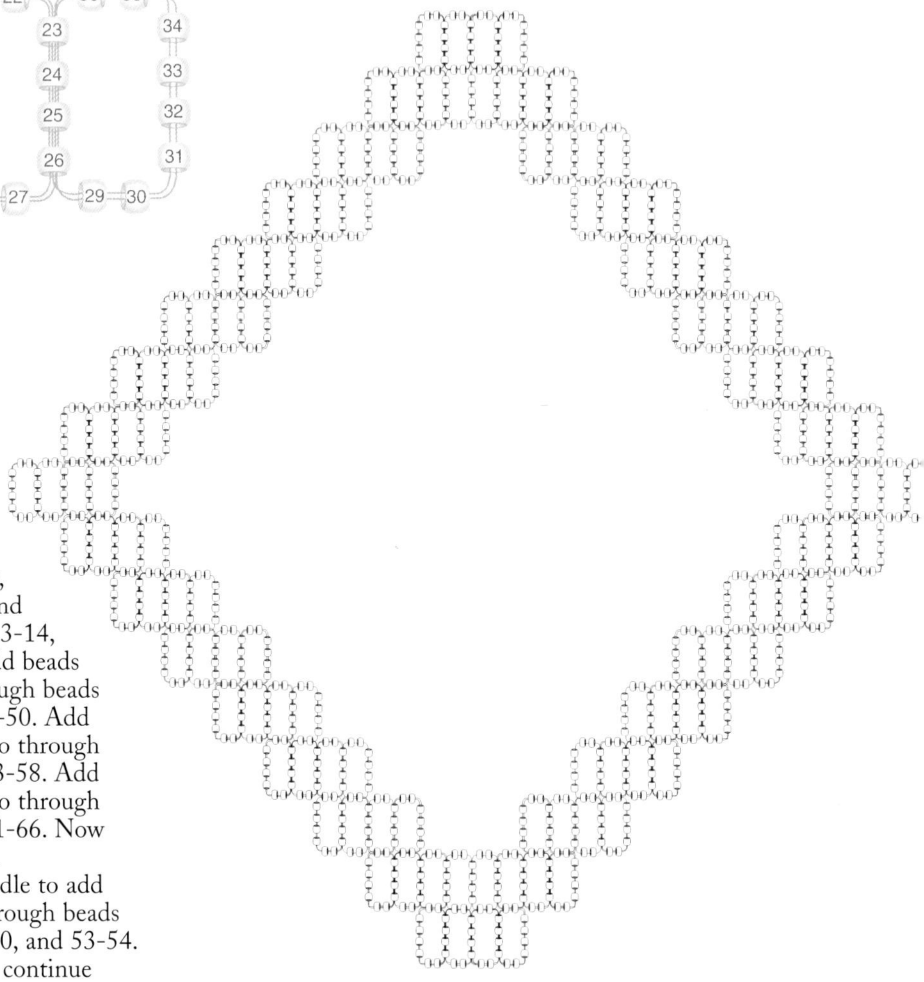

3 Following Figure 7, go through beads 3-6 and 13-18. Add beads 21-28, and go through beads 15-18 and 21-26. Add beads 29-36, and go through beads 23-26. Now the first row is in place.
4 Following Figure 8, reinforce the last rectangle in Row 1 by going through beads 29-36 and 23-26 again.
5 Row 2, and all subsequent rows, begin 2 rectangles in from the outer rectangle of the previous row. Position the needle to begin Row 2 by going through beads 27-28, 15-20,

3-6, and 13-14. Following Figure 9, add beads 37-46, and go through beads 13-14, 37-46, and 7-8. Add beads 47-52, and go through beads 43-46, 7-8, and 47-50. Add beads 53-60, and go through beads 47-50 and 53-58. Add beads 61-68, and go through beads 55-58 and 61-66. Now Row 2 is complete.
6 Position the needle to add Row 3 by going through beads 67-68, 55-60, 47-50, and 53-54. Add 10 beads, and continue working to finish Row 3.

FIGURE 10 ■ THE COMPLETED LOWER LAYER OF THE BORDER

THE CONNECTION AREA
(red beads)

According to Mary, connecting the double-layer border to the patterned diamond is "an inexact science at best," because "small changes in tension in either the border or the patterned diamond will create the need to change the number of beads" in the connections. In addition, the border is composed of beads sitting on two different planes, and this can also cause connections to vary. Although Figure 13 shows you how to make connecting rectangles composed of 2 vertical beads and 1 horizontal bead, you may have to make adjustments along the way, adding an extra bead here, or going through an extra bead or two there. The goal is to make

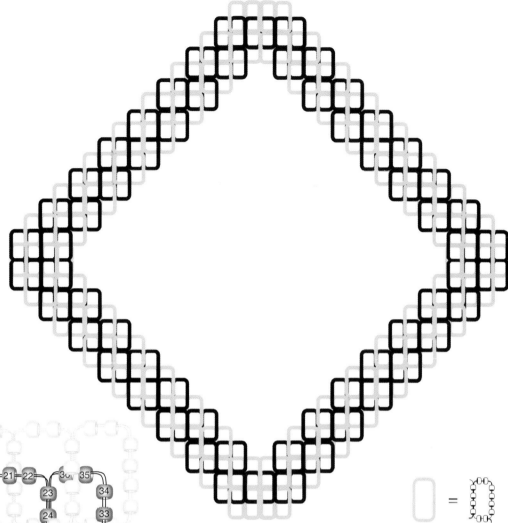

FIGURE 12 ■ THE INTERSECTING UPPER (BLACK) AND LOWER (WHITE) LAYERS OF THE BORDER

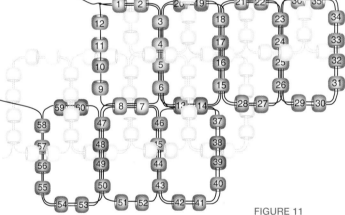

FIGURE 11

the beads in the connection area sit flat and look regular, but in reality, you may find that small inconsistencies are unavoidable. Mary doesn't worry about them. Instead, she believes that they make the piece more interesting.

1 Thread a needle ⅓ of the way down a 6′ length of thread. Following Figure 13, insert the needle up and down through several rectangles in the lower border area, leaving a 6" tail. Insert the needle through beads 1 and 2 of the lower layer, and add connecting beads 3-6. Reinforce by going back through beads 1-6, then beads 1-5. Add connecting beads 7-10, and go through beads 4-5 and 7-9. Go through beads 11

and 12 of the patterned diamond, and add connecting beads 13 and 14. Reinforce by going through beads 8-9, 11-14, and 8-10. Add connecting beads 15 and 16, and go through beads 17 and 18 of the patterned diamond. Add connecting bead 19, and go through beads 10, 15, and 16. Add connecting beads 20-22, and go through beads 3, 15-16, and 20-22. Go through beads 23-24 of the border's lower layer and beads 25-26 of the border's upper layer. Add connecting bead 27, and go through beads 21-26. Go through beads 28-31, and add connecting beads 32-34. Go through beads 28-34 and 27.

2 Continue working in this way until all of the connections are in place. Secure both ends of the thread, and snip.

FIGURE 13

AFRICAN AND MIDDLE EASTERN INSPIRATIONS

Pictured is a rear-view-mirror ornament made by male prisoners in the Cappadocia region of Turkey, ca. 1975, with a trio of songbirds worked in crochet and loomwork. Maşallah is an Arabic word meaning "may Allah ensure it," in this case, a safe journey.
3¼" wide x 7¾" high ■ Private collection
Tom van Eynde

As noted in "Highlights of Beadwork History," the world's oldest recorded beads, made of ostrich eggshell or marine shell some 40,000 or more years ago, come from Africa and the Middle East. This region has also provided the earliest definitive evidence of bead netting, which was known in Egypt by about 4,400 years ago and used to create the sumptuous wearable ornaments shown on the following pages.

Middle Eastern beadworking traditions are just as impressive as their African counterparts but not nearly as well documented. (Current usage varies considerably, but "Middle East" generally refers to countries extending from southwest and central Asia to North Africa, such as Afghanistan, Algeria, Cyprus, Egypt, Iran, Iraq, Israel, Jordan, Lebanon, Libya, Morocco, Pakistan, Syria, Turkey, and Yemen, and to countries in the Arabian peninsula, such as Bahrain, Kuwait, Oman, Qatar, Saudi Arabia, and the United Arab Emirates.) Even a brief glimpse reveals a dazzling variety of materials, techniques, objects, and cultures: aromatic cloves strung with coral or copal beads into multistrand necklaces among the Berber peoples of Morocco; glass beads netted to form a talismanic wall hanging among the Jews of Syrian Kurdistan; cast metal beads woven or twined into kohl containers among the Bedouin peoples of Saudi Arabia.

Another fascinating tradition emerged during World War I (1914-1918) among Turkish prisoners housed in jails in Egypt, Mesopotamia, Greece, and Britain's Isle of Man.

With European glass beads provided by camp authorities and knowledge of beading techniques obtained in camp classes, the prisoners crocheted beaded snakes and other items that were later sold through prison guards or in local shops (see the image on page 87). Beadwork was still being taught in Greek and Turkish prisons in the later twentieth century. In fact, the rear-view-mirror ornament shown to the left was collected from a prison in Turkey in the mid-1970s.

For many centuries cowrie shells (*Cypraea moneta* and also *Cypraea annulus*) have been used as beads in Africa and the Middle East. In some regions they are believed to ward off the evil eye; in others they symbolize fertility or wealth. In the Cameroon grasslands of western Africa, cowries were densely stitched to the surface of elephant masks, such as the one shown on the facing page, which were worn by members of secret societies during ritual dances that affirmed the power and prestige of the king. Long after the arrival of vast quantities of European glass seed beads in the nineteenth century, African and Middle Eastern beadworkers

continued to favor cowrie shell beads, as the Kirdi apron shown below, with its stark modern iconography, amply demonstrates. In some cases, however, cowrie shells lost out to glass beads, which came in sizes small enough to render the tapering contours of the Bakuba hat shown above with ease. What's more, European glass beads allowed African and Middle Eastern beadworkers to play with color as never before, as we will soon see.

BELOW The Kirdi peoples of Cameroon wove this mid-twentieth-century glass bead and cowrie shell apron, which sports unusual airplane motifs.
23" wide x 17½" high ■ Private collection
LARRY SANDERS

ABOVE This ingenious horned hat was made by the Bakuba peoples of the Democratic Republic of Congo (formerly Zaire) in the twentieth century of European glass beads netted over plaited canework.
18⅓" wide x 5⁷⁄₁₆" high x 12⅝" deep
Courtesy, The Field Museum, Neg. No. A114146c. Cat. No. 210195
DIANE ALEXANDER WHITE

RIGHT This is an early twentieth-century elephant mask of cowrie shells and cotton from the Bamileke peoples of the southern grasslands area of western Cameroon.
⅝" wide x 53⅛" high ■ Copyright, The Trustees of The British Museum Dept. of Ethnography. Given by the Wellcome Historical Medical Museum. Ethno. 1954, +23. 3445

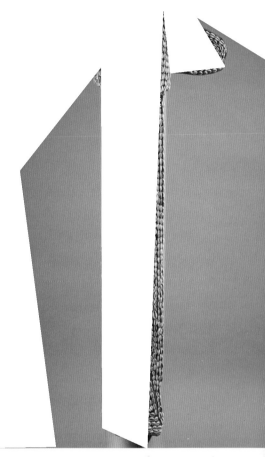

INSPIRATIONAL PIECE
Bracelets of Princess Sithathoryunet of Lahun, from the ancient Egyptian Middle Kingdom (2040-1640 B.C.E.)

ARTIST
Valerie Hector

TECHNIQUES
Peyote Stitch and Ladder Stitch

BEADWORK PROJECT
"Sithathoryunet" Bracelet I

1⅜" wide x 2¼" inner diameter

A majestic beaded belt was found intact in the tomb of Prince Ptahshepses of the Old Kingdom's Sixth Dynasty (ca. 2323-2150 B.C.E.). Ptahshepses is depicted in the clasp, which is inlaid with carnelian, obsidian, and turquoise. 1¾" wide x 35½" long ■ Courtesy, Egyptian Museum, Cairo. Cat. Gen. #87078

Long before the pyramids or the pharaohs who built them, the ancient Egyptians were doing beadwork, using techniques that have since become commonplace in many parts of the world. By about 4000 B.C.E., in the Badarian Period, Egyptian artisans were making simple belts by threading nine strands of beads, grouped in threes, through three-hole spacers.

Bead netting, involving the linking together of multiple rows or columns of beads with one or more threads, had developed by about 2500 B.C.E. in the Old Kingdom Period (2649-2134 B.C.E.). Judging by the bead-net dress shown on the facing page and its matching beaded broad collar, at least two netting techniques were in use: ladder stitch and an open diamond net. Bits and pieces of the dress were found with a matching beaded broad collar on the mummy of a female contemporary of King Khufu, or Cheops (ca. 2551-2528 B.C.E.), whose great pyramid still stands at Giza. Scholars believe such bead-net dresses may have been stitched to or slipped over plain linen garments. Many centuries after these dresses had gone out of fashion, Egyptian beadworkers used similar netting techniques to make mummy shrouds. (See the image on page 12.)

Another masterpiece of Old Kingdom beadwork is the Belt of Prince Ptahshepses, shown here, which features a panel of Egyptian faience, carnelian, and gold beads netted with gold wires and set in a gold band. The exact technique is not known, but the framing of a beadwork panel in gold suggests that the ancient Egyptians esteemed both materials equally. Thus, by about 2400 B.C.E., the Egyptians had mastered the craft of beadwork as it then existed, with at least three, and probably more, netting techniques at their disposal, and an aesthetic that favored lush colors and simple geometric motifs.

A very significant development, the emergence of three-dimensional beadwork, had taken place by the early Middle Kingdom Period (2040-1640 B.C.E.). One of the first examples is the Twelfth Dynasty (1991-1783 B.C.E.) Girdle of Senebtisy of Lisht (reign of Ammenemes I, 1991-1962 B.C.E.), which includes a long, tapering, zoomorphic tail of netted beadwork, possibly peyote stitch, over a wooden form. However, flat pieces of beadwork were still very common at this time.

Many fine fragments of Twelfth Dynasty beaded jewelry were recovered from the tomb of Princess Sithathoryunet of Lahun (reign of Ammenemes III, 1842-1797 B.C.E.) and later reconstructed to form exceptional pieces such as the bracelets shown on the facing page and a pair of matching anklets. In Sithathoryunet's lifetime, the use of multihole spacer plates was about two thousand years old. Dozens of small gold tube beads may have been threaded into her hair. She must have been radiant.

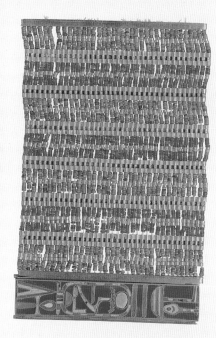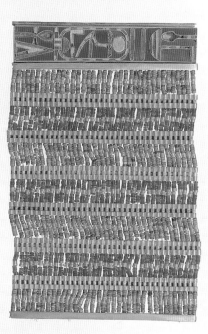

Pictured here are a pair of bracelets of ring beads from the Treasure of Lahun; Jewelry of Sithathoryunet. The clasps are inlaid with the cartouche of Amenemhat III.
From Lahun, BSA 8. Gold, carnelian, turquoise, blue and green paste.

Circumference: 12.5cm. Clasps, length: 8cm Courtesy, The Metropolitan Museum of Art, Rogers Fund and Henry Walters Gift, 1916. (16.1.8-.9). Photograph: Copyright 1983, The Metropolitan Museum of Art

EVERYTHING ABOUT THE BRACELETS of Sithathoryunet appeals to me but their flatness. I wanted to borrow the spacer structure for a bracelet of my own, but with greater dimensionality. Peyote stitch tubes seemed like an ideal material for this purpose. It was easy to make spacers from ladder-stitched peyote tubes and then connect the ladders with individual tubes. It was also easy to weave the tubes in peyote stitch, as I did in "Sithathoryunet" Bracelet II, shown on page 72.

Instructions for "Sithathoryunet" Bracelet I, also on page 72, follow. First, you will learn how to make the basic element, a four-bead-wide-by-fourteen-bead-tall peyote tube. Then you can follow the directions for the bracelet, adding or subtracting length according to the size of your own wrist or modifying the design to suit your own taste.

LEFT Bead-net dresses were fashionable in Old Kingdom Egypt. This reconstructed example, recovered from a Dynasty IV burial, is overlaid with a beaded broad collar and consists of about seven thousand Egyptian faience beads, now faded from their original blue.

Dynasty 4, reign of Khufu (2551-2528 B.C.E.) found at Giza, tomb G7440Z. 17⁵⁄₁₆" wide x 44 ½" high Museum of Fine Arts, Boston. Harvard University—Boston Museum of Fine Arts Expedition. 27.1548. Courtesy, Museum of Fine Arts, Boston. Reproduced with permission. Photograph © 2004 Museum of Fine Arts, Boston

"SITHATHORYUNET" BRACELET I

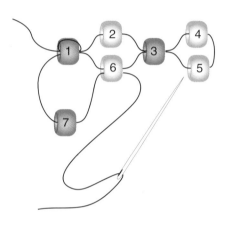

FIGURE 1

"Sithathoryunet" Bracelet I, the project bracelet, is shown to the right and II to the left.
Collection of the artist ■ LARRY SANDERS

TIPS

- *For the gold beads in my bracelet, I used 1.4mm hex-cut base metal beads with a 22-karat gold coating. Because these beads are expensive and hard to find, you might want to use cylinder seed beads instead, in a lined or galvanized gold, as called for in the instructions. They can be faceted or unfaceted. If you do use the 1.4mm hex-cut gold, you will need about four times as many of them as you would of the cylinder seed beads. Also, since the 1.4mm hex-cuts are smaller in size, you will have to create tubes that are 6 beads wide by 14 beads high.*

- *For the silver beads in my bracelet, I used antique French faceted aluminum beads. Whether faceted or not, lined or galvanized cylinder seed beads make an excellent substitute.*

- *For many years I have been using Coats & Clark brand cotton/polyester hand-quilting thread for all netting stitches, because it is strong, does not stretch, and comes in different colors. It is available at fabric stores. You can also use Nymo B thread.*

- *There are many kinds of elastic thread on the market. I found that Beadalon's 0.8mm "Elasticity" works well for these bracelets. It allows the bracelet to expand (but not too much), does not break easily, and knots well. The 0.5mm weight is too thin; the 1mm weight is too thick.*

- *The "Sithathoryunet" Bracelet should fit most medium-sized wrists. You can increase or reduce the sizes as needed.*

MAKING A PEYOTE RECTANGLE

There are two ways to make a peyote tube. You can start with a flat rectangle of peyote stitch and roll it into a tube, or start with a ring of beads and form the tube by working downward from the ring. I have always used the first method, because it works best for me. (You can learn the second method in Figures 1-3 on page 78).

1 To make a sample peyote rectangle, start with cylindrical seed beads in two colors, say turquoise and bronze. You will need 14 beads of each color. Thread a size 10 needle down a 24" length of thread, then wax and double the thread. String 4 beads— 1 turquoise, 1 bronze, 1 turquoise, 1 bronze—and slide them down to within 4" of the tail. Make an overhand knot around bead 1. You will undo this knot later. The beads you have just added will form Rows 1 and 2 of the rectangle. Due to the way peyote stitch works, beads 2 and 4 will make up Row 1, and beads 1 and 3 will form Row 2.

2 Following Figure 1, begin Row 3 by adding bead 5 in bronze and going back through bead 3. Pull tightly so that there is no extra thread between any of the beads. Add bead 6 in bronze, and go through bead 1. Again, check to see that the beads sit tightly against one another.

3 Start the next row by adding bead 7 in turquoise and going through bead 6. Add bead 8 in turquoise, and go through bead 5.

Row

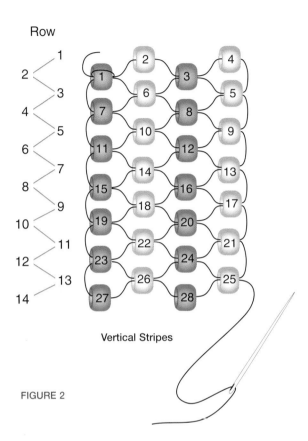

Vertical Stripes

FIGURE 2

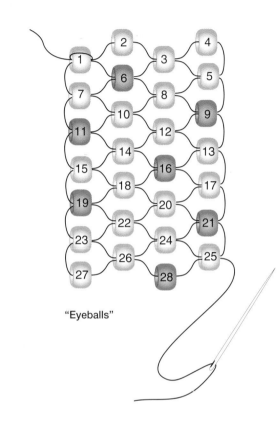

"Eyeballs"

4 Continue working in this way, and watch the pattern of vertical stripes emerge. (See Figure 2, left.) Stop working when you have added a total of 28 beads. Leave the needle on the working end of the thread while you anchor the tail end of the thread. To anchor the tail, first undo the knot around bead 1. Then thread a size 10 needle onto both threads of the tail, and go through beads 7, 10, 12, 13, 17, 20, and 22. Snip the tail threads close to the beads. The rectangle is now complete.

TURNING THE RECTANGLE INTO A TUBE

Now you are ready to turn the rectangle into a tube.

1 Bring the two serrated edges of the rectangle toward each other until they are nearly touching. Note how

perfectly the edges interlock. The next step is to close the seam by stitching in a zigzag pattern up and down from one edge to the next. Do this at least twice to make the seam secure.

2 Following Figure 3, insert the needle that is coming out of bead 25 through beads 4, 28, 2, and 27. Pull tightly. Make a second pass across the seam by going through beads 1, 26, 3, and 25. Pull tightly, making sure all beads are aligned properly and no extra threads remain between beads. Next, anchor the thread by going through beads 4, 3, 6, 7, and then 11, 14, and 16. Snip the thread. Check the tube: If it collapses, you have not used tight enough tension. The tubes for the bracelet should be as stiff as possible.

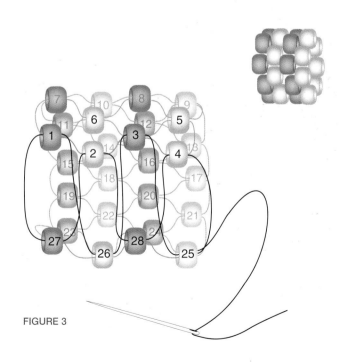

FIGURE 3

"SITHATHORYUNET" BRACELET I

The instructions below will make a medium bracelet that is $1^3/_8$" wide by $2^1/_4$" diameter. It expands to about $2^3/_4$" diameter. As you begin to assemble the bracelet, check to see if the size is right for your wrist. If not, you can add or subtract tubes accordingly.

MATERIALS

Cylinder seed beads

- 1.5 grams silver (lined or galvanized)
- 3 grams Ceylon beige
- 8.5 grams gold (lined or galvanized)
- 1.5 grams metallic light bronze
- 8.5 grams matte red aurora borealis
- 12 grams matte black
- 1.5 grams matte turquoise aurora borealis

1 spool cotton/polyester hand-quilting thread, black, or 2 spools Nymo B thread, black

1 spool 0.8mm Elasticity elastic thread, black

1 embroidery needle with an eye large enough to accommodate the elastic thread

size 10 needles

wax

MAKING THE PEYOTE STITCH TUBES

Make a total of 216 4-by-14 peyote stitch tubes in the following patterns. (See Figure 4.)

- 54 solid gold
- 36 Ceylon beige with matte black stripe
- 18 matte turquoise and bronze stripe
- 54 matte black with silver "eyeballs"
- 54 matte red with matte black "eyeballs"

MAKING THE 6-TUBE LADDER STITCH SPACERS

These 6-tube spacers are made very much like the bead ladders in Figure 1 on page 42 and Figure 1 on page 58. The only difference is that instead of using a single bead, you will be using a peyote stitch tube. Also, you will reinforce the ladder spacer by passing the thread through all six of the tubes a second time. All of the spacers are made of tubes worked in matte black with silver eyeballs. (See Figure 2, right side, on page 73.)

1 To make a ladder stitch spacer, thread a needle onto a 48" length of thread, then wax and double the thread to create a 24" length. String Tube 1, and slide it down to within 6" of the end. Tie an overhand knot around this tube, leaving a 6"-long tail. You will undo the knot later.

2 Following Figure 5, add Tube 2. Go back through Tube 1, then through Tube 2. (If you get confused, look again at Figure 1 on page 42 or Figure 1 on page 58, because the thread path is the same.) Add Tube 3, and go back through Tubes 2 and 3. Pull tightly, making sure the sides of the tubes press against one another. Continue working until you have added Tube 6 and gone back through Tubes 5 and 6.

3 To reinforce the ladder, you must make a second pass through each of the tubes. With the needle coming out of Tube 6, go back through Tubes 5, 4, 3, 2, and 1. Now anchor the working end of the thread by going back through Tubes 2 and 3 and making several overhand knots around

the thread that connects these tubes. Snip the thread. Anchor the tail end of the thread by first undoing the knot around Tube 1, then threading a needle onto the two strands of the tail. Next, go through Tubes 1 and 2, and make several overhand knots around the thread that connects these tubes.

4 Make a total of 9 ladder stitch spacers in this way.

STRINGING THE TUBES AND LADDER SPACERS

This bracelet consists of 6 rings composed of 27 colored tubes and 9 black/silver spacers, all connected with a long elastic thread that moves first clockwise, then counterclockwise, then clockwise again, changing direction at the start of every ring.

1 To begin Ring 1, cut a 68" length of elastic and thread an embroidery needle onto it. Following Figure 6, string 1 gold tube and slide it down to within 8" of the end of the thread. Make an overhand knot around this tube, which is Tube a of Row 1. You will undo the knot later. Insert

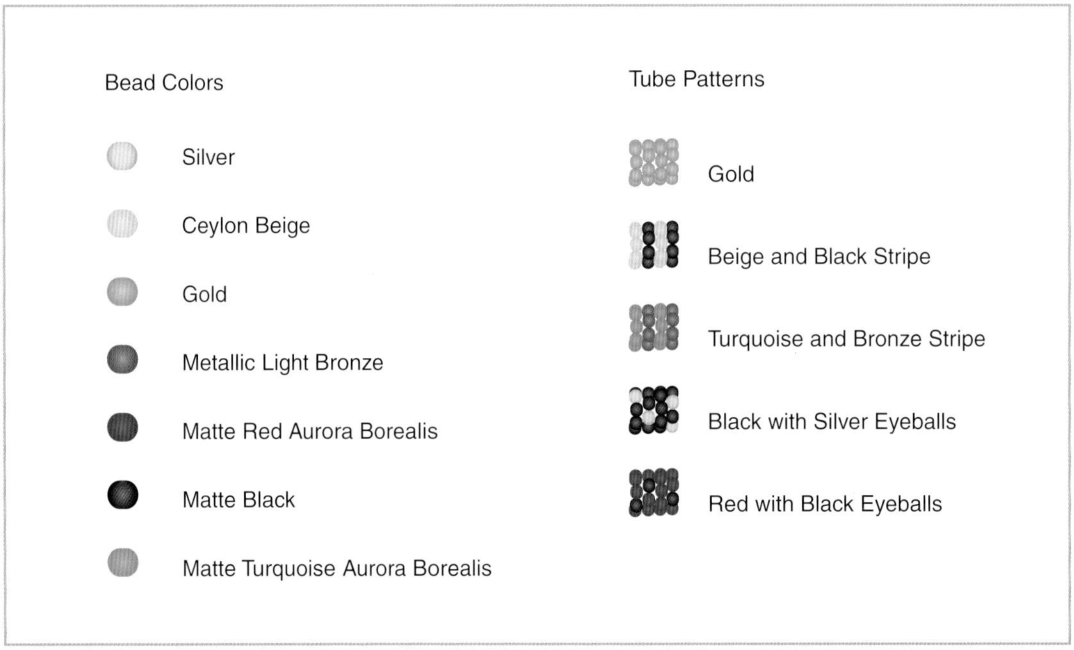

Bead Colors

Silver

Ceylon Beige

Gold

Metallic Light Bronze

Matte Red Aurora Borealis

Matte Black

Matte Turquoise Aurora Borealis

Tube Patterns

Gold

Beige and Black Stripe

Turquoise and Bronze Stripe

Black with Silver Eyeballs

Red with Black Eyeballs

FIGURE 4

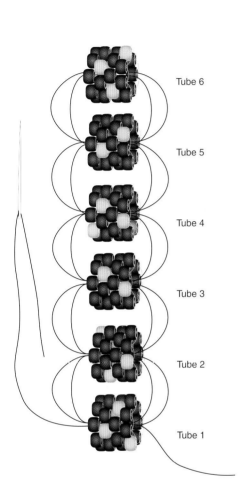

Tube 6
Tube 5
Tube 4
Tube 3
Tube 2
Tube 1

FIGURE 5

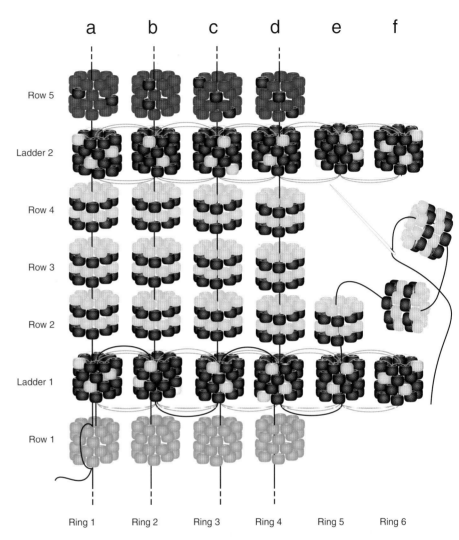

a   b   c   d   e   f

Row 5

Ladder 2

Row 4

Row 3

Row 2

Ladder 1

Row 1

Ring 1   Ring 2   Ring 3   Ring 4   Ring 5   Ring 6

FIGURE 6

the needle through Tube a in Ladder 1. String 3 beige/black tubes, and go through Tube a in Ladder 2. String 3 red/black tubes, and go through Tube a in Ladder 3. Pull tightly.

2 Continue working your way around the bracelet, adding 6 more ladder spacers and 6 more sets of 3 tubes each in these colors: gold, beige/black, red/black, gold, turquoise/bronze, red/black.

3 After you have gone through Tube a in Ladder 9, add 2 gold tubes, and go back through Tube a of Row 1. Then go through Tube a in Ladder 1 again. Insert the elastic down through Tube b in Ladder 1.

4 Begin working Ring 2 by going in the opposite direction from Ring 1. Add 3 gold tubes, and go through Tube b in Ladder 9.

5 Continue working your way around the bracelet until you have added Tube b of Row 2. Go down through Tube b in Ladder 1, then up through Tube c in Ladder 1.

6 Next, start Ring 3, moving in the opposite direction once again, by adding 3 beige/black tubes and going through Tube c in Ladder 2.

7 Continue adding rings until the bracelet is complete.

Anchor the working end of the elastic by going through the tubes in an entire ring and then making two overhand knots around the threads connecting 2 tubes in any ladder spacer. Anchor the tail by undoing the knot around Tube a of Row 1, threading a needle onto the elastic, and going through at least 9 tubes. Then knot the elastic around the threads between 2 tubes in any ladder spacer.

INSPIRATIONAL PIECE
*Hassock of King Tutankhamun
from the ancient Egyptian
New Kingdom (1550-1070 B.C.E.)*

ARTIST
Joyce Scott

TECHNIQUES
*Flat and Tubular Peyote Stitch
and Fringing*

BEADWORK PROJECT
"Bound" Earrings

*1¾" wide x 4⅛" high x ⅝" diameter
(dimensions of the figure)*

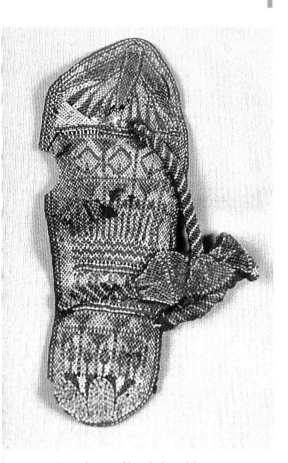

Several pairs of beaded sandals were recovered from the tomb of King Tutankhamun. The leather soles and straps of this intact example are covered with netted beads of Egyptian faience worked into lotus and papyrus plant and flower motifs. This technique may be what we would call peyote stitch.

8" high ■ Courtesy, The Egyptian Museum, Cairo. Cat. Gen. #85a

W hen did beadworkers first depict the human form? It is impossible to say. Although figurative beadwork had probably been invented hundreds of years earlier, no examples have yet been documented before the time of King Tutankhamun, who ruled Egypt from 1333-1323 B.C.E., during the New Kingdom (1550-1070 B.C.E.). King Tut was entombed with many pieces of beadwork, among them the hassock or footstool shown below. It depicts two captives shown in profile, with their necks and arms tied to their painfully arched backs. Their discomfort is palpable; we wince to see them suffer.

But this is not just the first recorded appearance in beadwork of the full human form. The hassock also represents the culmination of advances in beadwork techniques that facilitated not only the production of circular and three-dimensional formats, but also the curvilinear contouring needed to render the human body naturalistically. What's more, beadwork motifs were now liberated from their beaded backgrounds to become freestanding entities in their own right that could be applied, like the cobras to the right, to any surface. Thus, by 1323 B.C.E. beadwork had matured into a powerful medium for expressing many aspects of the human condition.

ABOVE, RIGHT Four faience-and-gold beadwork cobras, possibly worked in what is today called peyote stitch and symbolizing the cobra goddess Wadjet, adorned the linen headdress (now disintegrated) that King Tutankhamun wore to the tomb. Here, the cobras are shown atop the king's skull.
Photograph: Courtesy, The Griffith Institute, Oxford

BELOW, RIGHT Egypt's African and Asiatic enemies are recurring motifs of ancient Egyptian art. Here, they appear on a hassock made of netted Egyptian faience beads attached to a foundation of rushwork and linen found intact in the tomb of King Tutankhamun. This may be what is now called peyote stitch.
11⅜" diameter ■ Courtesy, The Egyptian Museum. Cat. Gen. #354

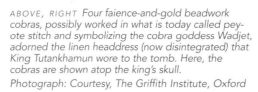

DESPITE ALL OF THEIR ACHIEVEMENTS, it seems that ancient Egyptian beadworkers never quite made the leap from producing flat, or two-dimensional, human figures to making them fully three-dimensional, or in the round. We don't know where or when that development took place. When it comes to modern figurative beadwork, the greatest artist of all is Joyce Scott, who uses peyote stitch both flat and in the round to create wearable art or sculpture showing human figures caught at revealing moments. In fact, Joyce single-handedly launched the American figurative beadwork movement in the late twentieth century.

Joyce traces her influences to the figurative beadwork of the Yorùbá peoples of Nigeria, whose primary technique was not peyote stitch, but sewing. Yet, while the Yorùbá, like the ancient Egyptians, deployed figurative beadwork to underscore political or religious authority, Joyce uses it to deliver biting social and political commentary. When asked to respond to King Tut's hassock with a piece of her own, Joyce Scott readily agreed, knowing it would allow her to revisit a theme of long-standing interest: man's inhumanity to man. Because some of her African-American ancestors were slaves, this theme has deep personal significance to Joyce, and she has touched upon it in numerous pieces over the years. In her "'Til All Are Free, None Are Free" Necklace, pictured here, she positions the wafer-thin body of a dark-skinned slave within the muscular grasp of a light-skinner master. She also brings the face of the master into the equation. But he is staring off into space, oblivious of the human whose life he controls. As usual, Joyce cleverly manipulates dimensionality, allowing the three-dimensionality of the master to affirm his dominance just as the two-dimensionality of the slave signals his powerlessness. Yet, in an ironic twist, the master is disembodied. Only his face and hands are shown; he is not fully human.

Again in her "Bound" Earrings, shown on page 78, Joyce plays with dimensionality and color symbolism to advance a similar message. If you have never worked with the human figure before, this is a great place to begin. As you craft these asymmetrical earrings, you will quickly catch on to the increases and decreases needed to breathe life into one of Joyce's human forms. Like most of us, they are often slightly imperfect. Joyce would not have it any other way.

As if to allow the wearer to feel the dehumanizing effects of slavery, Joyce Scott fashioned her "'Til All Are Free, None Are Free" Necklace of 2002—made of glass, plastic, and metal beads—slightly too small to wear comfortably. 11" wide x 12" high x 2½" deep Collection of the artist ■ LARRY SANDERS

Joyce Scott of Baltimore, Maryland, is a renowned visual and performance artist whose works address contemporary social, political, and personal issues. It was Joyce who first explored the use of three-dimensional peyote stitch to render armatureless, asymmetrical forms such as the human body; and her pieces are avidly collected. Over the years she has shared her techniques with hundreds of beadworkers. She is the author of *Fearless Beading*.

"BOUND" EARRINGS

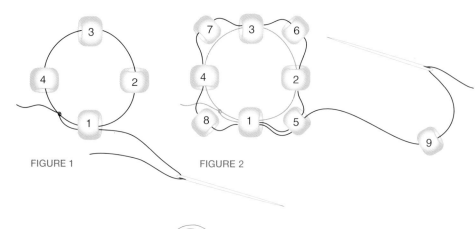

FIGURE 1   FIGURE 2

Shown are Joyce Scott's asymmetrical "Bound" Earrings, of glass beads, felt, sterling silver, and surgical steel.
Private collection ■ *LARRY SANDERS*

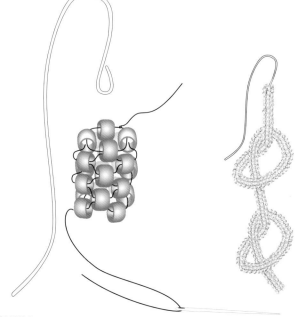

FIGURE 3

MATERIALS

Cylinder seed beads

    4 beads white pearl aurora
      borealis

    4 grams Ceylon beige

    39 beads gold luster
      transparent dark red

    5 grams matte metallic
      bronze

1 bobbin Nymo B thread

size 10 or 12 needles

wax

1 small disk felt or leather,
³/₈" diameter

2" 20 gauge round sterling silver wire, bent to the shape shown in Figure 3 and with ends filed smooth, or any commercial earring wire with a loop at the bottom

1 sterling silver or surgical steel earring post with a 10mm round pad (see Figure 12 on page 83)

1 sterling silver or surgical steel ear nut (See Figure 12)

To simplify the instructions, I have used these abbreviations.

    a = add

    gt = go through

    gbt = go back through

    sar = stitch across row,
      adding beads as usual

MAKING THE ROPE

The rope earring is made of one long peyote stitch tube knotted at two intervals. The entire rope is worked in Ceylon beige beads.

1 To begin, thread a needle onto an 80" length of thread, then wax and double it to form a 40" length.

2 Following Figure 1, string 4 beads, and make a square knot between beads 1 and 4. Leave a little slack between the beads or it will be hard to work the next few rows.

3 Following Figure 2, a bead 5, and gt bead 2. a bead 6, and gt bead 3. a bead 7, and gt bead 4. a bead 8, and gt beads 1 and 5. Now the first two rows are in place, but the rope still looks like a flat circle of beads.

4 Continue beading, adding bead 9 and going through bead 6, adding bead 10 and going through bead 7, adding bead 11 and going through bead 8, adding bead 12 and going through beads 5 and 9. The circle is turning itself into

a tube; help things along by adjusting the positions of the beads. Pull tightly at the end of each row, but try to leave some slack in the rope as it grows so that it will be supple enough to knot when the time comes. Keep adding rows until the rope is about 6¹/₂" long.

5 Leave the needle and thread in place. Following Figure 3, insert the ear wire down into the end of the tube nearest the needle, and stitch the wire in place. Form two open overhand knots in the rope as shown in Figure 3, and stitch them in place.

6 Undo the knot around bead 1, thread a needle onto the two threads in the tail, and anchor it by going through adjacent beads until it is secure. Then snip. Anchor the working end of the thread in the same way. Then snip.

MAKING THE FACE AND HAIR

1 The face is easy to make. To begin, thread a needle onto a 56" length of thread, then wax and double it to form a 28" length. String 12 matte metallic bronze beads, and move them down to within 6" of the end of the thread.

2 Make an overhand knot around bead 1, and follow Figure 4 to add beads 13-122. The only beads that will not be matte metallic bronze will be either white pearl for the eyes (beads 26, 27, 32, 33), or gold luster dark red for the nose (beads 71 and 73) and the mouth (beads 98, 103, 104, 109). When you are finished, anchor the thread by going through beads 118, 112, 111, 101, 89, and 88, and snip. Undo the knot around bead 1. Anchor the tail thread, and snip.

3 To add the hair, thread a needle onto a 20" length of thread, then wax and double the thread. Following Figure 5, insert the needle into bead 29, and gt beads 20, 18, 19, and 1. a beads 123 and 124, and gt beads 123, 1, and 2.a bead 125, and gt bead 4. a bead 126, and gt bead 6. sar until you have added bead 129. gt bead 12, and a beads 130-131. gt beads 130, 12, and 129. a bead 132, and gt bead 128.

4 Continue working in this way until you have finished the hair. Anchor both threads, and snip.

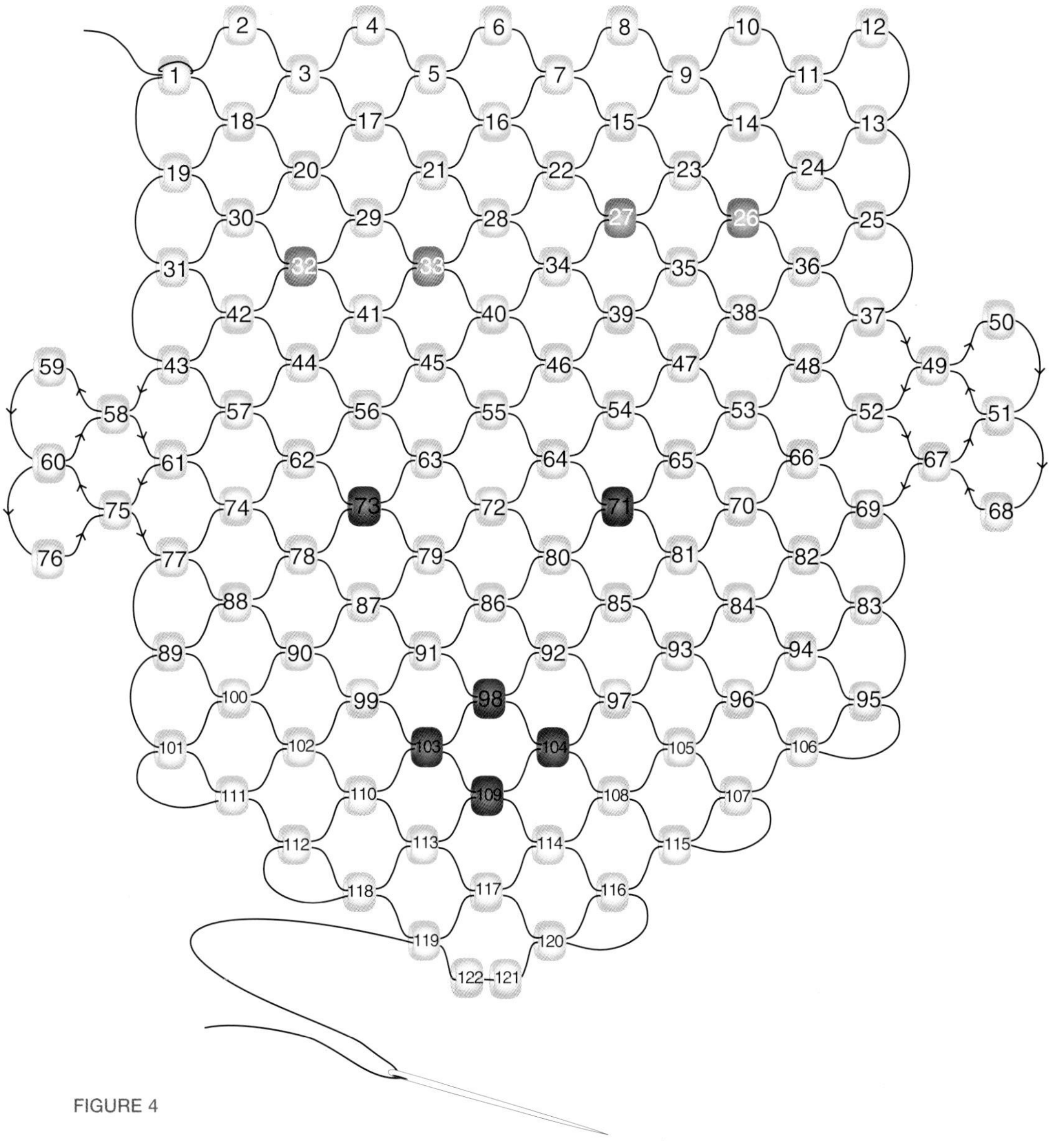

FIGURE 4

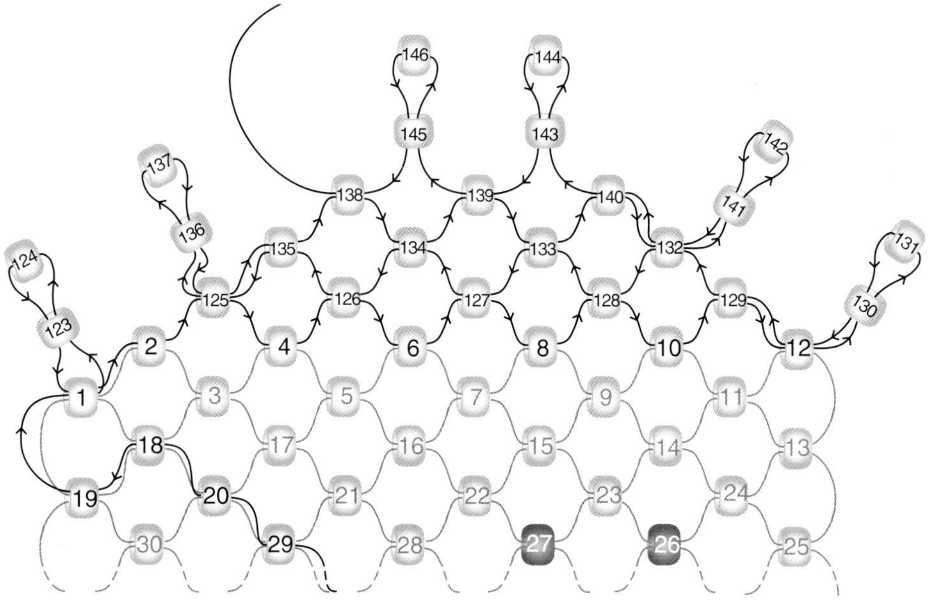

FIGURE 5

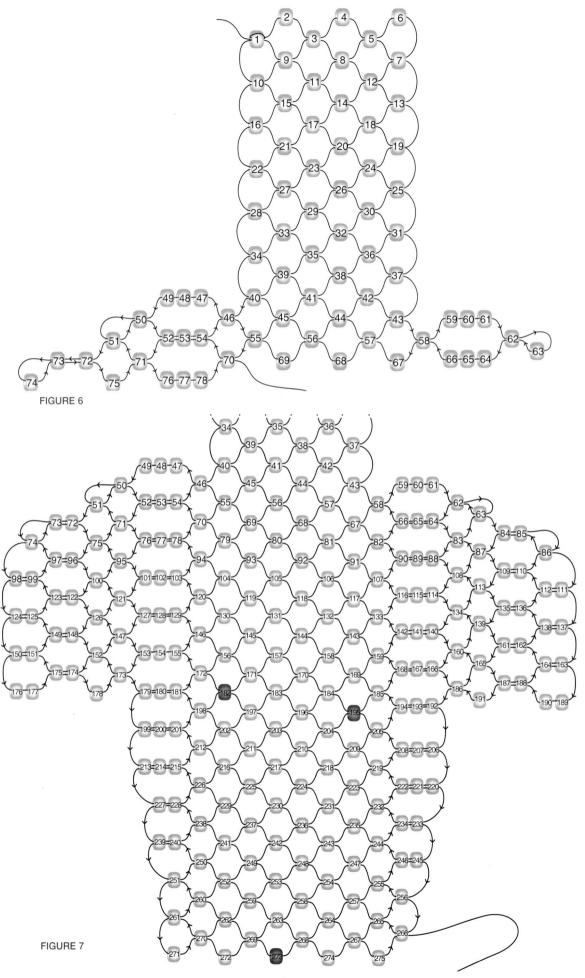

FIGURE 6

FIGURE 7

MAKING THE NECK AND SHOULDERS

Here you will learn how Joyce increases the width of rows by adding two or three beads per stitch. (It's a lot easier than it looks.) Like the face, the body is worked mostly in bronze beads, with occasional accents of red.

1 To begin, thread a needle onto a 76" length of thread, then wax and double the thread to form a 38" length. To begin, string 6 bronze beads, and move them down to within 6" of the end of the thread, making an overhand knot around bead 1.

2 Following Figure 6, a beads 7-40, pulling tightly after each row. To begin the left shoulder, a 46-51, gbt 50. Pull tightly after this and all steps. a 52-54, gt 46. sar. a 58-63, gbt 62. a 64-66, gt 58. a 67, gt 57. sar. a 70, gt 54-52. a 71, gt 51. a 72-74, gbt 73-72. a 75, gt 71. a 76-78, gt 70. Anchor the thread by going back through beads 55, 69, 56, 68, 57, and 67. Then snip. Undo the knot around bead 1, then anchor both threads, and snip.

MAKING THE TORSO

Here you will continue increasing until you have finished the shoulders and upper arms. Then you will begin decreasing as you approach the waist. You will add one bead per stitch in the center of the torso, and two or three beads per stitch at either side. Do not be surprised if threads are left showing above or below certain beads. If you follow the instructions carefully, you will have no trouble. All of the beads are bronze except for beads 182, 195, and 273, which are red.

1 To begin, thread a needle onto a 92" length of thread, then double and wax the thread to form a 46" length of thread. Following Figure 6, insert the needle from right to

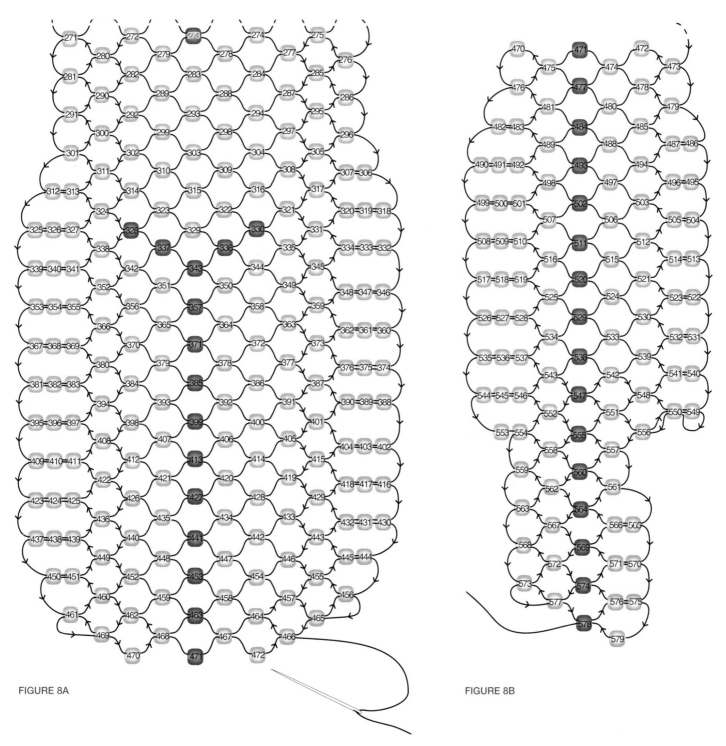

FIGURE 8A

FIGURE 8B

left through beads 30, 32, 35, 39, 40, and 46. Then go from left to right through bead 70, leaving a 6" tail from bead 30.

2 Following Figure 7, a 79, gt 69. sar. a 82, gt 66-64. a 83, gt 63. a 84-86, gbt 85 and 84. a 87, gt 83. a 88-90, gt 82. sar. a 94, gt 78-76. a 95, gt 75. a 96-97, gt 74. a 98-99, gt 97-96. a 100, gt 95. a 101-103, gt 94. sar. a 107. gt 90-88. a 108, gt 87. a 109-110, gt 86. a 111 and 112, gt 110-109. a 113, gt 108. a 114-116, gt 107. sar. a

120, gt 103-101. a 121, gt 100. a 122-123, gt 99-98. a 124-125, gt 123-122. a 126, gt 121. a 127-129, gt 120. sar. a 133, gt 116-114. a 134, gt 113. a 135-136, gt 112-111. a 137-138, gt 136-135. a 139, gt 134. a 140-142, gt 133. sar. a 146, gt 129-127. a 147, gt 126. a 148-149, gt 125-124. a 150-151, gt 149-148. a 152, gt 147. a 153-155, gt 146. sar. a 159, gt 142-140. a 160, gt 139. a 161-162, gt 138-137. a 163-164, gt 162-161. a 165, gt 160.

a 166-168, gt 159. sar. a 172, gt 155-153. a 173, gt 152. a 174-175, gt 151-150. a 176-177, gt 175-174. a 178, gt 173. a 179-181, gt 172. sar. a 185, gt 168-166. a 186, gt 165. a 187-188, gt 164-163. a 189-190, gt 188-187. a 191, gt 186. a 192-194, gt 185. Continue working in this way until you have added bead 275 and gone through bead 266. Anchor and snip.

MAKING THE LOWER TORSO AND LEGS

1 Thread a needle onto a 92"

length of thread, then wax and double the thread. Following Figure 7, insert the needle from left to right through beads 229, 237, 242, 248, 254, 257, 265, and 266, leaving a 6" tail from bead 229.

2 Following Figures 8a and 8b, add beads 276-597. Do not be surprised if threads show above or below beads. Work the shaded beads in red and all others in bronze. When you are finished, anchor both threads, and snip.

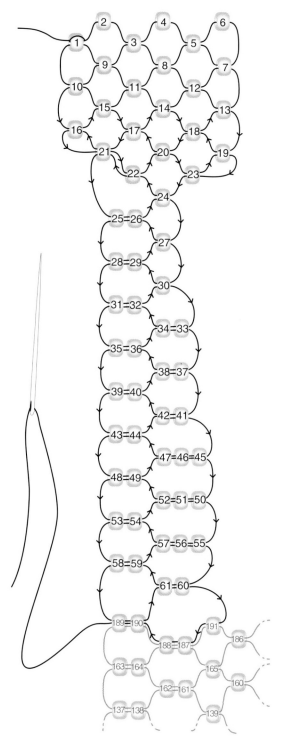

FIGURE 9A

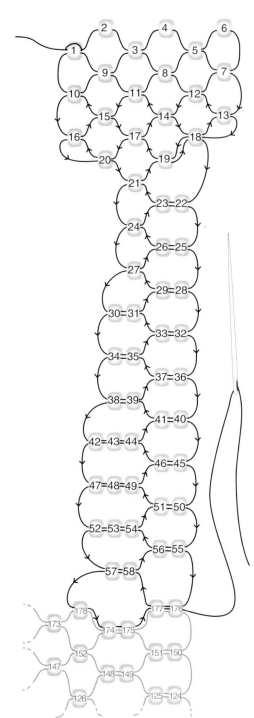

FIGURE 10A

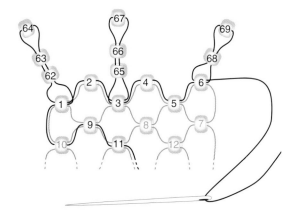

FIGURE 9B ■ FINGERS

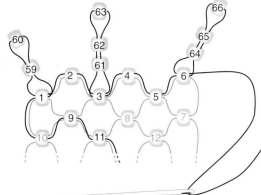

FIGURE 10B ■ FINGERS

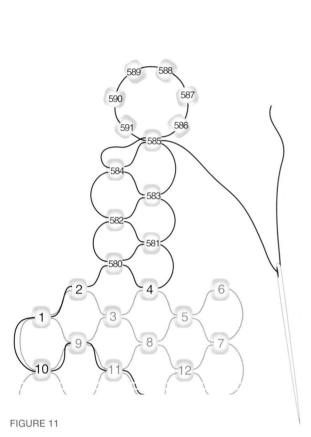

FIGURE 11

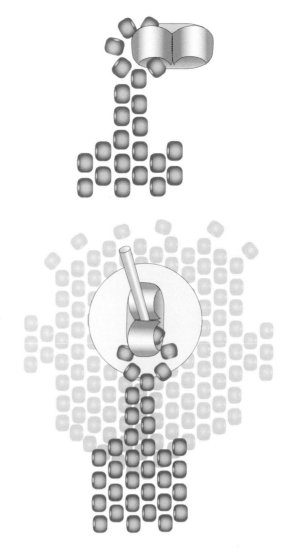

FIGURE 12

MAKING THE LEFT ARM, HAND, AND FINGERS

1 Thread a needle onto a 30" length of thread, then wax and double the thread. Following Figure 9a, make the left arm and then attach it to the left shoulder by stitching from beads 59-58 through beads 189-190, 61-60, 191, 187-188, and 190-189. Anchor the thread by going through beads 58-59, 57-55, 50-52, 49-48, and 43-44. Then snip. Undo the knot around bead 1, anchor, and snip.

2 To add the fingers, thread a needle onto a 20" length of thread, then wax and double the thread. Following Figure 9b, insert the needle through beads 11, 9, 10, and 1, leaving a 6" tail from bead 11. Add the fingers as shown, and anchor the thread by going through beads 7, 5, 8, 3, 9, 1, and 10. Then snip. Snip the tail end close to bead 11.

MAKING THE RIGHT ARM AND FINGERS

1 Following Figure 10a, pre-pare the right arm and stitch it to the right shoulder. Add the fingers as shown. Once the two arms are in place, bind the hands together. To do this, thread a needle onto an 18" length of thread. Wax and double the thread.

2 String 11 Ceylon beige beads, and work them down to within 4" of the end of the thread. Loop the 11 beads around one wrist, and make a square knot between the first and last beads. Add 35 beads, and form an 11-bead loop around the other wrist, knotting between beads 24 and 35. Anchor both threads, and snip.

MAKING THE NECK LOOP SUPPORT STRUCTURE

1 Add the neck loop support structure to the neck of the figure as shown in Figure 11.

ATTACHING THE EARRING POST AND BACKING

Joyce designed the findings so that the head is attached to the backing and the body is attached to the post. In this way, the head sits on the front of the earlobe and the body is at the back.

Yorùbá Beadwork, Nigeria

INSPIRATIONAL PIECE	ARTIST	TECHNIQUE
Yorùbá bag from twentieth-century Nigeria	NanC Meinhardt	Right Angle Weave

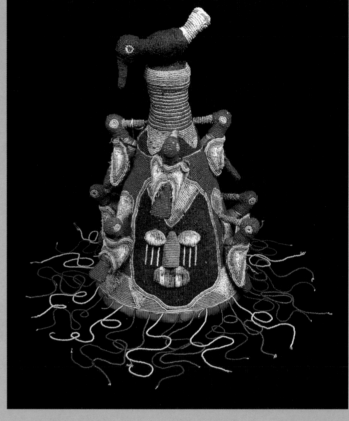

ABOVE *According to Yorùbá legend, Oduduwa, the supreme god, was the first to wear a beaded crown. This late twentieth-century crown features face and bird motifs worked in glass beads stitched to canvas.* 18" high x 10" wide x 10" deep ■ *Collection of NanC Meinhardt* TOM VAN EYNDE

LEFT *A Yorùbá king, the Élepè of Èpé, is shown with beaded crown, garments, fly whisk, and staff during the annual royal rites, Ìjèbú-Yorùbá, in 1982.*

Courtesy, Eliot Elisofon Photographic Archives, National Museum of African Art, Smithsonian Institution ■ HENRY JOHN DREWAL, *1982*

No matter how much or how little experience they have, all beadworkers periodically struggle with the same issue: how to come up with new designs. Some of us look outward for inspiration—to publications or workshops, to the world around us, or, as the artists in this book have been doing, to the beadwork of different times and places. Other beadworkers look within, drawing upon thoughts, feelings, experiences, or memories. In some cultures, beadworkers may turn to the spirit world for guidance, particularly when they are making items of great significance.

For Yorùbá beadworkers, fresh inspiration is critical. Traditional Yorùbá beadworkers work on commission to produce beaded clothing and ornaments for the various kings of Yorùbáland, which extends from southwest Nigeria into neighboring Benin and Togo. Every piece is important, because it will be worn or displayed on ceremonial occasions as proof of the king's authority. Yet the king's

beadwork signals far more than mere political power. Dressed in a beaded crown such as the ones shown above or seated on a beaded throne, the king demonstrates that he is favored by the gods and directly descended from them. Thus, for the Yorùbá, beadwork is a spiritually charged substance.

Traditionally, Yorùbá beadwork was made by male specialists trained from an early age by their fathers or other male relatives in their family's closely guarded techniques for sewing beads to canvas in plain two-dimensional or padded three-dimensional formats. The most talented beadworkers might be sought out by several different kings, each of whom might commission multiple pieces. Sometimes, a king would arrange a consultation with a famous beadworker to discuss the design of a crown, robe, chair, or stool; but it was up to the beadworker to combine the king's design ideas with his own to produce the final piece. If, after taking

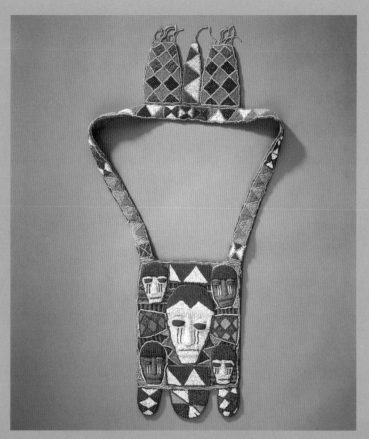

When faced with important matters, the Yorùbá consult a diviner to gauge the disposition of spiritual forces. Beaded necklaces and bags are essential elements of a diviner's regalia. This twentieth-century bag features five otherworldly faces with projecting noses, mouths, eyes, and brows.
35" high ■ © UCLA Fowler Museum of Cultural History, X96.3.3
DON COLE

In her "Diviner's Bag," made in 2002 of glass beads, Ultrasuede, linen, and cotton, NanC Meinhardt uses single-needle right angle weave to portray four aspects of artistic creation: wonder, anxiety, impasse, and the internal censor.
13½" high x 9½" wide ■ Collection of the artist ■ TOM VAN EYNDE

out his box of pattern templates and experimenting with various designs, the beadworker was still at a loss for inspiration, he might request guidance from the spirit world. As one Yorùbá beadworker explains, when he had no good ideas for a piece, he would take out a statue of the medicine god, which had been in his family for five generations. He would pray and offer sacrifices to the god and humbly request its help. That night in his dreams, if all went well, he would see the piece he was trying to make, complete with all of the colors and designs as they should be. The next morning, he would know just what to do, and his reputation would be saved.

NanC Meinhardt has thought a lot about the stages of the creative process. In her dual roles as beadwork artist and teacher, she understands the conflicts that arise when an artist's instincts are stifled by the negative comments of an internal or external censor. To become an effective artist, she believes, one must first turn off the internal censor. NanC relates easily to Yorùbá beadwork and owns several contemporary pieces. She chose to work

with the bag shown above, which was probably used by a Yorùbá diviner because, to her, an artist's work is similar to that of a diviner. By trial and error, both artists and diviners must walk a path from chaos and uncertainty to order and confidence. In the end, if all goes well, both make significant contributions to the world around them simply by trusting their instincts.

In her "Diviner's Bag," NanC portrays four basic emotions that all artists experience on a regular basis. The five faces on the Yorùbá bag, which evoke the diviner's all-seeing ability, seem remote, even otherworldly. In contrast, the four faces on NanC's bag are expressive and engaging.

NanC Meinhardt of Highland Park, Illinois,
worked in the health care field before discovering her true calling as a beadwork artist. Her studio now houses one of the country's foremost centers of beadwork education. For more information, see www.nancmeinhardt.com.

INSPIRATIONAL PIECE
Maasai beaded broad collars from twentieth-century Kenya

ARTIST
Flora Book

TECHNIQUE
Spiral Stringing with Spacer Plates

BEADWORK PROJECT
"Jayne's Cowl" Neckpiece

9¼" diameter x 2¼" high

Few of us would fail to recognize the beadwork of the Maasai peoples of the Great Rift Valley that spans southern Kenya and northern Tanzania. This is home to celebrated Mount Kilimanjaro, the tallest free-standing mountain in the world, and to formerly vast herds of zebras, giraffes, antelopes, and elephants. The Maasai make artful use of a profoundly simple beading technique in which parallel rows of beads strung on wire are connected either with multiholed spacer plates or wired interlacings. The Maasai seem to have an inexhaustible supply of ideas for using this ancient approach to fashion modern body ornaments.

Even when they use other techniques, such as sewing beads to an animal hide backing, the Maasai position them in simple parallel rows. Seldom if ever do they bother with more complicated structures such as weaving or netting. Since most Maasai groups are traditionally semi-nomadic, moving periodically with their herds of cattle in search of fresh grasslands, material possessions must be kept to a minimum. Simplicity in all things, even beadwork technique, is appropriate.

After they have finished milking the cows, collecting water and firewood, preparing food and tea, and tending to the children, Maasai women pick up their beadwork. They favor basic geometric designs such as dots, dashes, and stripes, and bold expanses of red, blue, white, and green, with small accents of yellow and other colors. Pictorial motifs just don't interest them. Although all Maasai wear beads and beadwork from childhood on, only on major occasions do the women encase their upper bodies in beadwork, layering five or six disk-shaped collars around their necks and donning elaborate earrings and headpieces. Most of these pieces may be more or less flat; but when worn together in layers, they take on a sculptural appearance and frame a woman's face in beadwork. Men's beadwork is far more restrained.

In this ca. 1975 photograph, a young Maasai woman is wearing enormous beadwork earrings, a button-embellished headdress, and several beadwork collars.
Courtesy, Robert Estall Photo Library
CAROL BECKWITH

RIGHT According to traditional belief, when an Oba, or ruler of Benin, dons his coral beadwork regalia, he instantly assumes divine powers. Here, King (Oba) Akenzua (1933-1978) is shown during a palace ceremony in 1964, wearing some 20 pounds of coral beads and beadwork.
Courtesy, Robert Estall Photo Library
WERNER FORMAN

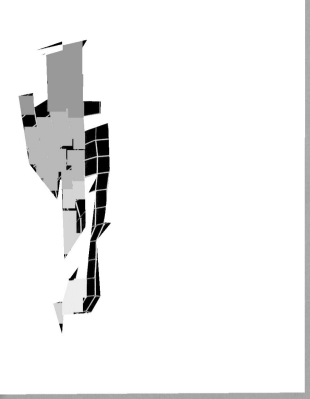

LIKE THE MAASAI, FLORA BOOK ALSO MAKES A VIRTUE of simplicity. She too lives in more than one place, spending part of the year in Seattle, part in London. So that she can work easily in either location, her beading materials have to be portable, her tools minimal. For her beads, Flora prefers sterling silver tubes that she buys commercially or cuts to size herself. Her thread is sturdy nylon fishing line. She limits her tools to a jeweler's saw, a tube cutter, a tumbler, and a cigarette lighter. What she does with these unpromising materials is astounding. Her work is instantly recognizable for the purity of its architecture.

Flora has long admired African beadwork and welcomed its influences in her jewelry. After seeing the image on the facing page of the Oba of Benin wearing an amazing coral beadwork jacket, she developed her own version with "Loretta's Vest," shown here. In Flora's hands, the dense, heavy, diagonal netting of the coral jacket becomes an open grid of streamlined squares.

Middle Eastern beadwork also fascinates her. Browsing in London's Portobello Road antique shops, she has found many pieces to add to her collection of Turkish prisoner-of-war beadwork (such as the one pictured below), of whimsical snakes, coin purses, and necklaces of World War I vintage. These pieces may not inspire her directly, but they enrich her understanding of the medium she loves.

In "Jayne's Cowl," shown on page 88, Flora creates her own kind of Maasai beaded collar. She makes vertical spacer plates support parallel rings, but her spacers are not rigid. Instead, they flex at their midpoints, where a small spacer joins a larger one. As a result, the seventeen sections of the cowl continually shift position, bending slightly in or out, according to the movements of the wearer. As the sections shift, the short tube beads that float on top of the long tubes also move slightly, making a gentle clicking sound and sparkling in ever-changing patterns. In a sense, Flora has invented an abacus-like Maasai collar, which is easily assembled using one long spiral of thread.

Flora Book's "Loretta's Vest," made in 1996 of sterling silver and nylon monofilament, was inspired by Benin coral beadwork garments such as the one shown on the previous page.
Collection of the artist ■ *Roger Schreiber*

Flora Book of Seattle, Washington, has long been influenced by the jewelry and beadwork of other cultures, particularly those of the Middle East and Africa. Although these influences sometimes surface in her own designs, she has developed an elegant, architectural approach to beading that is uniquely her own. Flora exhibits her work at several American galleries.

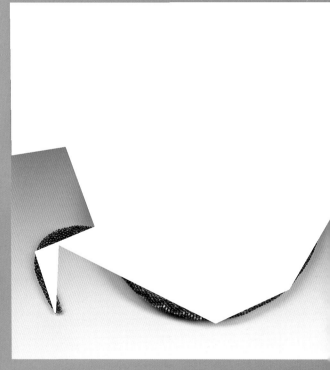

Crocheted beadwork snakes and other items were made by Turkish prisoners living in camps in Egypt, Mesopotamia, Greece, and Britain's Isle of Man during World War I. This snake bears the inscriptions "Souvenir" on its back and "Turkish Prisoners 1918" on its belly.
¾" wide x 71" long ■ *Collection of Flora Book*
LARRY SANDERS

"JAYNE'S COWL" NECKPIECE

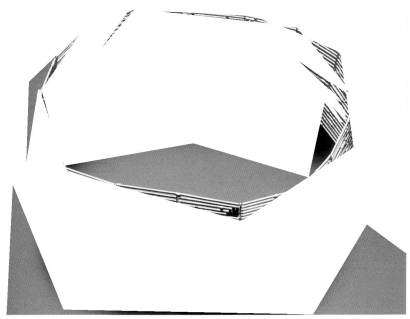

*Shown is Flora Book's "Jayne's Cowl" Neckpiece,
of sterling silver tube beads.
Collection of the artist* ■ ROGER SCHRIBER

MATERIALS

54' 2mm outer-diameter
sterling silver tubing

17 Long Spacer Plates
consisting of 17 15-hole
sterling silver spacer plates,
1½" long x ¹⁄₁₆" wide

17 Short Spacer Plates
consisting of 17 10-hole
sterling silver spacer plates,
1" long x ¹⁄₁₆" wide

3,026 (253 dozen) 2.5-3mm
outer-diameter sterling silver "float" beads, made of
plain tube or crimp beads

(or other beads with holes
large enough to slide over
the 2mm tubing)

25 yards 50-lb. test nylon
monofilament

jeweler's saw frame, fine
blades, and lubricating wax

jeweler's tumbler with
mixed-shape stainless steel
media

cigarette lighter

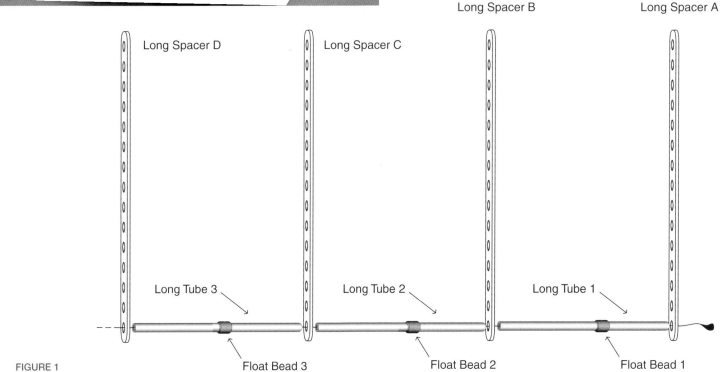

FIGURE 1

PREPARING THE LONG TUBES
1 Cut the 54' of 2mm tubing into 391 pieces, each measuring
1⁹⁄₁₆" long. Place the tubes into a tumbler, add water, and tumble
for 1-2 hours until the ends are smooth.

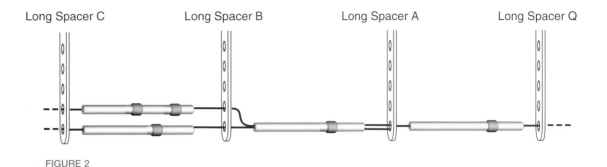

Long Spacer C   Long Spacer B   Long Spacer A   Long Spacer Q

FIGURE 2

BEGINNING TO STRING THE COWL

Using the cigarette lighter, melt one end of the nylon monofilament until a bead of plastic forms that is large enough to stop up the hole of a spacer. Do not leave a tail of thread; the thread will end in the ball.

1 Following Figure 1, take the working end of the monofilament and insert it through the first hole in Long Spacer A, the one with 15 holes. String 1 long sterling tube, and slide 1 sterling float bead over the tube.

2 Then go through the first hole in Long Spacer B. String another long sterling tube, slide another float bead over it, and go through the first hole in Long Spacer C. Pull slowly until the balled end of the monofilament sits against the first hole in Spacer A.

3 Continue stringing tubes, floats, and spacers until you have added the seventeenth long spacer, which is Long Spacer Q, and its long tube and float bead. Pull slowly until all of the thread is through, then pull tightly.

STRINGING RINGS 2-13

1 Now, to complete Ring 1 and begin Ring 2, after you have added the seventeenth long tube and float bead, go through the first hole in Long Spacer A, the first long sterling tube, and the second hole in Spacer B. See Figure 2. Add 1 long tube and 2 float beads. Work your way around the cowl in this

manner until you have gone through the second hole in Long Spacer Q. Add 1 long tube, slide 2 float beads over it, and go through the second hole in Long Spacer A. Add the seventeenth long tube in Ring 2 and 2 float beads. Go through the second hole in Long Spacer B, the next long tube, and the third hole in Spacer C. Attach Rings 3-13 in this manner, moving in a spiral and adding the correct number of float beads per ring as shown in Figure 3. Before going through the fourteenth hole in the next Long Spacer, read Steps 1-2 below.

STRINGING RINGS 14-23

1 Following Figure 3, increase the cowl's height by coupling Short Spacers and Long Spacers. Insert the monofilament through the first hole in a Short Spacer and then through the fourteenth hole in the next Long Spacer. Add 1 long tube and 10 float beads.

2 Continue working your way around the cowl, adding Rings 14-23, making sure to couple Long and Short Spacers in Rings 14 and 15. When you have finished adding the beads for the final segment of Ring 23, go through the last hole in the next Short Spacer. Pull tightly.

3 Leaving a tail of about $^1/_4$", snip the thread. Burn the end of the tail with a cigarette lighter until a ball of plastic forms. The ball should sit tightly against the final Short Spacer.

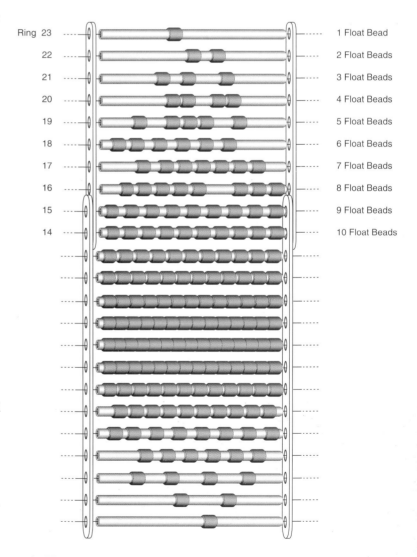

Ring 23 — 1 Float Bead
22 — 2 Float Beads
21 — 3 Float Beads
20 — 4 Float Beads
19 — 5 Float Beads
18 — 6 Float Beads
17 — 7 Float Beads
16 — 8 Float Beads
15 — 9 Float Beads
14 — 10 Float Beads

FIGURE 3

DINKA BEADWORK, SUDAN

INSPIRATIONAL PIECES
Dinka corsets

ARTIST
David Chatt

TECHNIQUE
Cubic Right Angle Weave

BEADWORK PROJECT
Samples of the structures used in David's "Dinka-Inspired" Bracelet shown on page 92

½" wide x 1⅜" high

Pictured is a fierce-looking Dinka warrior wearing a beaded corset that has been sewn around his torso, ca. 1975. The high spine indicates great family wealth; the bead colors identify the wearer's current age-grade.
Courtesy, Robert Estall Photo Agency
ANGELA FISHER

Like the Maasai of Kenya and Tanzania, the Dinka people of the Sudan are nomadic pastoralists who must carry their wealth with them when they move their cattle to new pastures. They are also ingenious beadworkers. Men and women encase their bodies in beaded corsets and bodices that resemble architectural structures. Long parallel strands of beads, connected with wire spines and interlacings, form the main panels of these ornaments and echo the shape of the torso underneath. Occasionally, the spines include beads united at right angles with multiple threads.

By their structure and color, these ornaments communicate the wearer's current age-grade or peer group and the family's prosperity. For example, a man's corset with an emphasis on red indicates a wearer in the fifteen-to-twenty-five-year-old age-grade. An unusually high spine indicates great family wealth. As the age-grade changes, the corset or bodice will change as well. Often these ornaments are stitched in place around the body, to be removed only when the wearer progresses to the next stage of life. A few corsets open and close with buttons attached to leather strips.

Sadly, Dinka beaded corsets may be things of the past. Battered by a decades-old civil war that has killed or displaced millions of people in southern Sudan, the Dinka have lost much of their traditional cattle-based lifestyle and many of the customs that went with it.

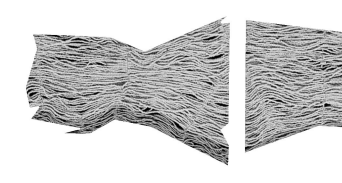

This twentieth-century Dinka corset opens and closes with plastic buttons.
33½" wide x 21½" high ■ Collection of Flora Book ■ DON TUTTLE

LEFT *Shown are samples of the sculptural forms that can be made within a few days of learning cubic right angle weave. It is easy to learn this technique using large, round beads such as the wooden ones I used here.*
tall green column: 1⅛" wide x 1⅛" deep x 3" high Collection of Valerie Hector ■ LARRY SANDERS

ONCE IN A WHILE AN ARTIST COMES along who revolutionizes an ancient technique. When that happens, as we saw with Joyce Scott (see page 77), we are all enriched. Now, David Chatt has done for right angle weaves what Joyce Scott did for peyote stitch. Right angle weaves, which orient beads at 90-degree angles, may not be as old as peyote stitch; but like peyote stitch, they turn up in many parts of the world. Unlike peyote stitch, which uses just one thread, most right angle weaves make use of two or more threads, which can make the beading process both cumbersome and slow.

David Chatt began working with flat right angle weave some fifteen years ago. He quickly discovered that its connections can be made as easily with one working thread end as with two. By itself this discovery was not revolutionary, but the next one was. Single-needle right angle weave, he realized, could be used to create large, three-dimensional structures consisting entirely of beaded cubes. Now, late twentieth-century Chinese beadworkers also toyed with cubic right angle weave, but they apparently never went beyond two layers of cubes or made pieces that were larger than a few inches.

In his "Dinka-Inspired" Bracelet, shown on page 92, David creates a kind of beaded corset for the wrist, with parallel, zigzag ropes that float between the clasp elements at either end. Following, you will learn how to make a cubic right angle weave tube built from cubes added one by one. Before long you can move on to more advanced structures, such as those used in David's "Dinka-Inspired" Bracelet.

A seemingly angst-ridden male face peers out from David Chatt's "Hanging on by a Thread" Marble Bag from 1998, made of glass beads, united in peyote stitch and right angle weave, and marbles of glass, wood, and felt.
8" diameter x 9" high ■ *Collection of Chris Rifkin* LARRY STESSIN

David Chatt is a Seattle artist and teacher who pioneered the use of cubic right angle weave to produce complex structures. His witty, award-winning pieces have been widely exhibited, and he is currently at work on a book. For more information, see www.davidchatt.com.

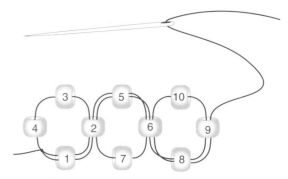

FIGURE 1

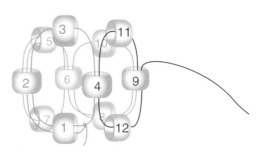

FIGURE 2

TIPS

■ *This technique will be easier to learn if you already know flat single-needle right angle weave. See Figures 2-4 on page 65.*

■ *Until you understand David's cubic approach it is best to work in 4-6mm round beads of glass, plastic, or wood. Using a permanent felt-tip marker, number the beads from 1-20 to make learning the first two cubes easier.*

■ *David's technique may look hard, but it is actually very easy if you keep in mind some basic principles:*

 • *Each cube has twelve beads that form six square faces.*

 • *There are four side faces, one top face, and one bottom face.*

 • *Each face contains four beads, all of which are shared with the neighboring faces.*

 • *No cube is complete until all six faces are in place and the top and bottom faces are stitched closed.*

 • *Neighboring cubes in a tube will share one face of four beads; neighboring cubes in larger structures may share more than one face.*

MATERIALS

(to make a short sample tube 4 cubes long by 1 cube wide)

36 6mm round beads of glass, plastic, or wood

1 small bobbin Nymo B thread

size 10 needles

wax

MAKING A SAMPLE TUBE 4 CUBES LONG

FORMING THE FIRST 12-BEAD CUBE

David likes to build the first cube by creating a right angle weave ladder and then stitching the ends together. (You learned this same structure using bugle beads and two working thread ends in Figures 5-6 on page 27.) David builds the additional cubes in a different way: one face at a time.

1 To begin, thread a needle onto a 60" length of Nymo B thread and double it to produce a 30" length. Wax the thread heavily. String beads 1-4. About 6" from the tail end of the thread, tie a square knot between beads 1 and 4.

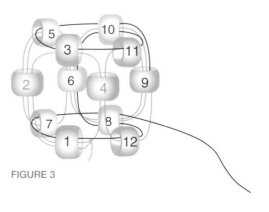

FIGURE 3

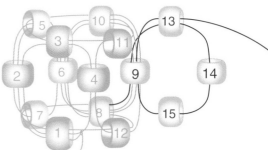

FIGURE 4

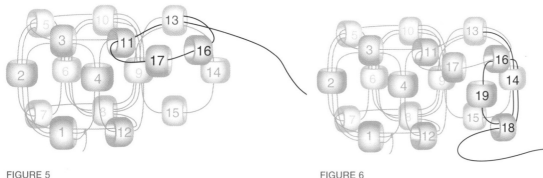

FIGURE 5

FIGURE 6

FIGURE 7

FIGURE 8

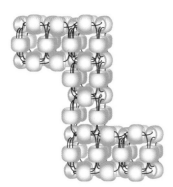

FIGURE 9

FIGURE 10

5 Now secure the top and bottom faces of the second cube by stitching around the 4 beads of each of those faces. If you have trouble, refer to Figure 3 again. Now the second cube is complete.

FINISHING THE SAMPLE TUBE

1 Continue beading until you have a tube that is 4 cubes long as shown in Figure 8. For a longer tube, add more cubes.

EXPERIMENTING WITH OTHER STRUCTURES

A ZIGZAG
After you understand the basic technique, try changing the direction of your tube to create a zigzag. See Figure 9 and the orange zigzag in the photograph on page 91.

A RECTANGULAR "O"
As you become more advanced, you can move on to more complex structures, where you add cubes in more than one direction. The Rectangular "O" in Figure 10 measures 4 cubes across by 5 cubes high by 2 cubes deep along its outer perimeter. You should be able to make it easily.

STRUCTURES WITH MORE DEPTH
Continue experimenting with other structures, such as the tall green column in the photograph on page 91, which is 3 cubes wide and 9 cubes high. Instead of following a rigid thread path, use your intuition, and remember the guiding concept: It is best to finish one cube before starting another, at least while you are learning.

EMBELLISHING
You can embellish structures in different ways. For example, try adding individual cubes in a "polka dot" fashion as David did in the "Dinka-Inspired" Bracelet.

2 Following Figure 1, go through beads 1 and 2. Add beads 5-7, and go through beads 2, 5, and 6. Add beads 8-10, and go through beads 6, 8 and 9.
3 Now you are ready to create the first cube. Following Figure 2, add bead 11, and go down through bead 4. Add bead 12, and go up through bead 9. Pull tightly.
4 All twelve beads of the first cube are now in place, but the top and bottom faces of the cube need to be stitched closed. Your needle

and thread should now be coming out of bead 9. Following Figure 3, go through beads 10, 5, 3, 11, and 10. The top of the cube is now closed. To close the bottom, go through beads 6, 8, 12, 1, 7, and 8.

BUILDING THE SECOND CUBE
1 Because the second cube will share its first face of four beads with the first cube, you only have to add 8 beads to build the second cube. To create the second face of the second cube, add 3 beads. To begin, follow Figure 4. Go up

through bead 9. Add beads 13-15, and go through beads 9 and 13.
2 To create the third face, follow Figure 5. Add 2 beads, 16 and 17, and go through beads 11 and 13.
3 To create the fourth face, follow Figure 6. Go down through bead 14. Then add 2 beads, 18 and 19, and go through beads 16, 14, and 18.
4 To create the fifth face, follow Figure 7. Go through beads 19, 17, and 4, and add 1 bead, 20. Go through beads 19 and 17 again.

INSPIRATIONAL PIECES
Photograph of Nelson Mandela and Mfengu (Xhosa) collar from twentieth-century Eastern Cape, South Africa

ARTIST
Valerie Hector

TECHNIQUE
Double-Layer Scallop Stitch

BEADWORK PROJECT
Sample of Double-Layer Scallop Stitch used in the "Red Ribbon" Necklace shown on page 96

1¾" wide x 1⅜" high
(dimensions of a sample measuring 22 beads across by 6 rows high worked in 8° beads)

In the fall of 1962, at the Old Synagogue Court in Pretoria, South Africa, Nelson Mandela was tried for treason for advocating armed resistance against the colonial government of the white Afrikaners, who had emigrated to South Africa from Holland starting in the mid-seventeenth century. Since the early 1940s, he had been an active member of an opposition party, the African National Congress, which promoted equal rights for South Africa's native blacks. Long before the white government's brutal *apartheid*, or "apartness," policy was established in 1948, blacks and other people of color had been kept apart from whites and subjected to intense racial, social, economic, and political discrimination. Forbidden to own land, forced to live in impoverished shantytowns and work for low wages, black South Africans had no way to improve their lives.

The trial opened on October 22, 1962. A hush fell over the crowded courtroom as Mandela entered, dressed not in the Western-style clothing of his white oppressors, but in the traditional attire of a South African chief. His feet were bare. For one whole minute, the judge sat in stunned silence. No one could fail to understand the significance of Mandela's appearance.

In this one dignified and defiant act, he silently asserted his high standing in an indigenous South African political system, his faith in traditional South African culture, and his rejection of the white man's abusive system. Two weeks later, he was sentenced to five years in prison. In 1964, he was tried for sabotage and sentenced to life in prison.

Not long before his treason trial, Mandela posed for the portrait shown at the left wearing traditional clothing and a wide beadwork collar common to men and women of his native chiefdom, the Thembu, and to other Xhosa-language-speaking peoples such as the Xhosa, Mfengu, and Mpondo. (Scholars generally refer to all Xhosa-language speakers as Xhosa or Southern Nguni.) As a mature Xhosa male, Mandela could have worn a few more of these collars, one on top of the other, and dozens of other pieces of beadwork as well. But in this case, less was more. A single collar sufficed to make his point. Ironically, the collar was made of the very European glass beads that had long been brought into South Africa by European traders and missionaries. Thus, Mandela was using an imported European trade good, transformed by the expertise of Xhosa beaders and worn against the backdrop of his bare African flesh, to subvert his formidable white adversaries.

Shown is an early 1960s portrait of Nelson Mandela wearing a Thembu beadwork collar. He probably wore a similar collar during his treason trail. He was released from prison in 1990, received the Nobel Peace Prize in 1993, and in 1994 became South Africa's first democratically elected president.
Courtesy, UWC-Robben Island Museum Mayibuye Archives, University of the Western Cape ■ ELI WEINBERG

Small lengths of single-layer scallop stitch make beautiful arcs and circles. By adding metal hoops and wool tassels, the Thembu turned them into earrings.
detail of earring: 2⅜" wide x 2¾" high; entire earring: 2⅜" wide x 2¾" high x 17⅜" long
Courtesy, The Field Museum, Cat. No. 222492. Neg. No. A114152c
DIANE ALEXANDER WHITE

THERE IS NOTHING UNUSUAL ABOUT THE SINGLE-LAYER scallop stitch used to construct Mandela's portrait-day collar and the earrings shown above. The same technique can be found in beadwork from western India, the Americas, and other parts of the globe. But the Xhosa invented a brilliant new variation by filling in the open spaces in one row with beads from the next row. (See the photograph to the right.) The rows do not merely interlink; they interpenetrate, producing a luxurious, double-layer kind of beaded fabric similar to the fabric produced by Mary Winters-Meyer's approach. (See Figure 11 on page 67.)

Trying to do justice to Nelson Mandela and the single-layer collar he wore for his portrait, my assistant Saing and I made about ninety 3-inch arcs of single-layer scallop stitch in various colors. We tried folding them, curving them, stitching them in pairs, and finally attaching them to wires; but nothing seemed right. So we gave up and went on to other projects. When I looked at the arcs six months later, however, I realized what was wrong. There were too many small parts, and even when combined, they seemed trivial. Not sure what would happen, I decided to make one long, narrow, double-layer ribbon, about the same width as a Xhosa beaded collar. I did not know at the outset that the longer it got, the more this ribbon would curl around itself. The "Red Ribbon" Necklace, shown on page 96, finally turned out to be just what I had been trying to make all along: the kind of substantial tribute that I felt Nelson Mandela and the beadworkers of the Eastern Cape deserved. Following, you will learn how to make a sample of the Double-Layer Scallop Stitch I used in my "Red Ribbon" Necklace.

Shown is a detail of a Mfengu collar worked in double-layer scallop stitch. The curve emerges as rows of interlocking loops are added to an initial line of beads. Note how tightly the layers interlock.
entire collar: 11⅜" diameter x ⅜" deep T
Courtesy, The Field Museum, Cat. No. 28789. Neg. No. A114148c
DIANE ALEXANDER WHITE

SAMPLE OF DOUBLE-LAYER SCALLOP STITCH

Shown is Valerie Hector's "Red Ribbon" Necklace, of cylinder seed beads. 3" wide x 73" long ■ *Collection of Natalie F. Hector* ■ RALPH GABRINER

TIPS

■ *It is best to learn this technique using two colors of 8° beads first. As you gain experience, you can progress to smaller beads in one color.*

■ *The amount of curve in a ribbon depends upon the number of beads per loop. I like to use 12 beads per loop, which is the number Alice Scherer and I found in the Xhosa collar we studied. For a sharper curve, try 14-16 beads per loop. For a gentler curve, try 8-10.*

■ *There are other ways of beginning new rows besides the ones we worked out by studying a Xhosa collar. Feel free to invent your own methods.*

■ *If possible, try to reinforce the long line of beads in Row 1 by going back through them with extra thread, as this line will take the most wear over time.*

■ *Tassels, whether simple or elaborate, are a great way to finish the ends of a "Ribbon" Necklace.*

Many Xhosa collars, such as the one Nelson Mandela wears in the photograph on page 94, were made with single-layer scallop stitch, a technique that resembles a lacy version of brick stitch (see the diagram below). Single-layer scallop stitch was also used to produce the earrings shown on page 95. Here, you will use double-layer scallop stitch to make a small sample of my "Red Ribbon" Necklace.

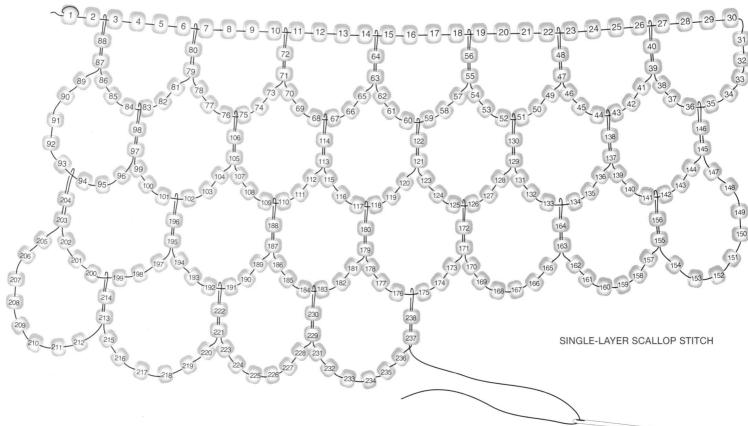

SINGLE-LAYER SCALLOP STITCH

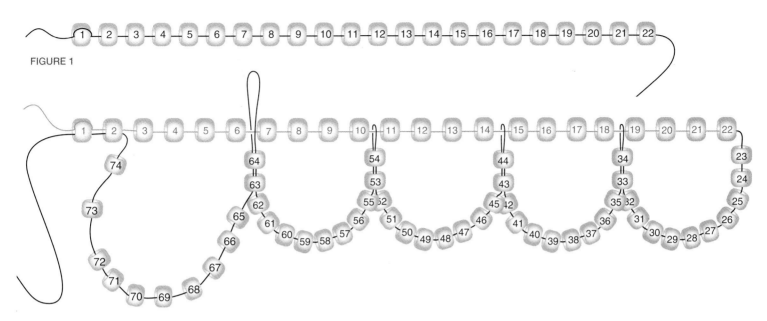

FIGURE 1

FIGURE 2

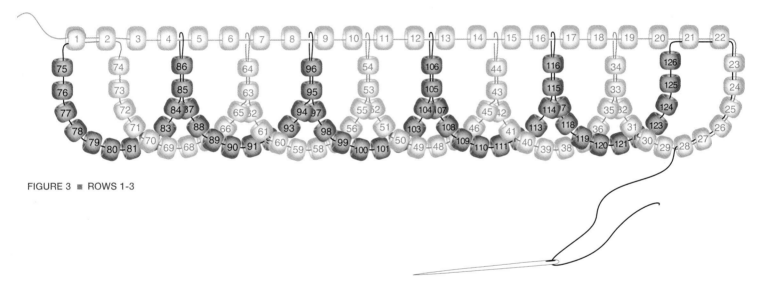

FIGURE 3 ■ ROWS 1-3

MATERIALS

(to make a small sample)

8° round glass beads

5 grams Color A

5 grams Color B

cotton/polyester hand-quilting thread

size 10 beading needles

wax

ROW 1

Your small sample begins with a Row 1 containing 22 beads.

1 To begin, thread a needle onto a 72" length of thread, double the thread to create a 36" length, and wax it. String 22 beads in Color A, and push them down to within 6" of the tail. Make an overhand knot around bead 1. (See Figure 1.)

ROW 2

In Row 1 you moved from left to right. In Row 2, which is also worked in Color A, you will move from right to left.

1 To begin, add 12 beads, 23-34, and loop around the thread that connects beads 18 and 19. (See Figure 2.) Go down through beads 34 and 33.

2 To create the second loop of 12 beads, add 10 beads, 35-44, then loop around the thread that connects beads 14 and 15, and go down through beads 44 and 43.

3 Continue adding loops until you have added beads 65-74 and gone through beads 2 and 1.

ROW 3

1 Row 3 is worked in Color B. Following Figure 3, with your thread coming out of bead 1, add 12 beads, 75-86. Cross under beads 71-69 of Row 2, and loop around the thread between beads 4 and 5. Go down through beads 86 and 85, and add 10 beads. Cross over beads 66-68, and then under beads 61-59. Loop around the thread between beads 8 and 9, and go down through beads 96 and 95.

2 Continue working until you have added beads 117-126 and gone through beads 21 and 22. As you add each new loop, be sure to cross under the left side of the loops in Row 2 and over the right side.

3 Prepare to start Row 4 by going through beads 23-28.

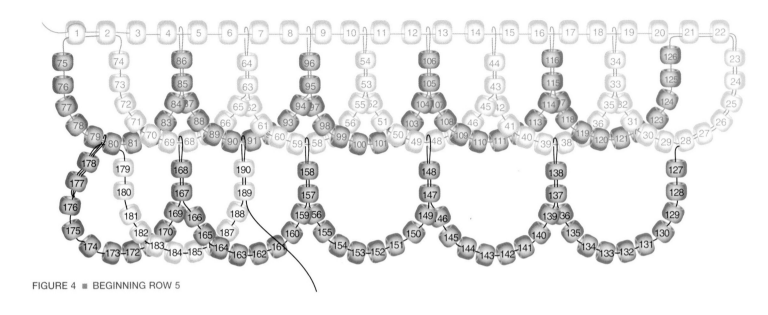

FIGURE 4 ■ BEGINNING ROW 5

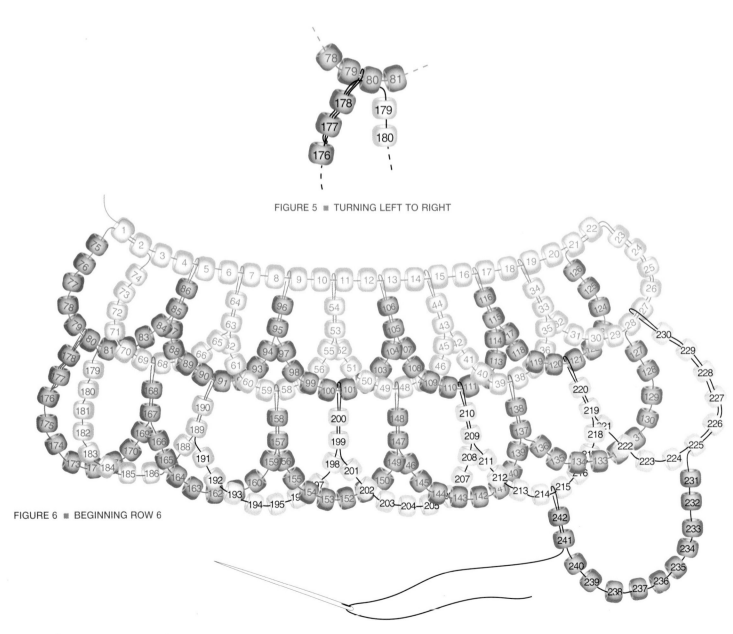

FIGURE 5 ■ TURNING LEFT TO RIGHT

FIGURE 6 ■ BEGINNING ROW 6

FIGURE 7

ROW 4

1 To start Row 4, which consists of single loops worked in Color B, add 12 beads, 127-138, and loop around the thread between beads 39 and 38. (See Figure 4.)

2 Continue working leftward until you have added beads 169-178.

3 Loop around the thread between beads 79 and 80, and go back down through beads 178 and 177. Make an overhand knot around the thread between beads 177 and 176, and then go back up through beads 177, 178, and 80. (See Figure 5.)

ROW 5

1 To begin Row 5, follow

Figure 4. Add 12 beads in Color A, 179-190, and continue working until you have added beads 221-230 as shown in Figure 6. Remember to cross over the right side of the loops in Row 4 and under the left side of the same loops.

2 Following Figure 6, loop around the thread between beads 28 and 27, and then go down through beads 230-225.

ROW 6

1 To begin Row 6, add 12 beads in Color B, 231-242, and keep working across this row until you have gone down through beads 272 and 271. (See Figure 7.)

2 To make the final loop of this row, add 10 beads, and

loop around the thread between beads 174 and 173. Keep working as usual.

CONTINUE WORKING THE SAMPLE

Continue working the sample if you wish, adding single loops in even-numbered rows and then interlocking them with new loops in odd-numbered rows.

REPRODUCING MY "RED RIBBON" NECKLACE

To reproduce the "Red Ribbon" Necklace, start with a Row 1 that is about 72" long. (It is best to count to be sure you have an even number of beads.) Then continue working to add 22 more rows (equals 11 interlocking rows) until the ribbon is about 3" wide. All told, it

should take about $^1/_2$ kilo of matte red aurora borealis cylinder seed beads and two to four weeks of full-time stitching to complete.

To make a shorter, thinner ribbon, start with a Row 1 that is about 48" long. By adding only 4 more rows (equals 2 interlocking rows), you will have a beautiful necklace to wrap or knot. Try varying the sizes of the beads—using 2 size 8° beads at the center of each loop, for example, and graduating down to cylinder seed beads at the edges.

INSPIRATIONAL TECHNIQUE
Ndebele Herringbone Stitch, as shown in the giraffe sculpture on the facing page

ARTIST
JoAnn Baumann

TECHNIQUE
Pyramidal Ndebele Herringbone Stitch

BEADWORK PROJECT
"Pyramid" Earrings

⅞" wide x 1⅞" high (including wires)

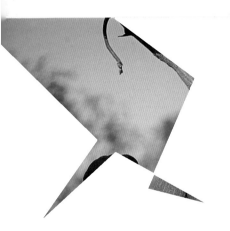

For the most part, beadwork is a woman's art form. In traditional cultures around the world, it often passes on through the generations as mothers patiently teach their daughters what their own mothers taught them. Ndebele beadworker Poppie Motshwene remembers learning from her mother when she was about fifteen years old. When Poppie did not understand a stitch, her mother would explain by drawing lines in the sand. Poppie's mother urged her to learn beadwork because it could provide her a good living. Her mother was wise. Today, in Nkosini, a small village about 2½ hours northeast of Johannesburg, South Africa, Poppie supports her eleven children by selling beadwork. Now in her mid-fifties, she still beads in the traditional way, while sitting against the trunk of a giant acacia tree, her dish of beads in her lap. Other women may join her, chatting as they work. All of her children know how to bead, but her son Frans helps her the most.

When Poppie began beading professionally many years ago, she made the traditional items of a Ndzundza Ndebele woman's costume, such as neck rings, headbands, armbands, aprons, and shawls. Elaborate fertility dolls, dressed in layers of beaded ornaments, also formed part of her offerings. Poppie would carry her wares in a basket on her head and take them to stores in Johannesburg, several long bus rides away. Or she would display her work on the ground at an impromptu roadside marketplace, hoping that passing motorists would stop and buy. Her customers would usually include people from races and cultures very different from her own, primarily white South Africans with whom she had little in common.

In 1992, to simplify her life, Poppie began selling her beadwork through a government-sponsored regional economic empowerment program. The beads were supplied, but she had to provide the needles and thread. Her first assignment was to bead a nontraditional item: a small wooden elephant and its baby, designed to be sold on the world market. More recently, Poppie has taken on other nontraditional assignments, beading giraffes and other animals that may take up to three weeks of full-time effort to finish. As her reputation has grown, Poppie has been invited to demonstrate in other countries. In 1997 she spent six weeks on a cultural exhibition tour in Switzerland, and in 1999 she demonstrated in Ohio. Thus, thanks to her beadworking talents, Poppie Motshwene has become a world traveler and an ambassador for the Ndebele.

Ndebele beadworker Poppie Motshwene, pictured here in 2002, taught her son Frans to bead by drawing lines in the sand, just as her mother taught her. Poppie and Frans often bead while sitting at the foot of a giant acacia tree near their home.
BRIAN LUSTIG

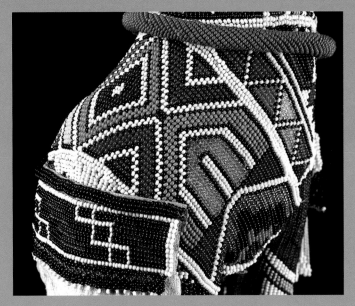

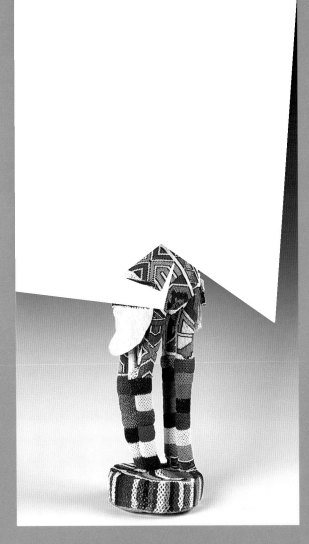

LEFT Poppie Motshwene beaded this wooden giraffe in Ndebele herringbone stitch in 2001. The motifs and colors are traditional, but the giraffe form was provided by a crafts cooperative that arranges export of Ndebele products.
8¾" wide x 44" high ■ Private collection ■ TOM VAN EYNDE

ABOVE This detail of the beaded giraffe shows Ndebele herringbone stitch. Other cooperative products include small beaded rhinoceroses.
Private collection ■ TOM VAN EYNDE

NDEBELE BEADWORKERS KNOW a number of stitches. One of them aligns beads in alternating rows of 45-degree angles, as seen in the detail photograph to the top right. It is hard to know exactly where this stitch originated, since other South African peoples such as the Zulu use it as well. But it was unknown in the United States until 1988, when Virginia Blakelock named it "Ndebele Herringbone Stitch" and published her instructions for it. Since then its popularity has increased, and leading American artists are using it in imaginative ways.

JoAnn Baumann uses it as an architect would, to devise intricate three-dimensional structures. For JoAnn, who taught herself how to do Ndebele herringbone stitch from a book, the most important part of the creative process is "playing" with the rules of a technique, and this requires letting go of the fear of making mistakes. More often than not, promising new variations start to suggest themselves. Following, JoAnn shares the secrets of her "Pyramid" Earrings, shown on page 102. These structures can also be used as elements in necklaces and bracelets.

JoAnn Baumann of Glencoe, Illinois, began beading many years ago while still pursuing a career in the gourmet food industry. Her beadwork has been featured in many publications, and she exhibits and teaches nationally. JoAnn also enjoys fabric collage as well as paper and fabric marbling. For more information, see www.jdesigns.org.

An avid beadwork student as well as a respected teacher, JoAnn produced this "Bracelet Stack" in 2004, after taking a netting class with Suzanne Golden. The secret to these airy yet durable structures lies in the use of Beadalon, a kind of nylon-coated stainless steel wire.
bracelet at left: 8½" diameter x 1" high
Collection of the artist ■ LARRY SANDERS

"PYRAMID" EARRINGS

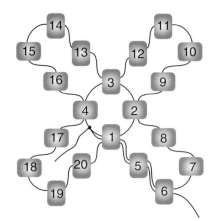

FIGURE 1

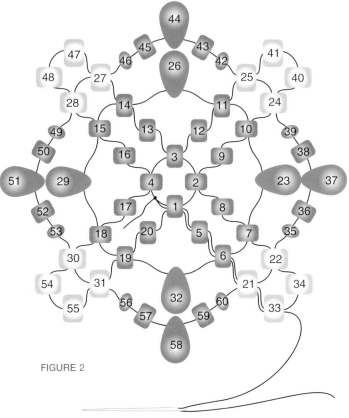

FIGURE 2

Shown here are six three-dimensional Ndebele herring-bone stitch earrings made by JoAnn Baumann in 2002. The project earring is at the top left.
Collection of the artist ■ LARRY SANDERS

MATERIALS

(for a pair of "Pyramid" Earrings)

Color A

    60 8° seed beads

    50 11° round seed beads

    24 5mm magatamas

    24 3mm magatamas

    2 5mm lentils or other disk beads

Color B

    96 8° seed beads

    8 11° round seed beads

    24 3mm magatamas

2 small sterling silver crimp beads

2 3mm sterling silver round beads

Silamide thread

size 11 or 12 beading needles

9" 20 gauge sterling silver round wire

wire-cutting pliers

chain-nose pliers

bead-crimping pliers

(optional) wax

To simplify the instructions, I have used these abbreviations.

    a = add

    gt = go through

    gbt = go back through

ROWS 1-3

The instructions that follow create a simplified four-sided pyramid with slightly fewer embellishments than JoAnn uses. Once you understand the basic structure, you can add embellishments of your own.

    All beads in Rows 1-3 are Color A 8°s.

1 To begin, thread a needle onto a 96" length of Silamide thread, then double the thread to produce a 48" length. You will make the entire earring with this thread. String 4 beads, and slide them down to within 6" of the end of the thread.

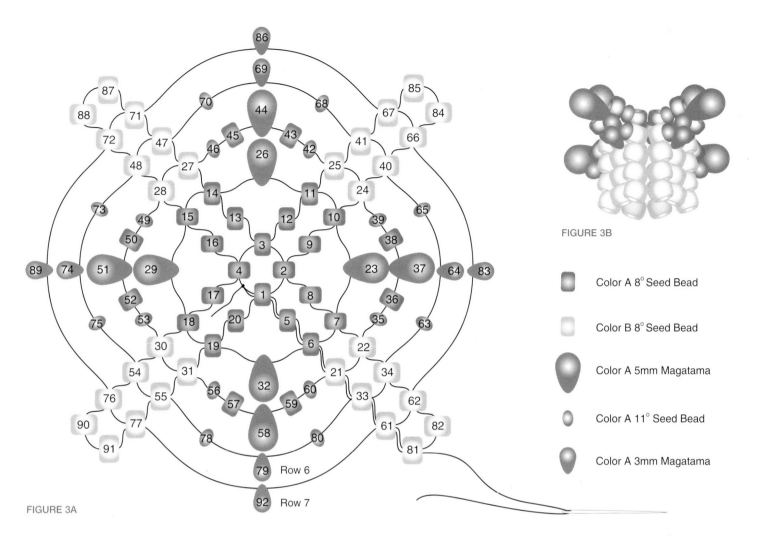

FIGURE 3A

FIGURE 3B

Color A 8° Seed Bead

Color B 8° Seed Bead

Color A 5mm Magatama

Color A 11° Seed Bead

Color A 3mm Magatama

2 Following Figure 1, tie the beads into a circle by forming a square knot between beads 1 and 4. This circle forms Row 1.
3 Next, a Rows 2 and 3 simultaneously. gt bead 1, and a beads 5-8. Pull tightly after every stitch. gt bead 2, and a beads 9-12. gt bead 3, and a beads 13-16. gt bead 4, and a beads 17-20. gt beads 1, 5, and 6. Now Rows 1-3 are in place and you are ready to start Row 4.

ROWS 4-5
Rows 4 and 5 are worked in a combination of Color A and Color B beads, in several sizes. The key to the right of Figure 3 will help you keep track.
1 Following Figure 2, a 2 8° beads, 21-22, in Color B, and gt bead 7. Pull tightly after each stitch. a bead 23, a 5mm Color A magatama, and gt bead 10. a 8° Color B beads 24-25, and gt bead 11. a bead 26, a 5mm Color A magatama, and gt bead 14. a 8° Color B

beads 27 and 28, and gt bead 15. a bead 29, a 5mm Color A magatama, and gt bead 18. a 8° Color B beads 30-31, and gt bead 19. a bead 32, a 5mm Color A magatama, and gt beads 6 and 21. Now Row 4 is in place and you are ready to start Row 5.
2 Row 5 forms the widest part of the pyramid and adds the 5mm magatamas that sit at the four corners of the pyramid. In Rows 5 and higher, it is very easy for the threads to tangle and catch. Pull tightly after each stitch to maintain firm tension, and wax the thread if necessary to prevent knots.
3 To begin Row 5, following Figure 2, a 8° Color B beads 33-34, and gt bead 22. a 5 Color A beads, 35-39 as follows: an 11°, an 8°, a 5mm magatama, an 8°, and an 11°. gt bead 24. a 2 8° Color B beads, 40-41, and gt bead 25.

a a second set of 5 Color A beads, 42-46, and gt bead 27. a 2 8° Color B beads, 47-48, and gt bead 28. a a third set of 5 varying Color A beads, 49-53, and gt bead 30. a 2 8° Color B beads, 54-55, and gt bead 31. a a final set of 5 varying Color A beads, 56-60, and gt beads 21 and 33. At this point, you will have a flat, circular panel of beadwork that will become three-dimensional as you continue to add rows.

ROWS 6-7
In Rows 6 and 7, the width of the pyramid begins to decrease as the sides of the structure get pulled together. Maintaining firm tension is crucial until the pyramid is complete, so pull tightly after each stitch.
1 To begin Row 6, following Figure 3a, g a 2 8° Color B beads, 61-62, and gt bead 34. a 3 Color A beads, 63-65, as follows: an 11°, a 3mm magatama, and an 11°. gt

bead 40. a 2 8° Color B beads, 66-67, and gt bead 41. a a second trio of Color A beads, 68-70, and gt bead 47. a 2 8° Color B beads, 71-72, and gt bead 48. a a third trio of Color A beads, 73-75, and gt bead 54. a 2 8° Color B beads, 76-77, and gt bead 55. a a fourth trio of Color A beads, 78-80, and gt beads 33 and 61.
2 To begin Row 7, still following Figure 3a, a 2 8° Color B beads, 81-82, and gt bead 62. a a 3mm Color A magatama, 83, and gt bead 66. Add 2 8° Color B beads, 84-85, and gt bead 67. a a 3mm Color A magatama, 86, and gt bead 71. a 2 8° Color B beads, 87-88, and gt bead 72. a a 3mm Color A magatama, 89, and gt bead 76. a 2 8° Color B beads, 90-91, and gt bead 77. a a 3mm Color A magatama, bead 92, and gt beads 61 and 81.
3 Now the pyramid has begun to take on its three-dimensional shape, as shown in Figure 3b.

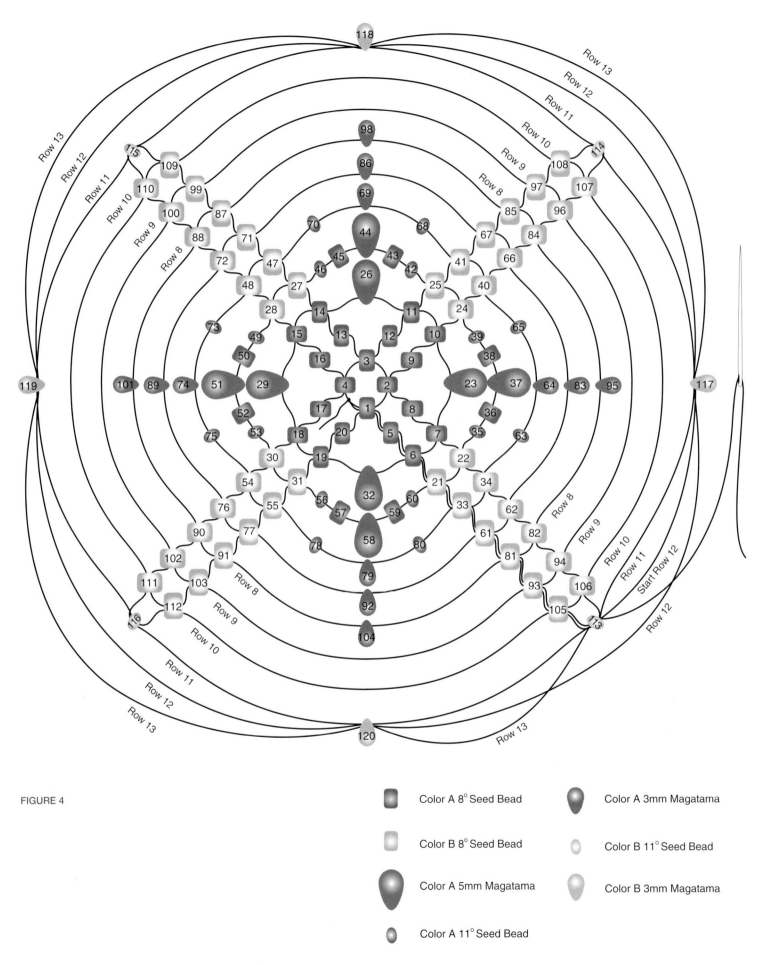

FIGURE 4

Color A 8° Seed Bead

Color B 8° Seed Bead

Color A 5mm Magatama

Color A 11° Seed Bead

Color A 3mm Magatama

Color B 11° Seed Bead

Color B 3mm Magatama

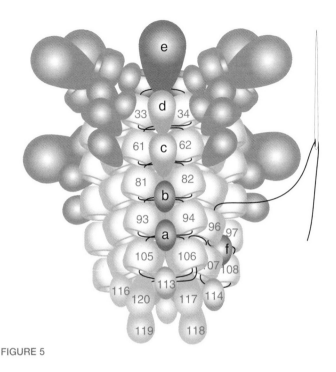

FIGURE 5

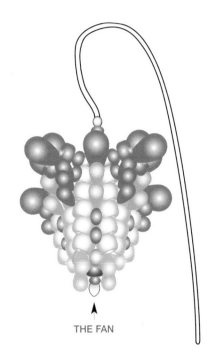

THE FAN

ROWS 8-12

In Rows 8-12, which decrease in width, you will form the bottom tip of the pyramid.

1 To begin Row 8, following Figure 4, a 2 8° Color B beads, 93-94, and gt bead 82. a a 3mm Color A magatama, 95, and gt bead 84. a 2 8° Color B beads, 96-97, and gt bead 85. a a 3mm Color A magatama, 98, and gt bead 87. a 2 8° Color B beads, 99-100, and gt bead 88. a a 3mm Color A magatama, 101, and gt bead 90. a 2 8° Color B beads, 102-103, and gt bead 91. a a 3mm Color A magatama, 104, and gt beads 81 and 93.

2 To begin Row 9, a 2 8° Color B beads, 105-106, and gt beads 94 and 96. a 2 8° Color B beads, 107-8, and gt beads 97 and 99. a 2 8° Color B beads, 109-110, and gt beads 100 and 102. a 2 8° Color B beads, 111-112, and gt beads 103, 93, and 105.

3 In Row 10, you will add only 4 11° Color B beads. To begin, a bead 113, and gt beads 106 and 107. a bead 114, and gt beads 108 and 109. a bead 115, and gt beads 110 and 111. a bead 116, and gt beads 112, 105, and 113.

4 In Row 11 you will add only 4 3mm Color B magatamas. To begin, a bead 117, and gt bead 114. a 118, and gt bead 115. a bead 119, and gt bead 116. a bead 120, and gt bead 113. Now all of the beads in the basic structure have been added.

5 Rows 12 and 13 are reinforcing rows. To complete Row 12, go from bead 113 through beads 117, 118, 119, 120, and 117. For Row 13, gt beads 118, 119, 120, and 113. Leave the thread in place until you are ready to begin embellishing.

EMBELLISHING THE PYRAMID

JoAnn's strategy is to embellish four of the "ditches," or grooves, that lie between two ridges of beads. Embellishing also strengthens the pyramid structure. You can embellish in a spiral path, working your way around the earring, or simply go from bottom to top and back down again in a figure-8 pattern, as shown in Figure 5.

1 To begin, go up through bead 106, a 11° Color B bead a, and go up through bead 93. a another 11° Color B bead, bead b, and go up through bead 82. a a 3mm Color A magatama, bead c, and go up through bead 61. a another 3mm Color A magatama, bead d, and go up through bead 34. a a 5mm Color B magatama, and go up through bead 33. Then work your way back down to the bottom of the pyramid as shown in Figure 5.

2 When you reach the bottom, move to the right to begin the next set of embellishments. To do this, go from bead 105 through bead 113, up through bead 106, down through bead 107, over through bead 114, and up through bead 108.

3 When you have finished embellishing four sides, anchor the thread by going through adjacent beads until it is secure, and snip.

THE EAR WIRES

1 Cut the 9" wire into two 4¹/₂" lengths. File them smooth at one end. Then take the chain-nose pliers and flatten these ends into a fan shape until it is wide enough to stop an 11° seed bead.

2 Slide the following onto each wire above the fan.

> 1 11° Color A seed bead
>
> 1 8° Color A bead
>
> 1 pyramid structure
>
> 1 5mm Color A lentil or disk bead
>
> 1 3mm sterling silver bead
>
> 1 sterling crimp bead

3 Press down hard on all elements, making sure there is no space between them, and use the bead-crimping pliers to squeeze the crimp bead around the wire. The crimp bead should not move. If it does, squeeze it some more.

4 With your fingers, bend the wires to form gentle arcs as shown in the photograph on page 102. Make the wires long or short depending upon your preference. Snip off the excess wire. File the ends smooth.

INSPIRATIONAL PIECES
Necklaces of tubular polygon stitch made by the Msinga of Kwa-Zulu Natal, South Africa, twentieth century

ARTIST
Valerie Hector

TECHNIQUE
Tubular Polygon Stitch

BEADWORK PROJECT
Samples of the technique used to produce the necklaces shown on page 108

Sample 1: ¼" wide x ¼" deep; Sample 2: ⁵⁄₁₆" wide x ⁵⁄₁₆" deep; Sample 3: ¼" wide x ¼" deep; Sample 4: ³⁄₁₆" wide x ³⁄₁₆" deep (using cylindrical seed beads and making 4"-long samples)

How are beadwork techniques invented? Why do they die out? And what do these techniques reveal about the cultures in which they had originated?

South Africa would be a good place to begin exploring these questions. It is home to some of the world's most ingenious beadworkers. They have invented a number of single-thread netting techniques such as Ndebele herringbone stitch, double-layer scallop stitch, and quadruple helix, to name a few. Most of these techniques were little known outside their places of origin until recently, when Western beadworkers discovered their enormous potential and began publishing them.

Tubular polygon stitch is another brilliant South African invention. Unlike any other technique in the world, it creates beaded tubes with three or more sides containing parallel rungs supported by vertical spines. The rungs can be closely spaced, with no air space between them, or loosely spaced, with plenty of air space. On rare examples, the rungs cross one another. I first came across this technique at Boyajiaan's Bazaar, a shop in Chicago's Hyde Park neighborhood. There, in the early 1980s, I found a rusty key chain with a 6-inch triangular beaded tube attached. The tag said "South Africa, $3.00." It was fascinating. I had never seen anything like it. A few years later, I found a square tube necklace. If three and four sides were possible, any number must be possible, I thought. But where had this technique come from, and how many other variations were there?

Zulu beadwork scholar Marilee Wood recognized it as a technique used by a Zulu group living in the Msinga District of KwaZulu Natal, South Africa. The sample Marilee found was called *indundu*, "braided leather cattle whip." She suspected that the technique was rare and that it had been invented in the first half of the twentieth century. Her colleague Frank Jolles had also documented square tubes called *ujantshi*, or "railway line," in the Msinga District. Because their research focused on other issues, neither Marilee nor Frank had collected more information on this technique.

Still hoping to learn more, I asked Phumzile Dlamini, a former student of Frank Jolles and a native Zulu speaker, to do a bit of informal fieldwork.

LEFT Msinga beadworker MaMyaka Sithole, of MaChunwini District, is pictured in 2002 with one of the beaded dolls she makes to sell. She was seventy-one when this photograph was taken.
PHUMZILE DLAMINI

RIGHT These hanging ornaments were made in 2001 of glass beads and copper wire by Msinga women living in the Mdukatshani tribal area of KwaZulu Natal. Msinga wirework is well known, but the idea for these beaded eggs came from Tessa Katzenellembogen, a British designer who helped the Msinga market their work abroad.
center: 2¼" diameter x 2¾" high
Private collection ■ LARRY SANDERS

In 2002, carrying my e-mailed questions and a few color photocopies, Phumzile went to the Msinga District and interviewed six women in their fifties, sixties, and seventies from different towns. All of the women agreed that the technique had originated in the vicinity of Weenen many decades ago and spread eastward. It had gone by different names, including *isitemela*, "train"; *ondlela*, "paths"; and *undlelaziye Goli*, or "way to Johannesburg." Apparently, the parallel rungs of the tubes reminded many Msinga of train tracks, and the broad bands of color on the tubes looked like individual train cars. Trains were important, because they went to distant places such as Johannesburg, where Msinga men traveled, looking for work. The women agreed that knowledge of the technique and its variations had died out in the preceding decades, as it became difficult to get the right beads and the Msinga gradually stopped making beadwork for themselves and started making it for sale on the world market. Still, the women expressed interest in learning the technique again; in fact, Phumzile e-mailed me in early 2004 to say that they were planning to study the diagrams in the book—which brings us all full circle.

Although the beadworkers' testimonies were invaluable, one major question remained. How was tubular polygon stitch invented? Did someone try to represent train tracks in beads? Possibly, but I think there is a better answer, which makes sense if we remember that the Zulu knew a number of techniques. Tubular polygon stitch could have developed by mistake or experiment, as a beadworker familiar with tubular Ndebele herringbone stitch modified the usual thread path. Wise enough to trust her intuition, she kept going, and a new technique was born.

Tubular polygon stitch may look difficult, but it is actually quite easy. Following, you will learn how to make tubes with three, four, and five closed and open sides. It is easiest to learn by using a different color for each side. Once you know the fundamentals, you can make tubes with any number of sides, in colors to suit your imagination. By adding clasp elements, you can turn the tubes into necklaces or bracelets. You can also make beaded beads, as Martha Hall does (see the photograph to the right).

TIPS

- *To prevent knots, it is best to keep waxing lightly as you work.*
- *If a bead looks to be out of alignment, take your needle and reposition it. If this fails, you may have made a mistake.*
- *Some polygon stitch tubes have a tendency to twist. This is especially evident in open-sided tubes worked in cylinder seed beads, but it can also occur in closed-sided tubes.*
- *Once you are experienced, you can try mixing bead sizes in a single tube. I like combining cylinder seed beads with*

1.4mm hex-cut metal beads, as you can see in the photograph to the left.
- *As noted, many tube variations are possible. In addition to varying the spacing between rungs, you can also vary the number of sides and the number of beads per side. But you must use the correct size dowel each time. Below are two tables that I developed for my studio to show which size dowel is required to produce which kind of tube for cylinder seed beads.*

For Closed-Sided Polygon Stitch Tubes in Cylinder Seed Beads

NUMBER OF SIDES	BEADS PER SIDE	DOWEL DIAMETER IN MM
3	3	2.5–3.0
3	4	3.5–4.0
3	5	5.0
3	6	6.0
3	7	7.0
4	3	3.5–4.0
4	4	5.0
5	2	3.0–3.5
5	3	5.0
6	3	6.0
7	3	7.0
9	3	11.0

For Open-Sided Polygon Stitch Tubes in Cylinder Seed Beads

NUMBER OF SIDES	BEADS PER SIDE	DOWEL DIAMETER IN MM
3	5	2.5–3.0
3	7	5.0
4	7	7.0

Shown are Valerie Hector's tubular polygon stitch necklaces in many variations, made in 2002 of glass and metal beads. Collection of the artist ■ *LARRY SANDERS*

MATERIALS

(to make 4" samples of the four tubes listed below)

cylinder seed beads in the following colors

- 5 grams Color A
- 5 grams Color B
- 5 grams Color C
- 2 grams Color D
- 1 gram Color E

6" wooden dowels in the following sizes

- 1 2.5-3mm diameter
- 1 3.0-3.5mm diameter
- 1 3.5-4.0mm diameter
- 1 5.0mm diameter

1 spool cotton/polyester hand-quilting thread, or other beading thread

size 12 beading needles

wax

FIGURE 1

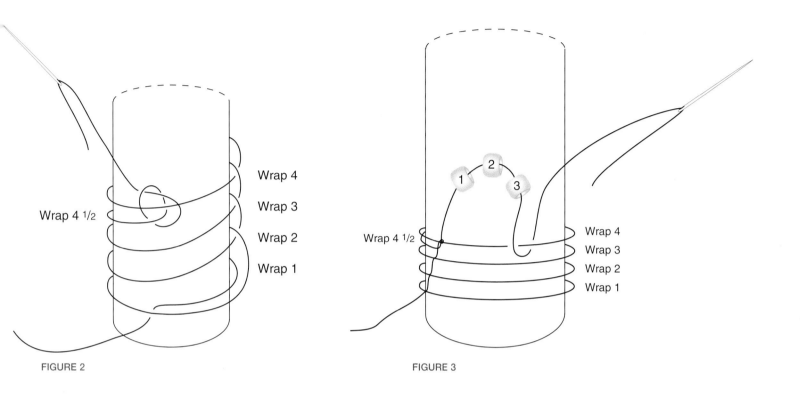

Wrap 4
Wrap 4 ½
Wrap 3
Wrap 2
Wrap 1

FIGURE 2

Wrap 4 ½
Wrap 4
Wrap 3
Wrap 2
Wrap 1

FIGURE 3

4" SAMPLE 1:
A CLOSED-SIDED TRIANGULAR TUBE WITH 3 BEADS PER SIDE
See Figure 1.
WRAPPING THE THREAD AROUND THE DOWEL
1 Thread a needle onto a 64" length of thread, then double the thread to create a 32" length. Wax lightly. Following Figure 2, loop the thread tightly around the dowel. Do not knot the thread at this point. Leave an 8" tail, which you can hold on to as you work.
2 Wrap the thread 3½ more times around the dowel, moving upward very slightly each time. Make one overhand knot around the fourth thread wrap. Pull tightly.
ROW 1
Each row will consist of three segments of 3 beads. In Row 1, you must anchor each

segment to the fourth thread wrap before adding the next segment.
1 To begin, following Figure 3, string 3 Color A beads, 1-3, and insert the needle under the fourth wrap about $\frac{1}{8}$" to the right of bead 3. Pull up tightly and press the beads against the dowel.
2 String 3 Color B beads, 4-6, and insert the needle under the fourth wrap about $\frac{1}{8}$" to the right of bead 6, as shown in Figure 4. Pull up tightly and press the beads against the dowel. The middle bead in each segment will sit slightly above the other two beads.
3 Finally, add 3 Color C beads, 7-9, and insert the needle under the fourth wrap. Pull up tightly. Adjust the segments around the dowel so there is equal space between each segment.

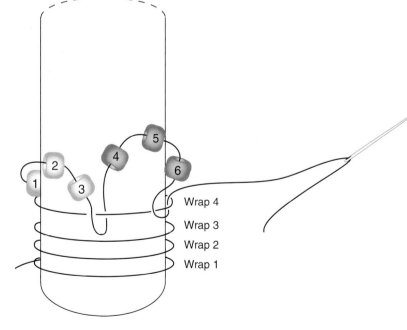

Wrap 4
Wrap 3
Wrap 2
Wrap 1

FIGURE 4

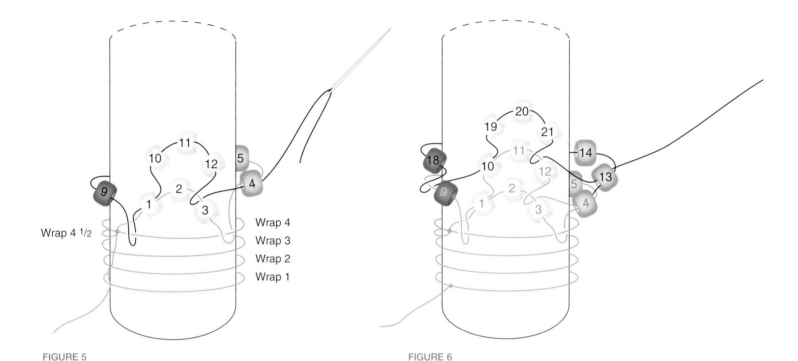

Wrap 4 1/2

Wrap 4
Wrap 3
Wrap 2
Wrap 1

FIGURE 5

FIGURE 6

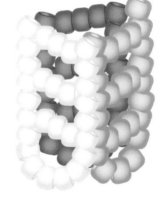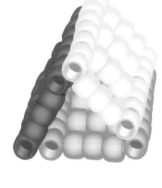

FIGURE 7

ROWS 2-3

1 After you have added beads 7-9 of the third segment of Row 1, again insert the thread under the fourth wrap. Following Figure 5, go up through bead 1.

2 Next, begin the first segment of the second row by adding beads 10-12 in Color A. Now, insert the needle under the thread that connects beads 2 and 3, and pull tightly. Use the thumb of one hand to press them up against the stick as your other hand pulls the thread taut. The beads should snap into place against the stick, directly above the beads below them. If you have trouble, check to be sure you have looped around the thread between beads 2 and 3.

3 To add the second segment of Row 2, go through bead 4, as shown in Figure 5. Next, add beads 13-15 in Color B, and insert the needle under the thread that connects beads 5 and 6. Pull tightly, using your left thumb to press beads 13-15 into place against the

stick, as your right hand pulls the thread taut.

4 To attach the third segment, go through bead 7, add beads 16-18 in Color C, and insert the needle under the thread that connects beads 8 and 9, as shown in Figure 6. Pull tightly. Following Figure 6, work Row 3 and all remaining rows in the same way as Row 2.

SLIDING THE BEADWORK DOWN THE DOWEL

You can bead long tubular polygons using a short dowel if you learn how to slide the beadwork off as you go.

1 After you have beaded about 75% of the dowel, undo the four thread wraps and slide the beadwork down until all but 2" of it has come off the dowel.

2 Next, as close to bead 1 as possible, make two overhand knots, which will prevent the work from coming undone. From now on, every time you finish beading about 75% of the dowel, slide off some of the beadwork. (You can also try using a long dowel, but if

you bead too much of it, it will be hard to remove the beadwork later.)

ADDING MORE THREAD

When the thread starts to run out, insert the needle down through 2-3 dozen beads in a nearby column. Pull tightly, and snip. Prepare a new length of thread. Find where you stopped working and insert the needle around a thread 2-3 dozen beads below that. Make an overhand knot around the thread, which you can undo later, and work your way up to continue beading.

4" SAMPLE 2: AN OPEN-SIDED TRIANGULAR TUBE WITH 7 BEADS PER SIDE

See Figure 7.

This is the tube that was attached to the key chain I found so many years ago. It is worked like the closed-sided tube, except that you insert the needle through the second bead of each segment, add 7 beads per stitch, and then loop around the thread that connects the third-to-last and second-to-last beads of each segment.

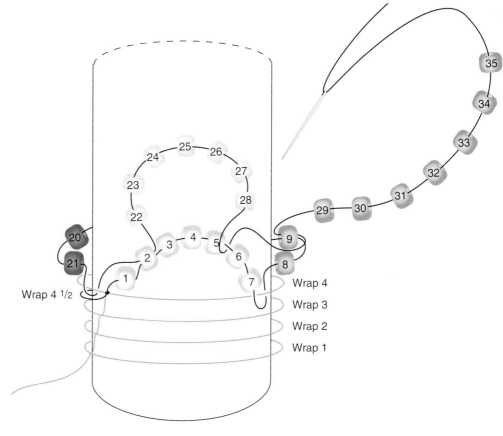

FIGURE 8

ATTACHING THE THREAD TO THE DOWEL

Follow Steps 1 and 2 in Sample 1 but use a 90" length of thread doubled to 45".

ROW 1

1 Follow the instructions for Sample 1, Row 1, but add 3 segments of 7 beads each, alternating Colors A-C as before.

ROWS 2-3

1 After you have added beads 15-21 of Row 1, insert the needle under the fourth thread wrap, then through bead 2. (See Figure 8.)

2 Add 7 Color A beads, 22-28, and insert the needle under the thread that connects beads 5 and 6. Pull sharply as you use your thumb to push the new segment up against the dowel until it snaps into place. Check to be sure you have looped around the thread that connects beads 5 and 6.

3 Next, go through bead 9, add 7 beads, and insert the needle under the thread that connects beads 12 and 13.

4 Continue beading in this way, sliding the beadwork down the dowel as needed.

4" SAMPLE 3:
A CLOSED-SIDED SQUARE TUBE WITH 3 BEADS PER SIDE

See Figure 9.

To make this tube, follow the instructions for Sample 1 with these exceptions:

- Use a 76" length of thread doubled to 38"
- Use Colors A-D
- Use a 3.5-4.0mm dowel
- Add four segments of 3 beads per row

4" SAMPLE 4:
A CLOSED-SIDED PENTAGONAL TUBE WITH 2 BEADS PER SIDE

See Figure 10.

To make this tube, follow the instructions for Sample 1 with these exceptions:

- Use a 68" length of thread doubled to 34"
- Use Colors A-E
- Use a 3.0-3.5mm dowel
- Add five segments of 2 beads per row
- Add 2 beads per stitch, and insert the needle under the thread that connects the 2 beads directly below them

FIGURE 9

FIGURE 10

As we have seen, the European continent is home to the earliest surviving tentative evidence of the art of beadwork, found in Eurasian Ice Age burial sites dating to 26,000-23,000 B.C.E. (See page 11.) One of the earliest fully intact examples is a small woven linen fragment stitched with seeds, recovered from a Neolithic site in Murten, Switzerland, dating to about 3000 B.C.E. Around 2000 B.C.E., elaborate multistrand necklaces were being made in what is now the United Kingdom from beads of organic materials such as Whitby jet and cannel coal. (See page 14.) Not until the thirteenth century C.E. do we find evidence of complex techniques such as bead netting. The first recorded examples of European glass seed beadwork also date to the medieval era, when sumptuous pieces were made for use in Christian churches and rituals.

European Jews also used beadwork to embellish religious textiles. The two panels shown to the left from a Torah mantle made in early eighteenth-century Prague display beautiful inscriptions in Hebrew characters, carefully stitched in tiny seed pearls. From the early seventeenth century on, both the number of beading techniques that appeared in Europe and the number of pieces made with them multiplied exponentially, for the simple reason that glass beads from Venice and other manufacturing centers became available in large quantities, appealing colors, and small sizes. (See page 15.) So many new aesthetic possibilities came along with these beads. They shimmered with reflected light in the sumptuous panels that Victor Hugo hung in Hauteville, his home on Guernsey, one of the Channel Islands, where he wrote some of his most celebrated works, while in religious exile from his native France. (One of the panels is shown on the facing page.)

Glass seed beads gave beadworkers new freedom to render complex pictorial motifs in astonishing detail. Rarely are these pieces signed or dated, but occasionally, as in the Spanish *trompe-l'oeil* panel shown on page 17, we see what may be their initials. In the nineteenth century and well into the twentieth, thousands of imaginative beaded bags were sewn, netted, crocheted, or knitted with European glass and metal beads. Popular motifs of the era included flowers, castles, formal gardens, windmills, and romantic couples; but designers also looked farther afield and adapted motifs from Oriental rugs or from ancient

Egyptian art and architecture. With its curious inscription in unreadable, or nonsensical, Arabic bordered by classic Greek "key" motifs, the knitted bag shown at the top right displays such an international design sensibility.

Beadwork is very much a going concern in Europe in the early twenty-first century. Verena Sieber-Fuchs of Zurich, Switzerland, for example, celebrated the new millennium with nontraditional bead materials such as foil "Happy New Year" platelets. (See page 17.) Contemporary European jewelry designers have also introduced decidedly new ideas, such as the "Arte Ziio" line of bracelets designed by Elizabeth Paradon in Milan, Italy. (See the photograph to the right.) This is only the beginning; there is much more to see in the sections that follow.

ABOVE, LEFT *This is one of five seventeenth-century embroidered panels, probably made in France or England, that hang in Victor Hugo's home on Guernsey. The floral motifs are worked in gold, copper, and chenille threads on a linen ground; white satin glass bugle beads fill the background.*
7' ½" wide x 8' 2" high (including frame)
© Photothèque des Musées de la Ville de Paris/Pierrain, No. 85. HUG 0588
J. M. MOSER

ABOVE, RIGHT *Oriental carpets inspired many beaded bag designs in late nineteenth- and early twentieth-centuries Europe and America. It is possible that the nonsensical Arabic inscription on this knitted bag with a silk drawstring closure was derived from such a source.*
8¼" wide x 9¼" high ■ *Barbara Siciliano*
PETER JACOBS FINE ARTS PHOTOGRAPHY

RIGHT *Elizabeth Paradon's "Arte Ziio" revolutionized wirework jewelry. Small looped wires attach glass, metal, and semiprecious stone beads to curved framing wires in these bracelets from 1999. The "Ziio" logo appears on the metal button clasps.*
left: 2½" wide x 7¾" long ■ *Private collection*
TOM VAN EYNDE

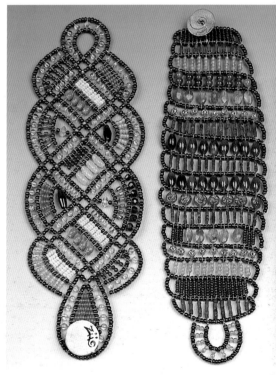

EUROPEAN INSPIRATIONS

SEVENTEENTH-CENTURY ENGLISH BEADWORK

INSPIRATIONAL PIECE
Seventeenth-century English basket

ARTIST
Karen Paust

TECHNIQUES
Tubular and Three-Dimensional Peyote Stitch and Free-Form Looping

BEADWORK PROJECT
"Dandelion Puff" Earrings

2" wide x 2¼" high

One of the most remarkable beading traditions of all time emerged in mid-seventeenth-century England. Venetian glass seed beads had recently begun arriving in England in small sizes and attractive colors, and aristocratic young ladies tired of embroidering with colorful silk threads were anxious to use them. These young women had considerable experience in the traditional techniques of two-dimensional embroidery, and in the latest trend toward three-dimensional "raised," "embosted," or "stumpwork," which required that floral and other motifs be made to project above the fabric to which they were sewn. In ways both obvious and surprising, these young ladies transferred their embroidery skills to beadwork, rendering the same objects and motifs they had been using all along, but adapting the techniques as needed to suit their exciting new raw materials.

Some of best examples of seventeenth-century English beadwork can be found in the three-dimensional baskets that were fashionable in the 1650s and 1660s. Several dozen baskets, such as the one shown here, survive in museums and private collections. A few bear the makers' names or initials, along with dates such as 1658 or 1663. While some look so much alike that kits may have been used, others appear to be strikingly original, even eccentric, one-of-a-kinds. Most are rectangular in shape, but a few are round or oval, with frames built of iron wires lashed together.

The niches between the wires invited endless strategies. Some beadworkers took a straightforward approach, making their baskets look more like trays by covering both the bottoms and the sides with bead-embroidered panels of silk or linen. Other beadworkers left the sides or the bottoms of the baskets open, to be filled with a mix of two- and three-dimensional elements. Often, the frameworks of these baskets were wrapped in stripes of blue or green and white beads strung on wire. The niches along the sides might be backed with a trellislike beaded net and then fitted with a number of three-dimensional sprays containing roses, daffodils, irises, pansies, and chrysanthemums, as well as lemons, oranges, blackberries, gooseberries, acorns, butterflies, and insects. Leaves in every shape and shade of green would complete the sprays and lend them fullness. Most of these floral elements were meticulously worked in peyote stitch, doubled-thread or multiple-thread right angle weave, but other off-loom netting and wireforming techniques also appear. No effort was spared to produce a dazzling conversation piece that might be placed on display in the home, offered as a commemorative gift, or used during christening ceremonies to hold a layette. Long before the end of the reign of King Charles II in 1685, these baskets had fallen out of fashion as tastes shifted to lighter forms of embroidery with motifs inspired by Chinese art.

This seventeenth-century English beadwork basket with an iron wire frame features three aristocratic ladies. One is holding a baby and standing on the grassy hillock of a garden near a fountain and an oak tree. The primary technique is what is today called peyote stitch. 19¹¹⁄₁₆" wide x 16½" high x 5⅞" deep ■ The Elizabeth Day McCormick Collection, 43.531. Courtesy, Museum of Fine Arts, Boston. Reproduced with permission. Photograph © 2004 Museum of Fine Arts, Boston

NO BEADWORKER OF OUR TIME MAKES finer beaded flowers than Karen Paust. She has devoted much of the last fifteen years to perfecting her art, which draws upon her interests in botany and gardening. Working in the garden allows her to observe "countless examples of color, light, and form" that influence what she does in the studio. Like her counterparts in seventeenth-century England, Karen takes no shortcuts, but constructs every petal, leaf, tendril, and insect of peyote, herringbone, and other needle-weaving stitches. Often she works in 14°, 15°, or 16° beads; but when she wants to achieve fine color shadings, she turns to the tiniest sizes: 18°-24°. A single flower may require thousands of painstaking stitches, but in the end, it will be a masterpiece of its kind.

After seeing the beadwork basket shown here, with its aristocratic figures amid opulent flowers and fruits, Karen decided to make a piece that would celebrate the humblest blossoms of all, the ones that grow at random along the fence in her alley. In her "Roadside Bouquet" Necklace, Karen plays up that randomness by positioning blossoms of different sizes and colors on each side of the necklace. On the right side, she places a pink hollyhock flower below a yellow dandelion and a white dandelion seed puff. On the left side, she places a white angel trumpet flower below its prickly seedpod and elongated bud. A bumblebee and a tiger swallowtail butterfly, rendered in the finest detail, complete the necklace. This is Karen's kind of opulence, and it is breathtaking.

Dandelions may be the quintessential weeds, but they make for fascinating beading. Following, Karen shares instructions for making her imaginative "Dandelion Puff" Earrings, shown on page 116. They feature some of the tiniest bugle beads available and involve three-dimensional peyote stitch for the base and seed wings that loop into one another to form a complex web.

Karen Paust of York, Pennsylvania, is a painter, fiber artist, gardener, and beadworker with a long-standing interest in botany. She combines all of these interests in her intricate beaded jewelry and sculpture, which can be found at leading galleries. Her work is widely published.

"DANDELION PUFF" EARRINGS

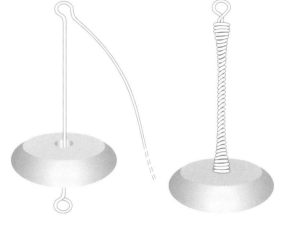

FIGURE 1

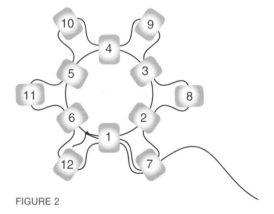

FIGURE 2

Shown are Karen Paust's "Dandelion Puff" Earrings, which she made in 2002. Collection of the artist ■ LARRY SANDERS

MATERIALS

(for a pair of "Dandelion Puff" Earrings)

14° beads

   1 gram matte translucent pale
   yellow-green

   2 grams opaque white luster

   2 grams opaque medium
   brown

2 grams 16° round seed beads,
translucent white opal

6 grams white satin or white-
lined clear bugle beads,
4mm long x 1mm diameter

2 wooden disk beads,
5mm diameter

2 2½" pieces 20 gauge sterling
silver round wire

2 sterling silver earring wires

1 spool white Nymo thread, size
O or OO

size 12 and 15 beading needles

7" fine-cut jeweler's flat or
half-round hand file

small piece 150 grit or finer
sandpaper

round-nose pliers

chain-nose pliers

wire-cutting pliers

wax

To simplify the instructions, I
have used these abbreviations.

   a = add

   gt = go through

   gbt = go back through

PREPARING THE ARMATURE

1 To form the stem of the armature, file and sand one end of a piece of 20 gauge sterling round wire until it is smooth. With round-nose pliers, form a small loop about ¹⁄₈" diameter at this end. (See Figure 1.) Slide a wooden disk bead down the wire until it sits atop the loop. Reduce the size of the loop as needed until it is just large enough to stop up the hole of the disk bead and remain hidden inside.

2 Next, about ³⁄₄" above the top of the disk bead, form another loop in the stem wire, also about ¹⁄₈" in diameter.

Following Figure 1, above, use your fingers to coil the remaining wire around the stem wire. Wrap somewhat loosely at the top and bottom of the stem and more tightly in the middle so that the coiling takes on a curving hourglass-like shape. When you reach the bottom of the stem, snip, file, and sand the end of the wire. Then use chain-nose pliers to push it against the stem.

BEADING THE CIRCULAR PEYOTE STITCH CAP AND THE STEM

A peyote stitch cap worked in white beads will cover the

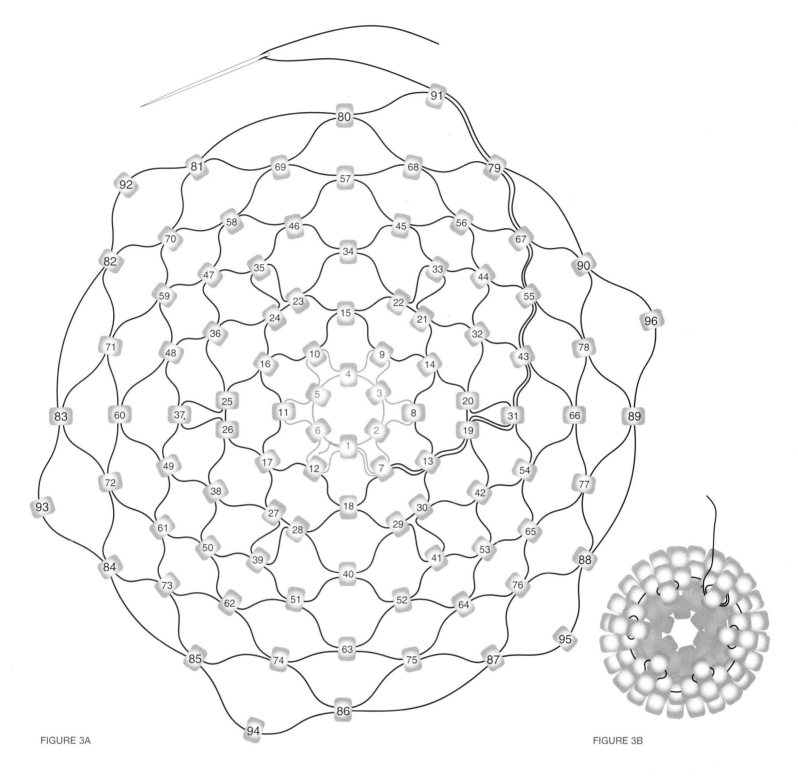

FIGURE 3A

FIGURE 3B

disk bead and serve as the base for the seed wings. The cap will gradually merge into the stem, which is peyote-stitched in yellow-green beads. Start at the bottom of the cap. Then increase and decrease the diameter of the cap so that it fits tightly around the disk bead.

1 To begin the cap, slide a needle onto a 20" length of thread. Do not double the thread. Following Figure 2, a

beads 1-6, and slide them down to within 4" of the tail. Tie a knot between beads 1 and 6. gt bead 1, and a bead 7. gt bead 2, and a bead 8. gt bead 3, and a bead 9. Continue working your way around the circle until you have added bead 12 and gone through beads 1 and 7.

2 Following Figure 3a, a beads 13-96. From beads 13-18, you will add 1 bead per stitch. After adding bead 18,

gt beads and 13. In the following row, from beads 19-30, continue increasing the diameter of the cap by adding 2 beads per stitch. After adding beads 29-30, gt beads 13 and 19. In the following row, return to adding 1 bead per stitch, starting with bead 31 and going through bead 20 before adding bead 32 and going through bead 21. After you have added bead 42, gt beads 19 and 31, and continue

with the next rows.

3 Starting with bead 91, decrease the diameter of the cap by adding 1 bead every other stitch. Still following Figure 3a, after adding bead 91, gt beads 80 and 81. a bead 92, and gt beads 82 and 83. Continue until you have added bead 96 and gone through beads 90, 79, and 91. At this point, your cap should resemble a shallow bowl. (See Figure 3b.)

EUROPEAN INSPIRATIONS

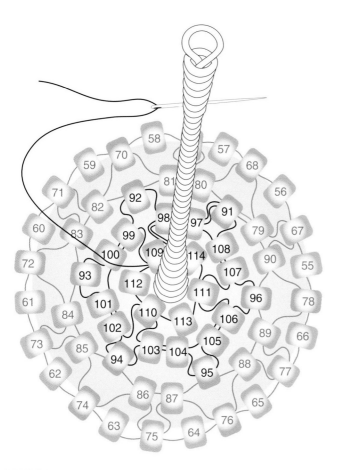

FIGURE 4

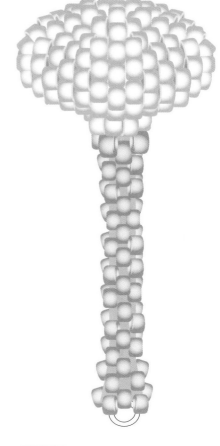

FIGURE 5

4 Next, insert the disk into the cap. The cap should cover the bottom, sides, and part of the top of the disk. If it covers less, you may have to add one or more extra rows at this point. Following Figure 4, work inward, decreasing the diameter of the cap further by adding beads singly or in pairs until you reach the stem. To begin, a beads 97-98, and gt bead 92. a beads 99-100, and gt bead 93. Continue working in this way until you have added beads 107-108 and gone through beads 91, 97, and 98.

5 In the next row, a 1 bead, and gt 4 beads. To begin, a bead 109, and gt beads 99, 100, 101, and 102. a bead 110, and gt beads 103-106. a bead 111, and gt beads 107-108,

97-98, and 109. To complete the final row, a bead 112, and gt bead 110. a bead 113, and gt bead 111. a bead 114, and gt bead 109.

6 Next, following Figure 5, cover the stem with yellow-green beads, adding 1 bead per stitch. When you have finished, anchor the thread by going down through $^3/_4$" of beads in the stem, and snip the thread. Anchor the tail thread at the bottom of the cap, and snip.

BUILDING THE SEED WING PUFF

The seed wings are made of seed and bugle beads attached to the peyote stitch cap. Each wing has a central stem supporting five spokes. The wings are connected at the tips of all five spokes in the center of the

seed puff and at the tips of two, three, or four spokes toward the edges. Karen used about 68 seed wings per earring, building them from the bottom center of the peyote cap outward to its edges.

1 To build the first wing, slide a needle onto a 28" length of thread, and wax the thread. Following Figure 6, insert the needle through at least 5 beads in the bottom of the peyote cap. The thread should stay in place when you pull on the needle. If it moves, go through a few more beads until the thread is securely anchored. a seed beads 1-4 in brown, bugle beads 5-7, beads 8 and 9 in 16° white opal, bugle bead 10, and bead 11 in 16° white opal. Use this same color pattern for

every seed wing and every spoke. Next, gbt beads 10 and 9, and a beads 12-14 of the next spoke. gbt beads 13-12, and a the remaining three spokes of this wing. To return to the peyote cap, go down through beads 8-1.

2 Build the next seed wing in the same manner except, after you add 16° beads 34 and 37, loop around the threads connecting beads 23 and 20.

3 Continue building seed wings and looping their spokes around the spokes of neighboring seed wings until you are satisfied with the volume of the puff. As you run out of thread, add new lengths.

4 To finish the earring, connect a sterling silver ear wire to the loop at the top of the stem. (See Figure 7.)

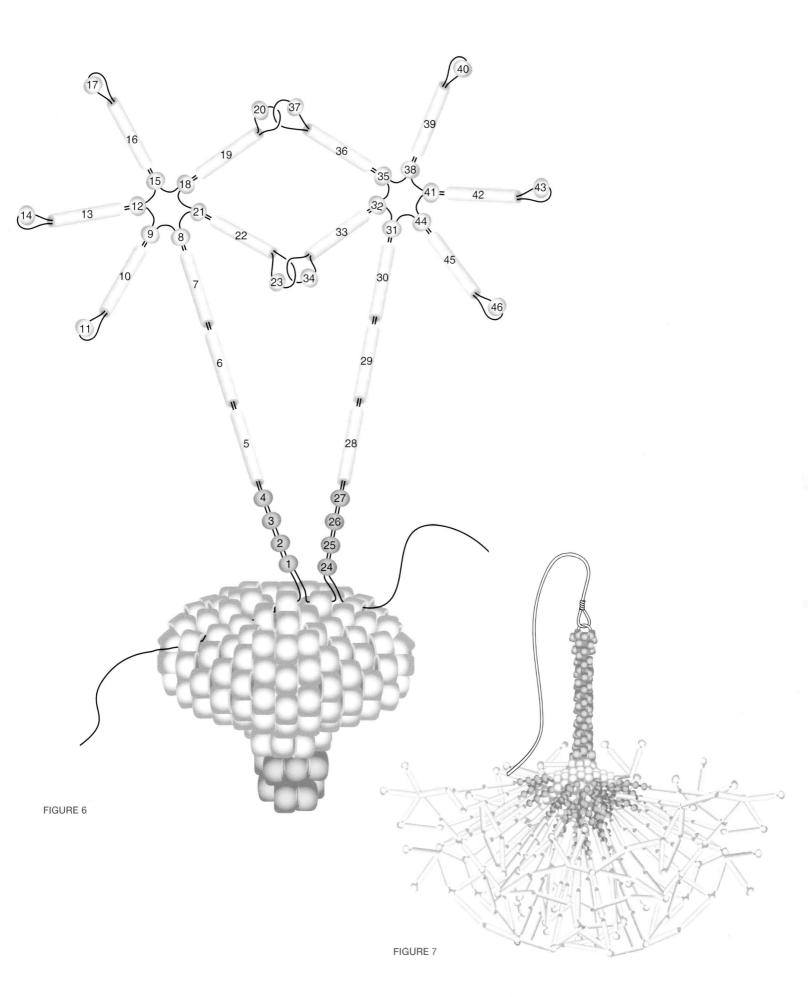

FIGURE 6

FIGURE 7

INSPIRATIONAL PIECE
Table with inlaid glass bead mosaic made in the workshop of J. M. van Selow, ca. 1750-1770, Braunschweig, Germany

ARTIST
Mary Kanda

TECHNIQUE
Mosaic Bead Inlay

The bead mosaic top of a wooden table from the mid-eighteenth-century factory of J. M. van Selow shows a Baroque formal garden replete with topiary trees, a gazebo, and a reflecting pool in front of a stately mansion. 26" wide x 37⅜" high (top only) ■ Städtisches Museum, Braunschweig
MONIKA HEIDEMANN

Besides the flat bead mosaic panels required for tabletops and cabinets, van Selow also worked in the round, making vases, urns, pedestals, and animal figures. Here, an exotic lavender bird on a wooden base strikes a naturalistic pose.
12⅜" wide x 13⅛" high x 6⅛" deep ■ Städtisches Museum, Braunschweig ■ MONIKA HEIDEMANN

More than once in the long history of beadwork, several artists have independently invented similar or identical techniques. They may be separated by hundreds of years or thousands of miles, but these artists are kindred spirits of a sort. Such is the case with Mary Kanda, who invented a way to inlay glass seed beads into sterling silver bezels filled with Portland cement, commonly known as tile grout. Her beaded leaves and flowers have made her famous to collectors of American designer jewelry, who eagerly seek her out at juried craft shows, hoping to take home a new necklace, bracelet, pin, or pair of earrings.

Mary did not learn that she had kindred spirits in mosaic beadwork until she had already mastered the technique on her own. She had always admired mosaics of every kind, especially those on the fences and walls of small towns in the southwestern United States. Wanting to capture the feeling of these mosaics in jewelry, Mary began studying Italian micro-mosaic jewelry, the delicate pictorial kind made in Venice, Italy. But it was hard to locate sources for the glass chips she needed; and when she did find them, they were irregular and difficult to work with.

Everything changed when she switched to prestrung Czechoslovakian glass seed beads, which are easy to handle and uniform. She could lay down strings of beads and then pull out the string once the beads were in place. This process was faster, and it allowed her to establish flowing curves with ease.

Mary's kindred spirits range from the jewelers of the ancient Indus Valley Civilization to the modern Huichol Indians of Jalisco, Mexico. (See pages 22 and 144.) But they used bugle beads, or set seed beads with the holes facing up.

Mary's approach is closest to that of Johann Michael van Selow, a maker of bead mosaic furniture and sculpture in eighteenth-century Germany. He too kept the beads on their strings as he placed them in their settings. He too liked pictorial formats. He would feature Chinese figures in exotic landscapes or bear trainers and their animals or splendid Baroque gardens. Unlike Mary, van Selow used wood or clay instead of sterling silver for his bases and putty instead of tile grout to set the beads. Eventually, he branched out into vases, cabinets, stands, and small animal sculptures. As fate would have it, Johann was

Many of Mary Kanda's bead mosaic pins and earrings are inspired by everyday flowers and leaves. Here is her "Tulip" Pin, made in 2002, of glass beads, sterling silver, tile grout, and a lamp-worked glass element. 1¾" wide x 3½" high ■ Collection of the artist ■ DEAN POWELL

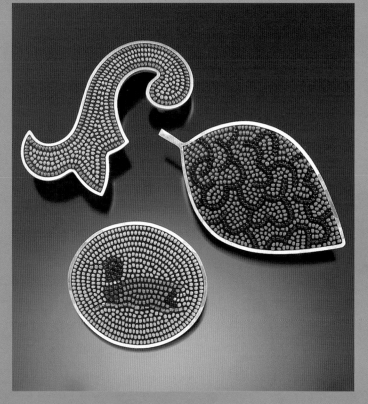

Mary Kanda made this trio of bead mosaic pins set in sterling silver in 2002 in response to motifs featured in the van Selow tabletop shown on the previous page to the left.
leaf pin: 1⅞" wide x 3⅜" high ■ Private collection ■ LARRY SANDERS

not nearly as successful as Mary. His creations never caught on with the buying public. Only a few years after establishing his small bead mosaic factory in Braunschweig, Germany, in 1756, he fell deeply into debt. In 1767, he reluctantly accepted a government-sponsored buyout of his inventory. The factory continued under new ownership, but finally closed in early 1772 or 1773. Today, of course, van Selow's pieces fetch large sums on the antique market, and museums treasure their van Selows as prime examples of eighteenth-century Rococo decorative art.

In response to the tabletop shown on the previous page, Mary created the trio of pins shown at the top right. The oval pin with its floating duck motif was inspired as much by the swans in the tabletop's reflecting pool as by the ducks that visit her property outside Santa Fe. Observing the scallop pattern on the pyramidal topiary trees led her to create a scallop-patterned leaf pin. For the third pin, with its broad, elegant arcs, Mary drew on the topiary bushes just below the pool.

Mary's process sounds straightforward enough. First, she solders and polishes a sterling silver bezel, then paints the inside bottom with an adhesive. After laying strings of beads into the adhesive, she removes the strings and presses tile grout into the beads. Then she wipes the surface clean with a sponge. But the nuances are many, the potential for failure great. If a bead moves out of place as the tile grout goes in, it has to be corrected. If the tile grout is not mixed properly, it will fail to adhere. In tight spaces, the beads have to be set one by one. And so on.

Lately, Mary has been adding small lamp-worked glass spirals that she makes herself. Curiously, van Selow also added prefabricated glass shapes to his pieces. Once again, to coin a phrase, great minds think alike.

Mary Kanda lives on a small ranch outside Santa Fe, New Mexico. She spent years perfecting her bead mosaic technique and is currently experimenting with making large-scale structures. Mary exhibits her work at galleries and juried art fairs around the country. For more information, see www.marykanda.com.

INSPIRATIONAL TRADITION
Wiener Werkstätte beaded jewelry

ARTIST
Jacqueline Lillie

Small flowers, leaves, and tassels add texture to this crocheted necklace designed in 1925 by Felice Rix for the Wiener Werkstätte. In contrast to the solidity and symmetry of the beaded balls, the secondary elements are light, playful, and asymmetrical.
17³⁄₄" diameter ■ Copyright Museen der Städt Wien, Inv. M 3.256
FOTOSTUDIO OTTO

Max Snischek designed this stylish crocheted rope necklace for the Wiener Werkstätte in 1920. Small local firms or individual craftspeople probably carried out much of the Werkstätte's beadwork production, leaving the designers free to work in a variety of media.
59" long ■ Copyright Museen der Städt Wien, Inv. M 3.258
FOTOSTUDIO OTTO

G reat artists in any medium are quick to absorb and transcend the things that inspire them. Beadwork is no exception, and Jacqueline Lillie is one of the great artists of our era. After three years of metalsmithing classes at the Academy of Applied Arts in Vienna, Jacqueline received a phone call from the owner of an antique shop in Vienna. A hatbox of tiny antique European glass beads had just come in, and the entire lot could be had for about fifty dollars. Jacqueline was skeptical. She had never worked with beads, and the price seemed high, so she split the lot with a friend. She took her half home and started doing research on old beading techniques. Eventually, she came across examples of Wiener Werkstätte beadwork from the 1920s. Suddenly she knew what she wanted to do with her cache of beads. Since there was no one to teach her, she started teaching herself.

The Wiener Werkstätte, or Vienna Workshop, was organized in 1903 as a guild for graduates of Vienna's prestigious School of Arts and Crafts. By 1905, it numbered close to a hundred professional artists and craftspeople who came and went, designing

and making ceramics, clothing, furniture, jewelry, metalware, and textiles. Rejecting the factory-made commodities of the day, the Wiener Werkstätte promoted the value of handmade things and advocated the complete union of form, function, and ornamentation—materials should be chosen for their aesthetic potential, not their economic value.

Long before she began beading, Jacqueline knew of these principles, and wholeheartedly agreed with them. However, even from the start, she never copied Wiener Werkstätte designs. Rather she reinterpreted them in her own style, going far beyond them in the process. She continued to use only the tiniest antique beads, because they yielded the most refined motifs and textures. She dramatically expanded the Werkstätte's repertoire of shapes from tubes, spheres, disks, and barrels to spirals, knots, bicones, and squares.

Jacqueline also expanded the vocabulary of patterns favored by Wiener Werkstätte beadwork designers. Like a gifted mathematician, she devised intricate geometric sequences that balance

Taking liberties with traditional Wiener Werkstätte necklace elements, Jacqueline Lillie separates the spheres with knots in this "Ball" Necklace from 1986, which, like all of her pieces, is worked in tiny antique European glass beads. The knottable clasp is an integral part of the design. 24" long ■ Private collection. Courtesy, Rosanne Raab & Associates, New York ■ ROBERT ZAHORNICKY

Jacqueline Lillie often finishes her beaded structures with sterling silver or stainless steel findings of her own design. In her "Fibula" Brooch, made in 1988, the simplicity of the sterling silver contrasts with the complexity of the spiraling finial and the beaded Perspex disk, giving the eyes a place to rest. 3⅝" diameter x 8" high ■ The Corning Museum of Glass, No. 89.3.7. Photograph: Corning Museum of Glass

continuity and change. In some pieces, such as the untitled necklace shown to the right, a sophisticated tension emerges between positive and negative, and this is yet another hallmark of Jacqueline's aesthetic.

Jacqueline has always preferred to keep her beading technique private. She acknowledges only that she knots each bead individually, thereby assuring the highest quality. We can only gaze at her masterpieces and marvel. She has been imitated but never surpassed.

Jacqueline Lillie of Vienna, Austria, was born in Marseille, France, and studied metalsmithing at the Academy of Applied Arts in Vienna. Jacqueline's pieces appear in numerous museum collections in the United States and Europe, and she exhibits with several American galleries. For more information, contact Rosanne Raab at www.rosanneraab.com.

Orange and red continually trade places in this untitled rope-and-disk necklace from 1996, shown here in a sculptural format. Before uniting the beads, Jacqueline Lillie first strings them in precise color sequences, an approach also used in bead crochet. 17¾" long ■ Private collection. Courtesy, Rosanne Raab & Associates, New York ■ KOHL-OLAH

123

INSPIRATIONAL PIECE
Funeral wreath, probably from France, ca. 1900-1930

ARTIST
Valerie Hector

TECHNIQUE
Wire Wrapping

BEADWORK PROJECT
"Floral" Pin

1¾" wide x 6½" long

In this stereocard published by Underwood & Underwood, more than a dozen beaded wreathes decorate the grave of Fernande Verbert in Laeken, Belgium. She died on March 22, 1888. French inscriptions on two of the wreathes read "To Our Little Niece" and "To My Goddaughter."
7" wide x 3½" high ■ Collection of Karen Hendrix ■ TOM VAN EYNDE

There is no realm of human experience that beadwork has not touched upon. Even death has been addressed, in ways that vary markedly by culture. As we have seen, for many millennia magnificent beaded pieces have been produced to commemorate the dead or to equip them for the afterlife. (See pages 10, 12, and 76.)

In the United States, when someone dies, fresh flowers are sent. But the flowers themselves soon wither and die. The French discovered a way around this problem. They made funeral wreaths out of glass beads, galvanized steel wire, and other durable materials that would last for months, even years, thereby countering the brevity of human life with the durability of human-made materials. For many decades, these wreaths were placed on graves in Catholic cemeteries in France, Belgium, and Germany.

It is hard to say exactly when the French first started making beaded funeral wreaths. But by the second half of the nineteenth century, they were so common that the famous French writer Emile Zola noticed how many styles there were. White wreaths, he tells us, marked the graves of women and children, and dark wreaths went to men. Some of the wreaths were personalized with inscriptions or with photographs placed under glass. Once a year, on November 1, All Saints' Day, the wreaths were repaired or replaced as the graves were tended. So great was the demand for these wreaths that at times French beadmaking factories were hard-pressed to maintain an adequate supply of the muted colors required.

The burgeoning French market for beaded funeral wreaths did not go unnoticed in Venice. Around 1880, two Italian sisters, Eulalia and Amelia Dorigo, supposedly spent several years in Paris studying every aspect of wreath manufacture. Upon their return to Venice in 1882, they established a wreath-making school that eventually attracted some two hundred students. Before long wreaths and wreath components destined for France were being made in cottage industry settings in Venice, home to a thriving glass seed bead industry and to legions of skilled women known as *impiraresse*, "bead stringers."

Beaded wreaths continued to be made well into the twentieth century. During World War I, they often appeared on the graves of fallen soldiers. Two large beaded wreaths, one light and one dark, once decorated the grave of Theodore Roosevelt's youngest son, Air Force Lieutenant Quentin Roosevelt, whose plane was shot down by German soldiers on July 14, 1918, in Chamery, northern France. When relatives could not be present to lay the wreaths on the graves of their loved ones, other people assisted, such as the two women

In a photograph dated February 9, 1918, two somber young women, members of the Women's Auxiliary Army Corps during World War I, distribute wreathes dedicated to fallen British soldiers at a cemetery in Abbeville in northwest France.
Imperial War Museum London, PCS25/6, Neg. No. Q8471

pictured above. Family members probably ordered these wreaths ready-made from funeral supply companies, which in turn ordered them from suppliers in Paris and elsewhere. Although beaded funeral wreaths were no longer made after World War II, even today they can occasionally be seen at cemeteries in France and Belgium, hidden away in darkened tombs as poignant emblems of love and loss.

To constuct this cross-shaped wreath, a framework of galvanized steel wire, designed to resist corrosion, was wrapped with paper or floss that was in turn wrapped with long strands of beads strung on wire. Wirework spirals and flowers complete the ensemble.
25" wide x 38" high
Architectural Artifacts, Chicago, IL
DAVID WILKES

THIS STAR-SHAPED WREATH, with its little porcelain cherub, signaled the death of a child. Did the child die of natural causes or as a result of war? Was this wreath ever used, or had it been sitting around some old warehouse all these decades? It is impossible to say. My eyes kept returning to the serrated edges of the wreath. At first these edges seemed innocuous, like abstract leaves or petals, and I made the curving, wreathlike pin in orange beads shown on page 126. (Instructions for making this pin follow.) Later I began to see the serrations as saw blades or ominous shards of shrapnel. The purple pin, also pictured on page 126, resulted from this darker perspective.

Faded plastic (possibly celluloid) flowers surround a somber porcelain angel and add a strangely upbeat note to this twentieth-century funeral wreath of glass beads, cotton, and galvanized steel wire.
19" diameter x 3" deep ■ Private collection ■ TOM VAN EYNDE

"FLORAL" PIN

Shown are two of Valerie Hector's "Wreath-Inspired" Pins. The project pin is shown at the left. A continuous strand of knotted loops of beads, tightly wrapped around a sterling silver armature, was used in the pin at the right. Collection of the artist ■ LARRY SANDERS

TIPS
- *The instructions given here will produce a large pin 1¾" wide by 6½" long. If you want a pin half that size, you can reduce the length of the four sterling wire segments by half.*
- *The ribbon lengths provided in the Materials list are generous. You will use more ribbon if you space your wraps closer together than if you space them farther apart.*
- *It is important to wrap tightly and establish consistent spacing between wraps.*

MATERIALS

12 grams 15° glass beads, opaque red, pink, or wine luster

12 yards 4mm-wide silk or synthetic ribbon, dark rose or color to match beads

6' 8" sterling silver or brass round wire, cut into 4 20" lengths

1 spool 26 or 28 gauge black-coated craft wire

1 bobbin cotton/polyester hand-quilting thread, red or other matching color

1 commercial 3-hole pin back with attached pin stem

size 10 needles

small piece 150 grit or finer sandpaper

round-nose pliers

chain-nose pliers

cutting pliers

7" jeweler's fine-cut flat or half-round hand file

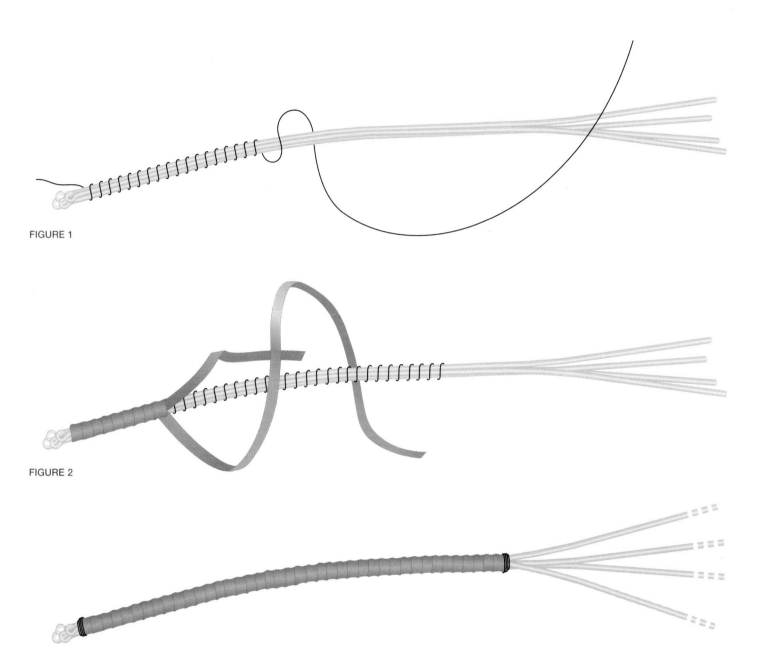

FIGURE 1

FIGURE 2

FIGURE 3

FORMING THE STEM

The stem consists of four sterling silver wires bound together by a length of black wire covered by ribbon.

1 To begin, file and sand both ends of each sterling silver or brass wire until they are smooth. With needle-nose pliers, form a loop at one end of each wire. With chain-nose pliers, squeeze each loop a little to flatten it. Pick up the wires and arrange them so that the loops are touching.

2 Cut off a 24" length of black wire (or leave it on the spool if you prefer). Leaving a $^1/_4$" tail, begin wrapping the four silver wires together, starting at their loops. (See Figure 1.) Continue wrapping until you have covered about 6" of the silver or brass wires. Snip the wire $^1/_4$" away from the last wrap. Finish wrapping the tail wire, and snip it.

3 Take a length of ribbon 3 yards long (or leave it on the spool if you prefer). Following

Figure 2, begin wrapping tightly around the wire nearest the loops. Leave a 2-3" tail. Wrap tightly over at least 2" of the tail of the ribbon to hold it in place. Snip off any excess tail ribbon. Continue wrapping until the 6" of binding wire are all covered with ribbon.

4 Next, heading in the opposite direction, wrap another layer of ribbon around the first layer all the way down to the loops. Then add a third layer of ribbon, moving away from

the loops and toward the four loose wires. Snip off the extra ribbon, leaving a 2" tail.

5 Pressing down on the ribbon to keep it in place, wrap a 2" length of black wire tightly 3-5 times around the ribbon to secure it. (See Figure 3.) Snip off the tail as close to the black wire as possible. Take another 2" length of black wire and wrap it tightly 3-4 times around the ribbon nearest the loops. Now the stem ribbon is secure.

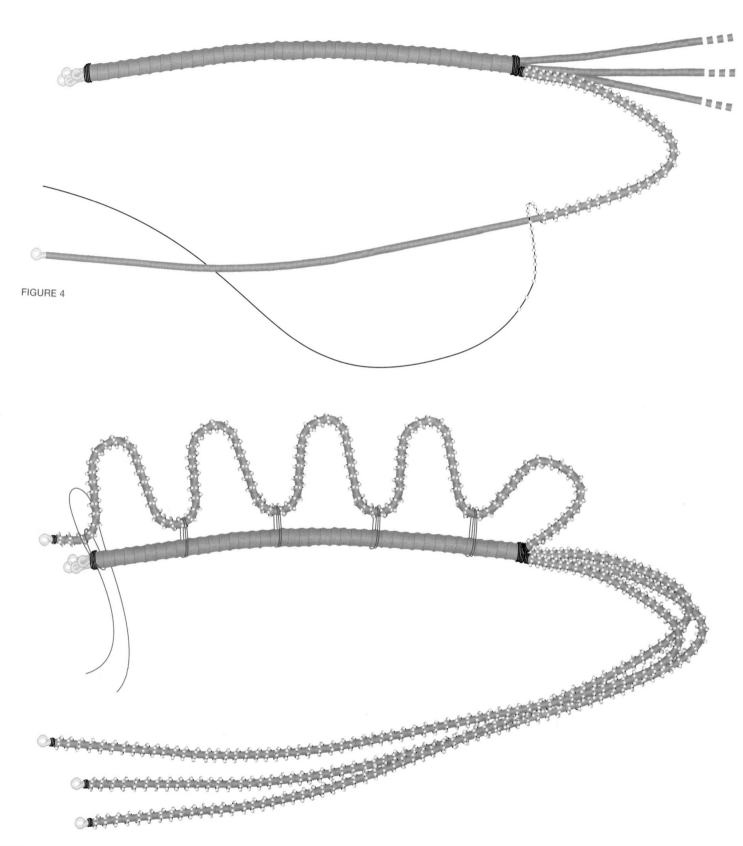

FIGURE 4

FIGURE 5

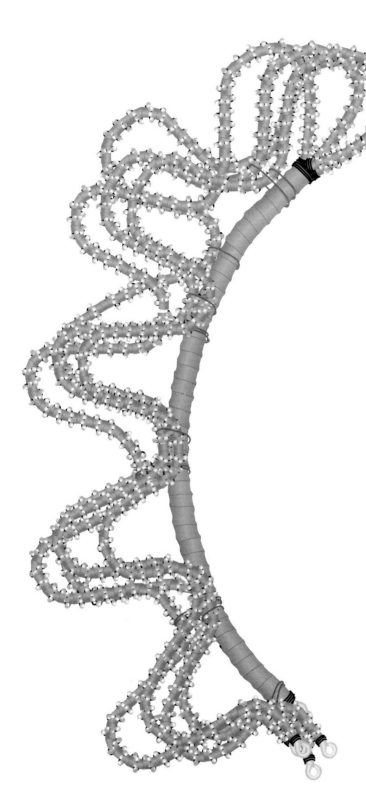

WRAPPING RIBBON AND BEADS AROUND THE BRANCHES

1 Next, tightly wrap one layer of ribbon around each of the four branches. You will need about $2^{1}/_{4}$ yards of ribbon for each branch. When you are finished, secure the opposite ends of each branch with black wire just as you did for the stem.

2 Next come the beads. Thread beads onto 1 yard of the spool of black wire. Secure the wire by wrapping $^{1}/_{2}$" of it several times around the ribbon nearest the stem of the first branch.

3 Slide the beads down the wire, and start wrapping them tightly over the ribbon. (See Figure 4.) Continue wrapping until you reach the loop end of the wire. To secure the beads, wrap about $^{1}/_{2}$" of black wire around the end nearest the loop, and snip.

4 Repeat until all the remaining branches are beaded.

SHAPING THE BRANCHES AND ATTACHING THEM TO THE STEM

Form each branch with your hands so that it snakes down the stem. You can use needle-nose pliers to help you, but you run the risk of cracking a bead.

1 Shape the first branch as shown in Figure 5, so that the end of the branch aligns with the end of the stem. Make six scallops. Each will be about 1" tall and 1" wide at its base.

2 Next, slide a needle down a 2-yard length of thread, and double the thread. Loop the thread around the base of one of the center scallops, and tie a knot around the scallop. Stitch into the ribbon in the stem, and pull the scallop close to the stem. Loop around the scallop again, and stitch into the stem several times until the scallop is secure. Snip the excess thread.

3 Form the other branches in the same way, making six, seven, or eight scallops per branch. Then stitch them into the stem. You can also stitch the branches to one another. Figure 6 shows the completed piece. Shape the branches as desired.

ADDING A PIN STEM

1 Stitch a pin stem to the back of the stem.

FIGURE 6

AMERICAN
INSPIRATIONS

I n North, Central, and South America and in the Caribbean—as in other parts of the world—beadwork was created as beads were added to strung, sewn, netted, twined, plaited, and woven textiles and baskets. Beadworkers of the Americas expertly harnessed the potential of a wide variety of organic bead materials, ranging from pine nuts and juniper berries; to animal bones, claws, and teeth; to abalone, dentalium, and other marine shells. Beads of inorganic materials such as stone and metal were also deployed to maximum effect. In the Americas as elsewhere, beadwork researchers face the same problem: Very few early pieces have survived.

ABOVE This early sixteenth-century Taíno zemi, a kind of spiritually charged object associated with shamans and the ruling elite, depicts what may be the face of a bat or an ancestral human skull. The face of a living human may be depicted on the other side.
19½" wide x 32" high ■ Courtesy, Archivio Fotografico del Museo Preistorico Etnografico "Luigi Pigorini," Rome, No. 4190 ■ DAMIANO ROSA

RIGHT "Powhatan's Mantle," ca. 1608, is one of the earliest surviving examples of North American Indian beadwork, and it is a masterpiece composed of Marginella roscida shells meticulously stitched in concentric circles or parallel rows to a deerskin ground.
59" wide x 92" high ■ Ashmolean Museum, University of Oxford, PHIGH 4329

One of the earliest extant examples is "Powhatan's Mantle," shown to the right, which is worked entirely in Marginella shells on a deerskin ground. Powhatan was chief of the Virginia Algonquians in the early seventeenth century. Presumably, he is represented as the central figure of the mantle, surrounded by thirty-four circles that represent chiefdoms under his control.

The arrival of European glass beads into the Americas and the Caribbean in the late fifteenth century radically altered the beadworking landscape by introducing new possibilities of color, texture, detail, and light reflectivity. Glass beads also eliminated the hand labor required to shape and perforate beads of indigenous materials such as shell. Almost instantly after they obtained European glass beads, the indigenous peoples of the Americas and Caribbean started incorporating them into their beadwork compositions.

Instead of clashing with existing bead materials, European beads complemented them. An excellent example of this productive synthesis can be

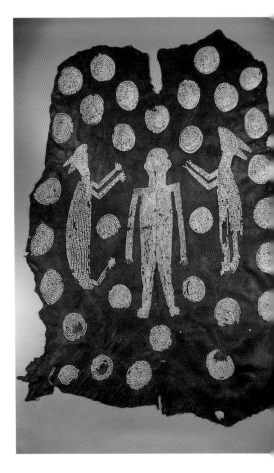

LEFT *Pictured here is Ashuca Losano of Tuncarta, Saraguro, Ecuador, making a beaded collar for sale to other women in her community, ca. 1978. She uses a single-thread netting technique and a zigzag motif similar to that used by Chimú beadworkers in Peru several centuries earlier.*
LYNN MEISCH

BELOW *"Marassatrois," or "The Twins That Are Three," is a Vodou flag made by Eviland Lalanne of Port-au-Prince, Haiti, ca. 1990, of sequins and beads stitched to cloth. This flag honors the spirits of the Marasa, or "Sacred Twins," who, along with the child born after them, are believed to have magical powers.*
30" wide x 38" high ■ Collection of Marilyn Houlberg ■ DIANE ALEXANDER WHITE

seen in the *zemi* shown on the facing page, made by the Taíno peoples of the Greater Antilles in the early sixteenth century, only a few years after the arrival of Christopher Columbus and his men in the area in 1492. The body of the *zemi* is worked in organic materials indigenous to the region, including seeds and conch shell beads crocheted, braided, and stitched with cotton thread over a wooden hemisphere. The Taíno loved European glass beads the moment they saw them and integrated them effortlessly into the *zemis*' arms (or wings) and eye sockets. European mirrors made perfect eyes and ear spools. Somehow, these and other disparate elements work together beautifully. Sadly, by the mid-sixteenth century, the Taíno had been wiped out, largely by European diseases.

One of the most vibrant beadworking traditions of our time flourishes in Haiti, where artists create beaded and sequined flags, such as the one shown to the right, to honor the saints and spirits of the *Vodou* religion. *Vodou* is a syncretic religion that blends elements of Christianity with elements of the African religions that were brought to

Haiti by slaves from West and Central Africa. African slaves were used to farm the cocoa, cotton, sugarcane, and coffee plantations of the French colonists. Originally, *Vodou* flags were made for use in nighttime temple ceremonies, where they flashed with reflected light. After being taken from a temple storeroom, the flags were unfurled, attached to a portable flagstaff, and danced with by the *laplace*, or senior-ranking *Vodou* member. Now, they are also made for sale by a number of artists. However, this is not strictly a commercial undertaking, because the artists are also practitioners of *Vodou* who are sincere in their wish to honor a particular saint or spirit. The making of a flag is a meditative process, requiring, on average, some 18-20,000 plastic sequins and glass beads, stitched individually with the help of one or more assistants.

Plains and Plateau Beadwork

INSPIRATIONAL PIECES
*Photographs of Nez Perce warriors
and skyline of Portland, Oregon*

ARTIST
Marcus Amerman

An early twentieth-century example of traditional Plains pictorial beadwork, this wool-and-muslin bag depicts a lone horse and rider on one side and a simple tepee scene on the other. It may be the work of the Lakota or Western Sioux.

8" wide x 8" high ■ Mitchell Museum of the American Indian, Kendall College, Evanston, IL, Cat. No. 88.31 ■ DIANE ALEXANDER WHITE

LEFT Marcus thinks of his "Chief Minthorn" Bracelet from 1993 as a beaded wrist painting. It is made of glass beads, rubberized cotton, leather, and a color photocopy of a photograph of the chief.
2" wide x 7" long ■ Collection of Misa Joo
MARCUS AMERMAN

In their own powerful way, Marcus Amerman's beaded pictures speak volumes about the North American Indian experience. A Choctaw by descent, Marcus was born in Phoenix, Arizona, and raised in Pendleton, Oregon. He started his training early, watching as family members practiced traditional Native American Indian arts such as painting, carving, silversmithing, and beading. Marcus vividly remembers attending the Pendleton Roundup rodeo in the 1960s, where he saw North American Indians dancing in brightly beaded costumes and cowboys riding broncos. Many of the Native Americans attending the Roundup came from nearby Plains or Columbia Plateau tribes such as the Nez Perce, Umatilla, and Yakima. They brought with them spectacular pieces of woven and sewn beadwork, such as the bag shown to the above right, which featured geometric or simple pictorial motifs including deer, elk, bear, bald eagles, flowers, trees, mountain scenes, warriors on horseback, women holding infants, and American flags. Marcus was fascinated. At age ten, he began doing beadwork. By the time he was fifteen, he had his own table

at the Roundup, and it did not take him long to sell his first piece. Little did that customer know that Marcus was destined to become an artist of international renown.

Eventually, after pursuing classes in math and physics at Whitman College in Walla Walla, Washington, Marcus changed his major to fine art and began studying painting and sculpture. Following graduation, he attended the Institute of American Indian Art in Santa Fe, where he also studied filmmaking and photography. It was in Santa Fe that he first began making beaded portraits of famous Native American leaders such as Geronimo (1829-1909) of the Apache and Chief Joseph (1840-1904) of the Nez Perce. Marcus would photocopy an old photograph, glue the copy to a piece of rubberized cotton, and stitch beads in parallel lines over the copy, using the beads as a kind of paint to emphasize certain aspects of the photo. In effect, he had invented a kind of photo-realist beadwork that allowed him to bring together his interests in painting, beadwork, and film, while honoring North American Indian cultural heroes whose

ABOVE "The Gathering," a bead painting created by Marcus Amerman in 1999, reflects the complexity of Native American life in late twentieth-century America, where skyscrapers dominate a horizon once filled with trees, mountains, and sky.

17" wide x 10" high ■ Portland Art Museum, Portland, Oregon. Marcus Amerman, "The Gathering," 1997, beadwork, 10" high x 17" wide, Pratt Fund Purchase

LEFT Eleven mounted Nez Perce warriors, some wearing feather headdresses and beaded regalia, line up as if preparing for battle. They were photographed on the Umatilla Reservation in Oregon by Major Lee Moorhouse on July 4, 1906.

National Anthropological Archives, Smithsonian Institution, Neg. No. 2987-B-12 ■ MAJOR LEE MOORHOUSE

courageous lives and deeds are too seldom remembered.

To create "The Gathering," shown above, Marcus collaged three photographs from different time periods. The first, shown here, which he placed in the foreground, was taken in the early twentieth century. The second, which appears in the background, was taken in the 1990s and shows skyscrapers in downtown Portland. The third photograph, also recent, shows Mt. Hood, which looms in the distance beyond the city. Each photograph energizes the other, and the combination produces a brilliant work of art that can be interpreted in various ways. Astride their horses on a small but prominent patch of grass, the warriors seem to be asserting their rights to the ancient lands that were taken from them. They are still the landlords, very much alive in the present and proudly maintaining their culture. This is what Marcus had in mind as he was making the piece.

As an artist Marcus straddles two worlds, melding two kinds of formal art training—one Western, the other North American Indian. Whether he is painting, beading, or engaging in performance art, he sees himself as a kind of warrior whose purpose is to educate Americans of all races and backgrounds about "the beauty and power of our Indian culture." He feels a spiritual kinship with all North American Indians and a sense of responsibility to formulate the truth as it appears to him. Yet he is also comfortable taking for his subject matter familiar icons of pop culture such as Marilyn Monroe, Michael Jackson, and various *Star Wars* characters. Once beaded, their images look somewhat North American Indian, an irony Marcus relishes.

Marcus Amerman of Santa Fe, New Mexico,
is a renowned visual and performance artist of Choctaw Indian heritage who has been beading seriously since he was a child. Traditional and contemporary influences blend seamlessly in Marcus's beadwork, which can be found in museum and private collections.

INSPIRATIONAL PIECE
Beadwork bag of the Achomawi or Atsugewi tribe, Pit River Region, northern California, ca. early twentieth century

ARTIST
Don Pierce

TECHNIQUE
Loomweaving

BEADWORK PROJECT
"Quail on the Mountain" Evening Bag

5" wide x 8" high
(dimensions of the body of the bag, closed)

ABOVE *An unknown American Indian woman, possibly a Fox, may be preparing to weave beads in this late nineteenth- or early twentieth-century photograph. The top ends of her warp threads are attached to a tree and the bottoms appear to be loose. White beads sit on a nearby cloth.*
Courtesy, Denver Public Library, Western History Collection/Geneology Dept., X-33896

RIGHT *Shown are details of three late nineteenth- or early twentieth-century Great Lakes beaded sashes with pulsating motifs rendered in complex color harmonies. The top and middle sashes were probably woven by the Wisconsin Potawatomi and the bottom by the Chippeway. The beads are European glass.*
top sash: 4⅛" wide x 76" overall
Courtesy, Benson L. Lanford Collection
LARRY SANDERS

Beads have evidently been woven into textiles since at least the mid-second millennium B.C.E. True beadweaving typically involves a weft thread that moves horizontally across a set of vertical warp threads. It is the weft thread that usually carries the beads, depositing one or more of them between warp threads; but there are exceptions to this rule. Beads may be used sparingly—to accent areas of the textile—or in such great abundance that they nearly obscure the threads used to hold them together. A loom is not necessary. The warp threads need only be secured at one end by attaching them to a board, stake, tree, or other object. In such "loose warp" techniques, the lower ends of the warp threads hang freely. In "fixed warp" techniques, on the other hand, the lower ends are secured in some way—either to the waist of the weaver or to a bar, loom, or other device—thereby creating tension and making the weaving process more efficient.

Many cultures have practiced beadweaving over the centuries, but few have been as prolific as the North American Indians of the Subarctic, Plateau, Great Basin, Plains, Great Lakes, Woodlands, and Southeast. It is impossible to know when beadweaving began in these regions. One of the earliest surviving examples may well be the "Hiawatha" Wampum Belt, shown on the facing page, which, according to native tradition, was completed before the arrival of the white man. Other wampum belts were recorded starting in the 1620s. In the nineteenth and twentieth centuries especially, using vast quantities of European glass seed beads and both loose and fixed warp techniques, North American Indian beadweavers pursued high standards of artistic and technical achievement. This is to say nothing of their contributions in bead sewing, netting, plaiting, twining, and basketry.

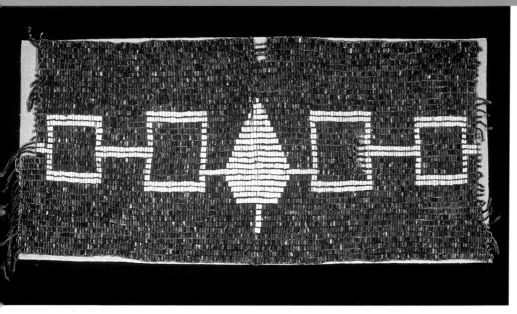

The famous "Hiawatha" Wampum Belt, woven with cylindrical mollusk shell beads, commemorates the centuries-old Haudenosaunee, or "People of the Long House" alliance between the five Indian nations that the French called "Iroquois." According to oral tradition, the stylized pine tree at the belt's center represents the Onondaga Nation and the Tree of Peace. From east to west, the open squares represent the Mohawk, Oneida, Cayuga, and Seneca.
10½" wide x 21½" long ■ New York State Museum, Albany, NY, Ref. No. E-37309, now curated at The Onondaga Nation. Used with permission of The Council of Chiefs, Onondaga Nation

One artist's interpretation of what is probably the "quail feather" motif is featured in this detail of a bag made by the Achomawi or Atsugewi peoples of the Pit River Region, northern California, ca. early twentieth century.
6 9/16" wide x 26½" long ■ Denver Art Museum Collection: Native Arts acquisition fund, 1948.135. © Denver Art Museum 2002

DON PIERCE DID NOT TAKE UP beadwork until the mid-1980s, when he was in his fifties. He found himself looking over his wife's shoulder, suggesting ways she could improve her beadweaving. One day, half in jest, she challenged him to make his own piece. So he began reading books and studying the work of other loomweavers. Within ten years he had emerged as a major artist in his own right.

Like the beadweavers of northern California's Achomawi and Atsugewi tribes, Don favors strong, simple geometric patterns. One of their woven bags caught his eye, and he decided to adopt its motifs for a bag of his own. Never one to generate designs by computer, he worked out the specifics on graph paper. After finishing his bag, he happened upon an artist at the Indian Market in Portland, Oregon. She was from the Yurok, another northern California tribe, and her prints featured the same motif that Don had seen on the Achomawi/Atsugewi bag. She told him that the motif is also traditional among the Yurok, who call it "Quail on the Mountain." Don interpreted this coincidence as a blessing of sorts, and named his bag accordingly. Following, he shares instructions for making his "Quail on the Mountain" Evening Bag, shown on page 136.

Don Pierce of Coos Bay, Oregon, began loom beading in 1987 after seeing the work of Virginia Blakelock and other artists at "The Bead Goes On," an exhibit of contemporary beadwork in Eugene, Oregon. Today he is widely respected as a beadwork artist and educator. He is the author of *Beading on a Loom* and *Designs for Beading on a Loom*. Don teaches and exhibits his work nationally. For more information, see www.donpierce.com.

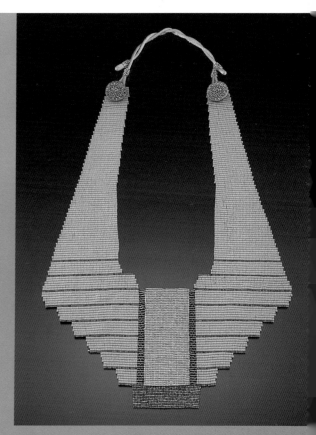

Don Pierce's 1998 "El Castillo: Turquoise" Neckpiece was inspired by El Castillo, an ancient Mayan pyramid at Chichén Itzá in the Yucatán peninsula of Mexico, and loomwoven with porcelain, glass, and metal beads.
9¾" wide x 13¼" high ■ Collection of the artist
LARRY SANDERS

"QUAIL ON THE MOUNTAIN" EVENING BAG

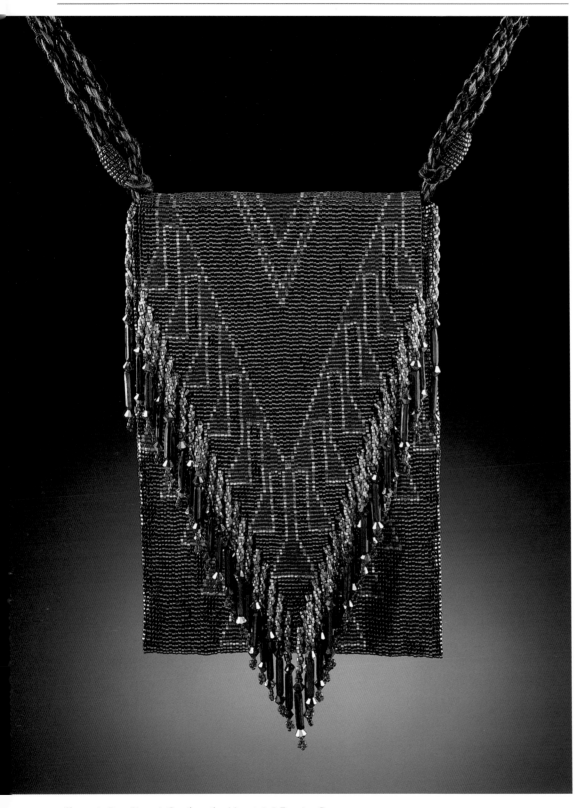

Shown is Don Pierce's Quail on the Mountain" Evening Bag.
Collection of the artist ■ LARRY SANDERS

MATERIALS

Cylindrical seed beads

    13 grams galvanized gold

    6 grams violet iris

    40 grams metallic black violet

Other beads

    86 ⅝" x ⅛" glass bugle beads, matte metallic midnight blue-purple

    172 6mm Arium 2X (2-cut) bicones

2-3 size 12 beading needles

132 yards Nymo D thread

1 yard thick polyester cord, black (for the strap)

¼ yard polyester satin fabric, black (for the lining)

beading loom

WARPING THE LOOM AND TYING ON THE WEFT THREAD

1 Attach 97 warp threads to the loom. Each thread should be 42" long. To prepare the weft thread, slide a needle onto a 60" length of thread. Do not wax or double the thread. About 6-8" down from the top end of the warp threads tie an overhand knot around the first warp thread, leaving a 6" tail. (If your loom is in the upright position, make a knot around the left side warp 6-8" above the bottom ends of the warp threads.)

ROWS 1-222

1 For Row 1, string 96 beads in the following order: 47 metallic black violet, 2 galvanized gold, and 47 metallic black violet. Stretch the weft thread below the warp threads so that you have one bead between every two warp threads. (See Figure 1.)

2 When you reach the end of the row, loop around and over the outer warp thread. With one hand, press beads 96, 95, and 94 up between their respective warp threads, and use the other hand to insert the needle through these beads. Pull the thread firmly.

3 Keep working your way across Row 1 in this way, going through 2-3 beads at a time until the needle is coming out of the first bead you added. Pull firmly. (See Figure 2.)

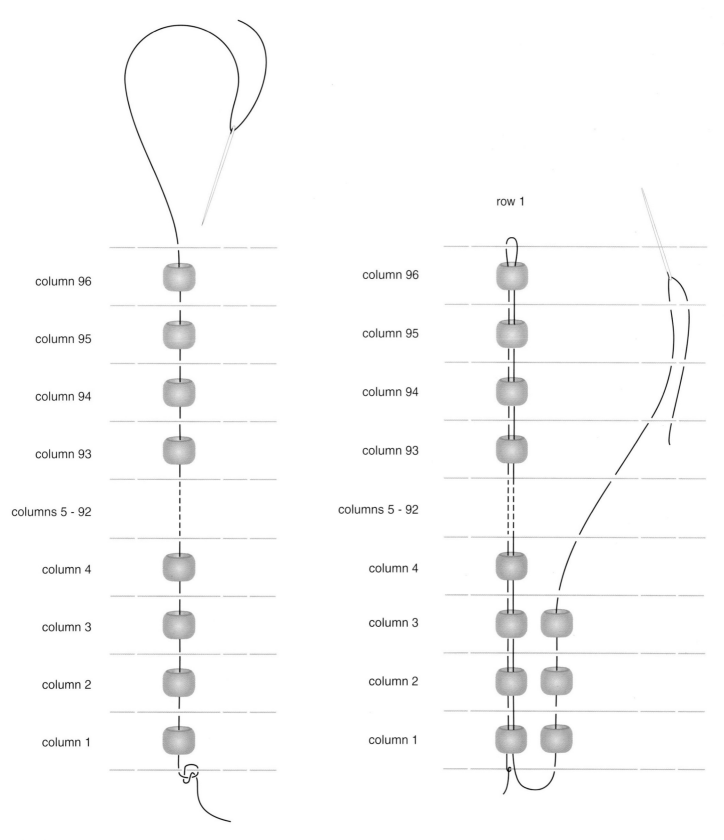

column 96

column 95

column 94

column 93

columns 5 - 92

column 4

column 3

column 2

column 1

FIGURE 1

row 1

column 96

column 95

column 94

column 93

columns 5 - 92

column 4

column 3

column 2

column 1

FIGURE 2

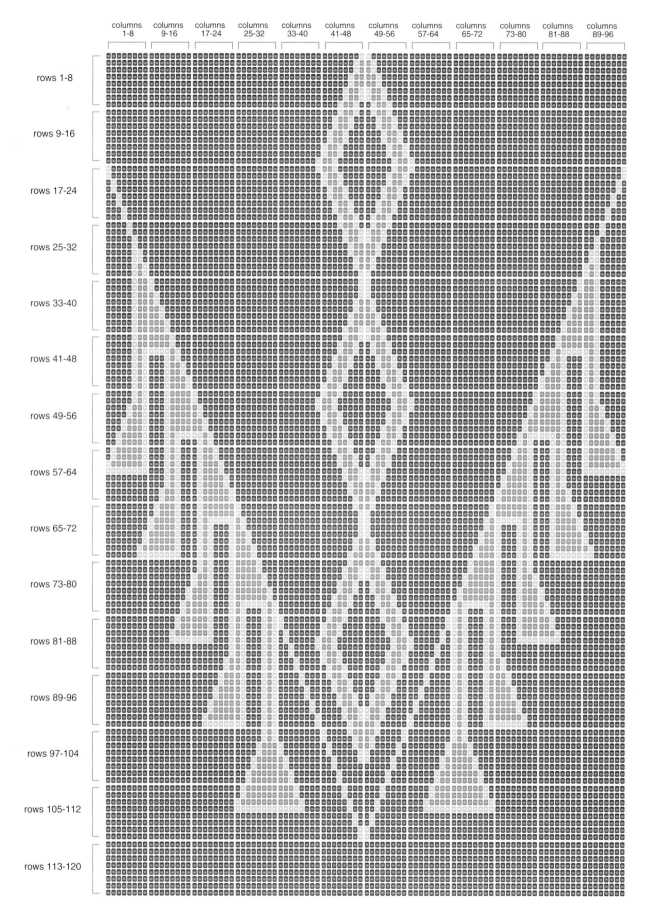

columns 1-8 columns 9-16 columns 17-24 columns 25-32 columns 33-40 columns 41-48 columns 49-56 columns 57-64 columns 65-72 columns 73-80 columns 81-88 columns 89-96

rows 1-8

rows 9-16

rows 17-24

rows 25-32

rows 33-40

rows 41-48

rows 49-56

rows 57-64

rows 65-72

rows 73-80

rows 81-88

rows 89-96

rows 97-104

rows 105-112

rows 113-120

FIGURE 3

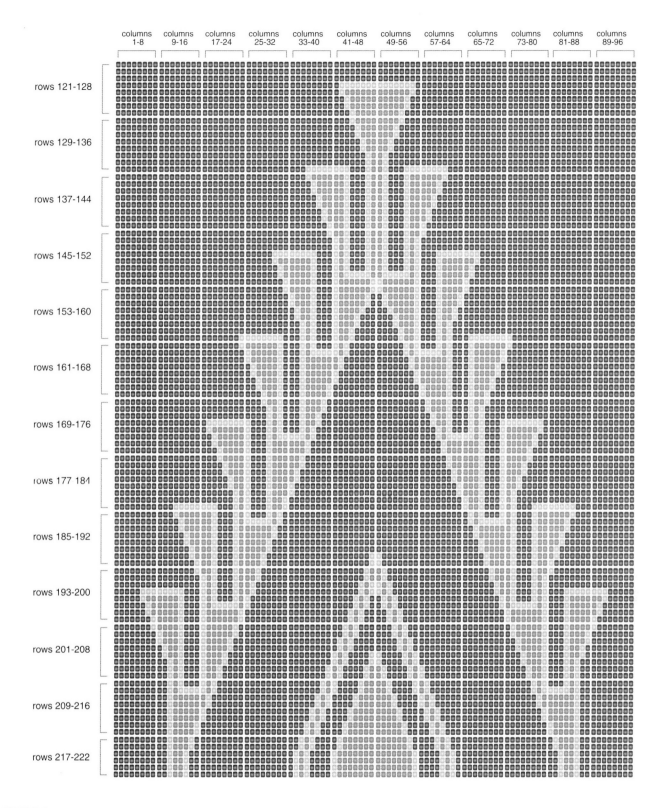

columns 1-8 columns 9-16 columns 17-24 columns 25-32 columns 33-40 columns 41-48 columns 49-56 columns 57-64 columns 65-72 columns 73-80 columns 81-88 columns 89-96

rows 121-128

rows 129-136

rows 137-144

rows 145-152

rows 153-160

rows 161-168

rows 169-176

rows 177-184

rows 185-192

rows 193-200

rows 201-208

rows 209-216

rows 217-222

FIGURE 4

4 Loop around and below the outer warp thread, and begin Row 2. Following the graphs in Figures 3-4, add rows 2-222. You will run out of weft thread several times. When you have only 8-10" of weft thread left, pass the needle back into the previous row through several beads. Make an overhand knot around a nearby warp thread, then pass the needle through several more beads. Pull tightly, and snip. Prepare a new 60" weft thread. Insert the needle through several beads in the last row worked, knot around a warp thread, and go through more beads until you come out through the last bead you added. Continue working.

ROWS 223-248

At Row 223, begin to decrease the width of the rows by 5 beads on the left and 5 beads on the right.

1 After you have finished Row 222, pass the needle around the outside warp thread, go through the first 5 beads of Row 222, and then loop around the sixth warp thread. To loop around a warp thread, see Figure 5.

2 Following the graph in Figure 6, add the 86 beads of Rows 223. Maintain this new width until you have added Row 248.

ROWS 249-327

1 Starting with Row 249, every fifth row, continue decreasing by 2 beads on the left and 2 beads on the right until you have reached the triangular tip of the bag. Follow the graph in Figure 6.

2 When you are finished, work the weft thread back through 4-5 rows, go through several beads, make a knot, go through several more beads, and snip.

FINISHING THE SQUARE END OF THE BAG

At this point you can remove the work from the loom by cutting and knotting the warp threads.

1 Finish the square end of the bag by anchoring the warp threads, one by one, in the body of the panel. Knot if necessary, then snip.

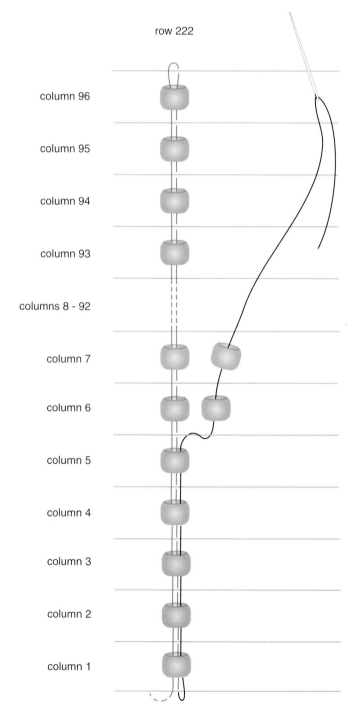

row 222

column 96

column 95

column 94

column 93

columns 8 - 92

column 7

column 6

column 5

column 4

column 3

column 2

column 1

FIGURE 5

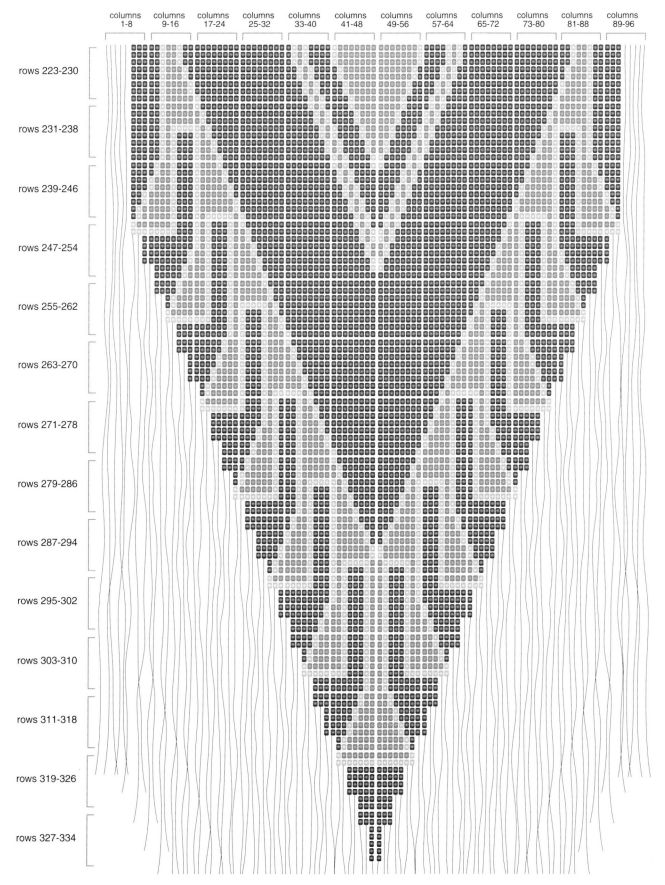

columns 1-8   columns 9-16   columns 17-24   columns 25-32   columns 33-40   columns 41-48   columns 49-56   columns 57-64   columns 65-72   columns 73-80   columns 81-88   columns 89-96

rows 223-230

rows 231-238

rows 239-246

rows 247-254

rows 255-262

rows 263-270

rows 271-278

rows 279-286

rows 287-294

rows 295-302

rows 303-310

rows 311-318

rows 319-326

rows 327-334

FIGURE 6

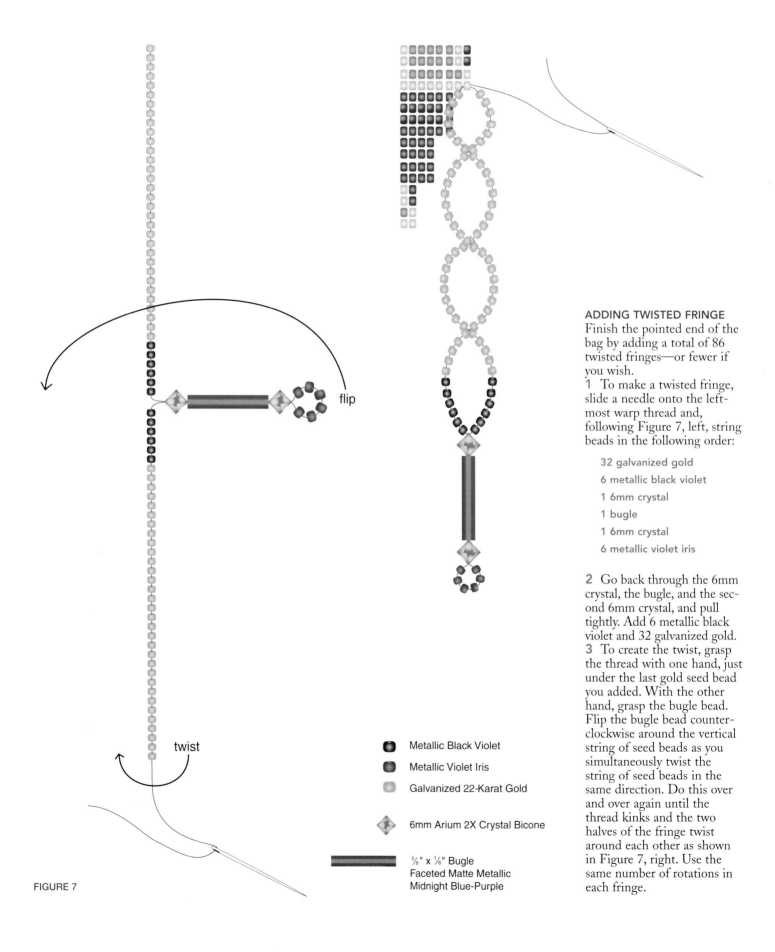

flip

twist

ADDING TWISTED FRINGE

Finish the pointed end of the bag by adding a total of 86 twisted fringes—or fewer if you wish.

1 To make a twisted fringe, slide a needle onto the left-most warp thread and, following Figure 7, left, string beads in the following order:

   32 galvanized gold

   6 metallic black violet

   1 6mm crystal

   1 bugle

   1 6mm crystal

   6 metallic violet iris

2 Go back through the 6mm crystal, the bugle, and the second 6mm crystal, and pull tightly. Add 6 metallic black violet and 32 galvanized gold.

3 To create the twist, grasp the thread with one hand, just under the last gold seed bead you added. With the other hand, grasp the bugle bead. Flip the bugle bead counter-clockwise around the vertical string of seed beads as you simultaneously twist the string of seed beads in the same direction. Do this over and over again until the thread kinks and the two halves of the fringe twist around each other as shown in Figure 7, right. Use the same number of rotations in each fringe.

Metallic Black Violet

Metallic Violet Iris

Galvanized 22-Karat Gold

6mm Arium 2X Crystal Bicone

⅝" x ⅛" Bugle
Faceted Matte Metallic
Midnight Blue-Purple

FIGURE 7

4 It may take as many as 100 rotations for the twist to take hold. Once it does, hold the twist in place while you insert the needle back into the body of the bag. Pull tightly, knot around a warp thread, go through a few more beads, and snip.

5 Move on to the next twisted fringe.

LINING THE BAG, ADDING THE CORD, AND STITCHING THE SEAMS

1 To prepare the lining, cut a piece of satin that is $5\frac{1}{2}$" wide by $8\frac{1}{2}$" high. Beginning at the bottom of the bag, fold $\frac{1}{4}$" of the satin under and begin stitching the satin to the beadwork. (The flap of the bag will not be lined.) Do the same with the left and right sides of the lining.

2 Position the cord as shown in Figure 8, and stitch the looped ends in place. Position the middle of the cord so that it forms a line across the top of the bag, under the satin lining. Stitch the cord to the beadwork as shown in Figure 8. Stitch the satin, edges folded under, over the cord and to the beadwork. Finally, fold the bag over so that the top and bottom edges of the lining meet, and stitch across the left and right sides of the bag. (If you wish, you may wrap a strand of violet iris beads over the tops of the cord loops to cover the seam, as shown in Figure 8.)

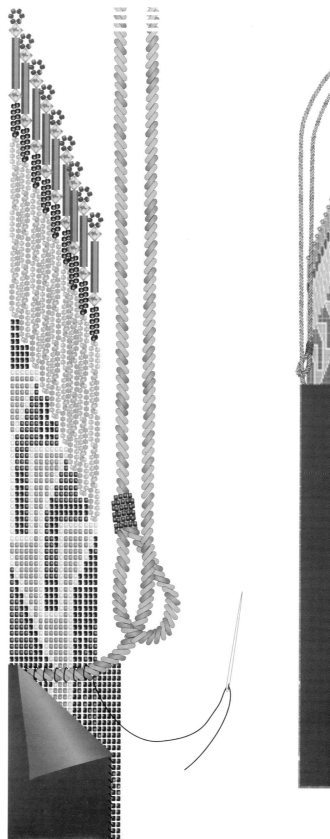

FIGURE 8

HUICHOL BEADWORK, MEXICO

INSPIRATIONAL PIECE
Gourd from the Huichol of Jalisco, Mexico, late twentieth century

ARTIST
Robin Bergman

TECHNIQUE
Square Stitch

BEADWORK PROJECT
"Trio of Earrings to Mix and Match"

Ribbon Earrings: ⅝" wide x 4" high; Full Flower Earrings: 1" wide x 1½" high; Half Flower Earrings: 1" wide x 4" high (excluding wires)

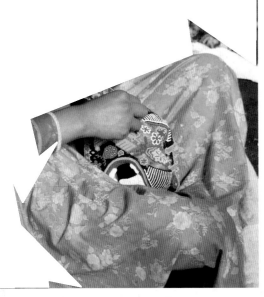

Huichol beadworker Maximina Hernandez Mijares of San Andrés Cohamiata, Jalisco, inlays beads into a wax-lined gourd destined for sale, ca. 1985. The wax and beads were supplied by Jesse Hendry, an American who has long helped the Huichol market their pieces abroad.

COURTESY, JESSE HENDRY, PUERTO VALLARTA, MEXICO

Not many beadworkers invite us to look into the holes of their beads. Bead holes are usually functional, not ornamental, aspects of a piece, meant to carry the threads that hold it together. Yet the Huichol peoples of western Mexico deliberately press their threadless beads, holes facing up, into a wax compound that they spread over the surface to be beaded. Often this surface is a dried gourd or a piece of carved wood. Rather than detract from the appearance of a piece, the holes make it that much more interesting, as they draw our attention to the impossibly tiny rings of color that define each motif. The same cannot be said for Huichol beaded earrings, bracelets, necklaces, and bags, which are worked in netting techniques that by their very nature hide the bead holes.

Although their beadwork has become a valuable commodity sold in stores all over the world, the Huichol do not view beading as a strictly commercial activity. For most Huichol beadworkers, it is still partly religious in nature, a form of prayer that expresses and strengthens traditional Huichol beliefs and values. By living in rugged, inaccessible parts of the Sierra Madre Occidental, the Huichol have managed to maintain their ancient culture despite the pressures that followed the Spanish conquest of Mexico starting in the early sixteenth century. To this day, Huichol beaded gourds that are not made for sale are made as offerings to the gods and goddesses in the belief that the beaded motifs will act as visual prayers. On yearly pilgrimages to *Wirikuta*, the Huichol's mythological homelands in distant San Luis Potosi, these beaded votive gourds are deposited in locations that the ancestors are believed to have visited. The Huichol hope that just as humans drink water from plain gourds, the gods will "drink" the prayers that beaded gourds contain and grant them abundant crops and good health. For at least a hundred years, and probably much longer, the Huichol have been praying in this same way, although beaded gourds made a century ago are much simpler than those made for sale today. Looking at the gourd shown on the facing page is like looking through a kaleidoscope at modern versions of the most important symbols in Huichol culture: the deer, the maize plant, and the peyote cactus flower. Together, they form a trio of sacred, life-giving symbols that recur in Huichol art, myth, and ritual.

Also embedded in the landscape of the gourd are other important symbols, such as the sun, the snake, the ceremonial arrows, the bird, and the *toto* flower. A sophisticated sense of spatial relationships governs their placement, orienting the white deer and the red snakes diagonally and the maize plants and large yellow flowers vertically around a large, six-pointed star that encircles a six-petaled flower in the center of the gourd. Another kind of complementarity is established between the larger motifs, which are symmetrical, and the smallest motifs, which are not. All of these elements are so expertly integrated that we notice their harmony as much as their complexity. This may be no accident, for the Huichol value harmony and the unity that it brings to human relationships, which can be very complex. When unity is achieved, they believe, a kind of paradise follows.

ABOVE This is a detail of the beaded gourd shown to the right. There may be dozens of motifs in a single Huichol gourd, and they are all perfect. Not one bead is out of place.
Private collection ■ LARRY SANDERS

RIGHT An advanced sense of spatial relations permeates this Huichol beaded gourd made for sale in the early twenty-first century. The white deer and red snakes are oriented diagonally and the maize plants and yellow flowers vertically around a large six-pointed star in the gourd's center.
11" diameter x 2¾" high ■ Private collection ■ LARRY SANDERS

ROBIN BERGMAN IS ONE OF THE COUNTRY'S leading knitwear designers, known for her lush colors and asymmetrical patterns. Not surprisingly, her textile design expertise and her background in painting serve her well when it comes to beadwork. Square stitch is a favorite technique because it allows her to design on a computer in a grid format and to improvise, something she felt was impossible in loomwork.

In her "Trio of Earrings to Mix and Match," shown on page 146, Robin picks up on the intriguing spatial relationships in the Huichol gourd, on Huichol color sensibility, and on the Huichol's love of floral and animal motifs. There are four design elements in the Trio: the Half Flower, the Full Flower, the Arrow, and the long blue Ribbon. Robin assembles them with ease, repeating some elements and inverting others until the symmetries and asymmetries are perfectly, and playfully, in balance.

Following are instructions for making the Trio. You can wear the earrings asymmetrically; or, to be symmetrical, make one or more matching pairs.

Robin Bergman of Concord, Massachusetts, is an award-winning knitwear designer who trained as a painter in college. She never lost her childhood love of beadwork, however, and always has at least five or six major beading projects under way. For more information, see www.robinoriginals.com.

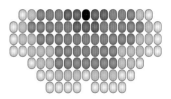

Half Flower

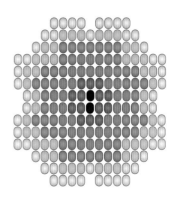

Full Flower

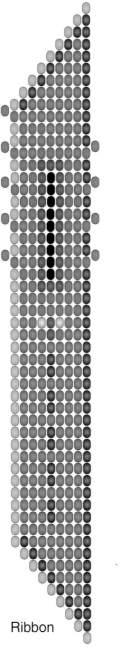

Ribbon

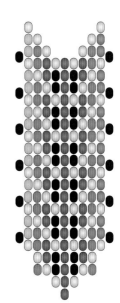

Arrow

Shown are Robin Bergman's "Trio of Earrings to Mix and Match."
Collection of the artist ■ LARRY SANDERS

MATERIALS

(to make the "Trio of Earrings to Mix and Match")

Cylinder seed beads

   4 grams matte opaque dyed Capri blue

   2 grams opaque dyed squash

   1 gram matte opaque dark blue

   2 grams matte opaque light blue

   2 grams opaque red

   1 gram opaque maroon

   1 gram opaque matte black

Other beads

   6 4mm lentil beads, translucent or opaque red

   3 8° lined turquoise/red striped beads

   3 3mm matte black magatamas

3 sterling silver French ear wires

Nymo B thread, black

size 12 beading needles

There are four square-stitch elements in the "Trio of Earrings": the Half Flower, the Full Flower, the Arrow, and the Ribbon. (See Figure 1.) You will need to make:

   4 Half Flowers

   3 Full Flowers

   1 Arrow

   2 Ribbons

If you are not familiar with brick stitch, practice making the Half Flower first, which involves both increasing and decreasing rows. Then you can make the other elements.

MAKING A HALF FLOWER

1 Slide a needle onto a 40" length of thread, and double the thread to create a 20" length. Wax the thread. Leaving a 6" tail, string the 15 beads of Row 1. Follow the color pattern for the Half Flower in Figure 1. Tie an overhand knot around bead 1.

2 Following Figure 2, add bead 16, and go clockwise through bead 15. Go through

● Opaque Matte Black

● Matte Opaque Dark Blue

● (Dyed) Matte Opaque Capri Blue

● Matte Opaque Light Blue

● (Dyed) Opaque Squash

● Opaque Red

● Opaque Maroon

FIGURE 1

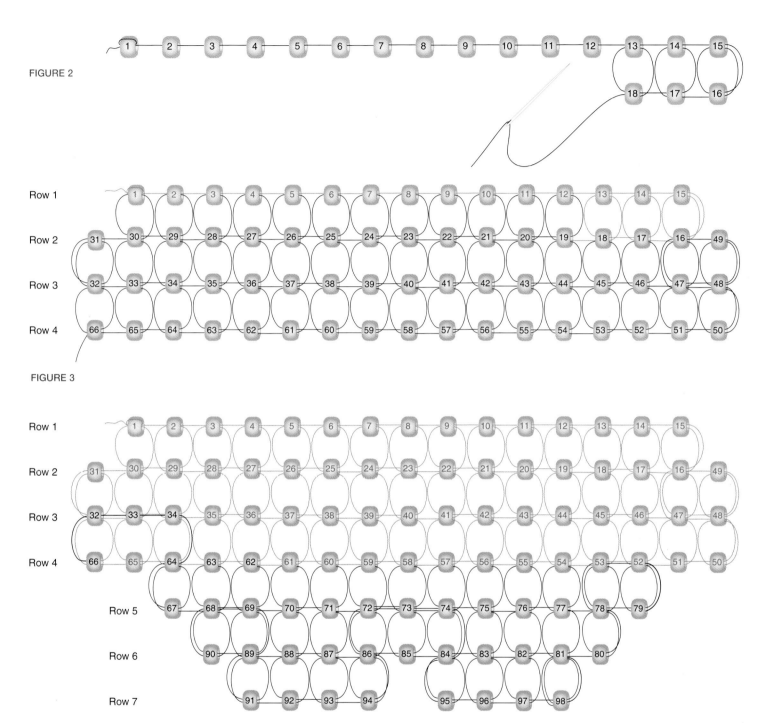

FIGURE 2

FIGURE 3

FIGURE 4

bead 16 again, and add bead 17. Go clockwise through beads 14 and 17. Add bead 18, and go clockwise through beads 13 and 18.

3 Finish Row 2 by adding bead 31. (See Figure 3.)

4 To begin Row 3, add bead 32. Go counterclockwise through beads 31 and 32, and add bead 33. Continue working until you have added bead 48. Add bead

49 to finish Row 2, and go through beads 16, 47, and 48. Add bead 50, and continue until Row 4 is complete.

5 In Rows 5-7, decrease the number of beads in each row. (See Figure 4.) First, you must get into position to begin Row 5 2 beads in from Row 4.

6 After you have added bead 66 and gone through beads 32 and 66, go through beads 32-

34 and 64. (See Figure 4.) Complete Rows 5 and 6 in this way.

7 Row 7 has a space in the middle, which requires that you skip a bead. To do this, after you have added bead 94 and gone through beads 86 and 94, go through 86 again, and then through 72-74 and 84. Now you are in a position to finish Row 7.

8 Make 4 Half Flowers in this way, and set them aside.

MAKING A FULL FLOWER

1 To make a Full Flower, thread a needle onto a 74" length of thread, then double and wax the thread. First make a Half Flower, then turn it upside down and make another one exactly as you made the first. For the Full Flower pattern, see Figure 1.

2 Make a total of 3 Full Flowers.

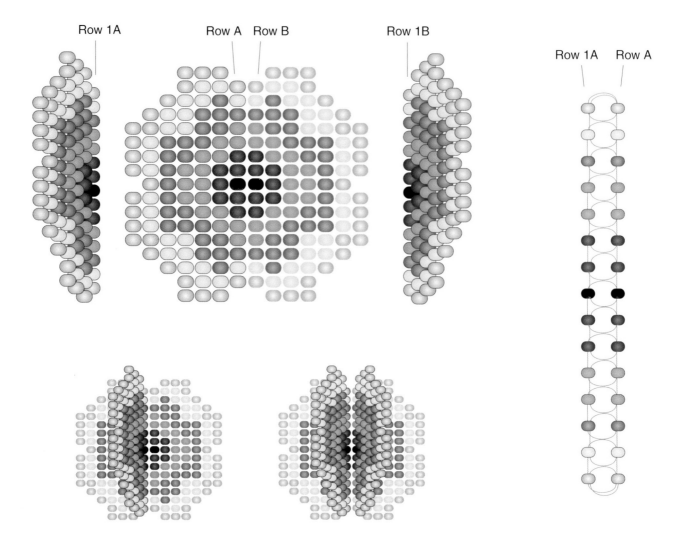

FIGURE 5

MAKING THE ARROW
The easiest way to make the Arrow is to start in the middle and work your way down. Then turn the Arrow upside down and work in the other direction. In this way you will be decreasing, which is generally easier than increasing. Add the edge beads as you go, or after the Arrow is finished. For the Arrow pattern, see Figure 1 on page 146. Make 1 Arrow.

MAKING THE RIBBON
The easiest way to make a Ribbon is to begin in the middle and work your way down. Then turn the Ribbon

upside down and finish the other half. You will need to tie off and add on thread at some point. (See Figures 5-6 on page 19). For the Ribbon pattern, with its "Red Bug" motif, see Figure 1 on page 146. Add the edge beads as you go, or after the Ribbon is finished. Make 2 identical Ribbons.

ATTACHING THE HALF FLOWERS TO THE FULL FLOWER
The Flower Earring has a Full Flower at its center and 2 Half Flowers projecting off of it on each side, for a total of 4 Half Flowers.

1 To attach 4 Half Flowers to the Full Flower, follow Figure 5.
2 Square stitch Row 1A to Row A, and Row 1B to Row B. Then flip the Full Flower over and do the same on the other side.

ATTACHING THE ARROW TO THE FIRST RIBBON
The Arrow arches above the surface of the Ribbon.
1 Follow Figure 6 to stitch Point 1A to Point A, 1B to B, and 1C to C. Be sure to orient the first Ribbon with the Red Bug facing down, exactly as shown in Figure 6.

ATTACHING THE FULL FLOWERS TO THE SECOND RIBBON
1 Orient the second Ribbon as shown in Figure 7, with the Red Bug at the top. Square stitch 1 Full Flower to one side of the Ribbon as shown, so that Rows 1A and 1B line up with Rows A and B on one side of the Ribbon. Stitch the second Full Flower to the other side of the Ribbon so that Rows 2A and 2B line up with Rows A and B on the other side of the Ribbon.

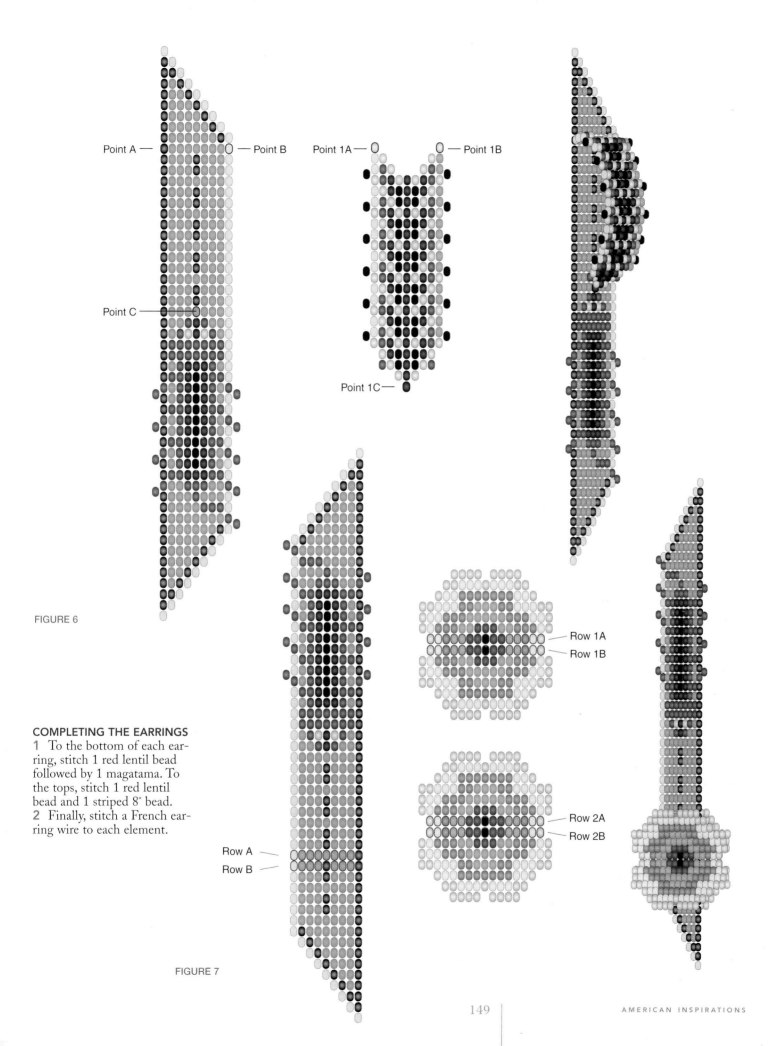

Point A —   — Point B

Point C —

Point 1A — O   O — Point 1B

Point 1C —

FIGURE 6

COMPLETING THE EARRINGS
1 To the bottom of each earring, stitch 1 red lentil bead
followed by 1 magatama. To
the tops, stitch 1 red lentil
bead and 1 striped 8° bead.
2 Finally, stitch a French earring wire to each element.

Row A —
Row B —

Row 1A
Row 1B

Row 2A
Row 2B

FIGURE 7

AMERICAN INSPIRATIONS

CHIMÚ BEADWORK, PERU

INSPIRATIONAL PIECE
Pectoral from the Chimú peoples of Peru, ca. late fifteenth/early sixteenth century

ARTIST
Madelyn Ricks

TECHNIQUES
Flat and Pyramidal Peyote Stitch

BEADWORK PROJECT
"Triple Diamond" Brooch

4" wide x 3⅛" high x ¾" deep

We owe most of our understanding of ancient beadwork to the archaeologists and museum professionals who recover and reconstruct pieces that have typically spent the last five or more centuries in fragments on the floor of a tomb or over a skeleton. Because threads had broken or disintegrated over time, a number of pieces shown in this book were reconstructed from such fragments. (See pages 10 and 71.)

In the late 1980s, archaeologists discovered more ancient beadwork fragments in tombs nestled inside pyramids built by the Moche Civilization (ca. 100-800 C.E.) near the village of Sipán in north coastal Peru. In Tomb 1, dating to about 300 C.E., archaeologists painstakingly unearthed the remains of two beaded tunics, two turquoise bead bracelets, and eleven shell bead pectorals, or wide bib necklaces, on or near the skeleton of a man about forty years old. While the tunics were made of gilded copper platelets stitched to a woven cotton cloth, the bracelets and pectorals were made of parallel strands of beads held together by perforated copper spacer plates. (As we have seen, spacer plates have been used by beadworkers in many parts of the world from 4000 B.C.E.). (See pages 14 and 71.)

The uppermost pectoral in the tomb, shown on the mannequin pictured here, features two crouching animals facing each other on a white ground. Scholars believe that this pectoral and the other objects in Tomb 1 belonged to an aristocratic warrior-priest who presided at the Sacrifice Ceremony, where prisoners of war were ritually decapitated and their blood drunk from shell containers. Elaborate depictions of this ceremony, showing the warrior-priest in action, have been found on Moche ceramics, and it may be that the Sacrifice Ceremony was widespread in Moche culture.

More than a thousand years later, beaded pectorals were still being made in coastal Peru, but motifs, techniques, and materials had apparently grown more sophisticated. In contrast to the strung pectorals found in Tomb 1 at Sipán, netted pectorals were reportedly recovered from tombs in Chan Chan, the northern capital of the Chimú culture, which flourished from ca. 800-1470 C.E.—until the Inca conquest of the Chimú in the 1460s. More beaded pectorals, slings, pillows, and small bags were found farther south, at sites in the Huari and Chancay Valleys. It is not known precisely how these pieces were used, but it is clear that the Chimú were great bead connoisseurs who used spiny oyster shells to obtain orange beads; other shells to obtain purple, yellow, and white beads; malachite to make green beads; and jet or shell to make black beads. Iridescent mother-of-pearl platelets also appear in at least one Chimú pectoral. (See the photograph on the facing page at the top right.)

Pictured is a mannequin wearing copies of clothing and ornaments found in Tomb 1 at Sipán, ca. 300 C.E. Gilt copper platelets embellish the tunic. The necklaces include a multistrand shell bead pectoral.
Image Courtesy, Dr. Chris Donnan/UCLA Fowler Museum of Cultural History ■ SUSAN EINSTEIN

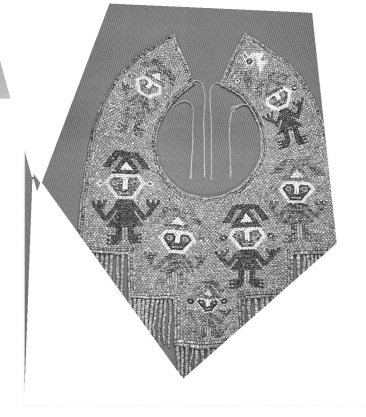

A late fifteenth- or early sixteenth-century pectoral found at Chan Chan shows seven mysterious figures resembling those on Chimú woven textiles. 17" wide ■ © American Museum of Natural History, No. 3479(2) J. BECKETT

This pectoral with energetic zigzag or wave motifs was reportedly found with the one to the left. It is worked with cotton threads and beads of spondylus shell, mussel shell, and jet. Mother-of-pearl platelets ring the edge of the pectoral. 13¾" wide x 13½" high ■ © American Museum of Natural History, No. 2574(3) ■ R. P. SHERIDAN

SEVEN STYLIZED HUMAN FIGURES WITH outstretched arms and elaborate headdresses dominate the stepped and tasseled pectoral to the top left. Two small birds are poised at one end. To Madelyn Ricks, the human figures looked like costumed jugglers with balls in midair. She also noticed the birds. Wanting to work from the motifs in the pectoral, yet project a sense of playfulness, she designed the pectoral shown to the right, with three contemporary showgirls juggling birds and diamond-shaped balls. In keeping with the showgirl theme, she chose brighter versions of the colors used in the Chimú pectoral. Madelyn worked the background in peyote stitch, but found it too flat. To achieve a more dynamic effect, she made some of the motifs project outward by using an innovative technique that combines flat and pyramidal peyote stitch and square stitch. Like so many of Madelyn's pieces, "Juggles with Birds" is both exotic and lighthearted. Her mastery of motif and technique is all the more remarkable given that she has been doing beadwork for less than ten years.

Madelyn designed the "Triple Diamond" Brooch shown on page 152 specially to show how she makes her projections. As you will see when making the brooch, the projections are hollow inside. The pin has three pyramidal projections, but you might want to experiment with other shapes as well.

Madelyn Ricks of Naples, Florida, spent years pursuing her first medium, ceramics, before she discovered beadwork. She uses two- and three-dimensional peyote stitch to produce both wearable and nonwearable works of art with colorful, complex graphics. Madelyn exhibits her often-published work at national juried art fairs.

Madelyn Ricks made her "Juggles with Birds" Pectoral in 2002. It features three showgirls in short, multilayered dresses juggling diamond-shaped balls worked in pyramidal peyote stitch rising from a flat peyote stitch ground. 10¾" wide x 15¼" high ■ Collection of the artist ■ LARRY SANDERS

"TRIPLE DIAMOND" BROOCH

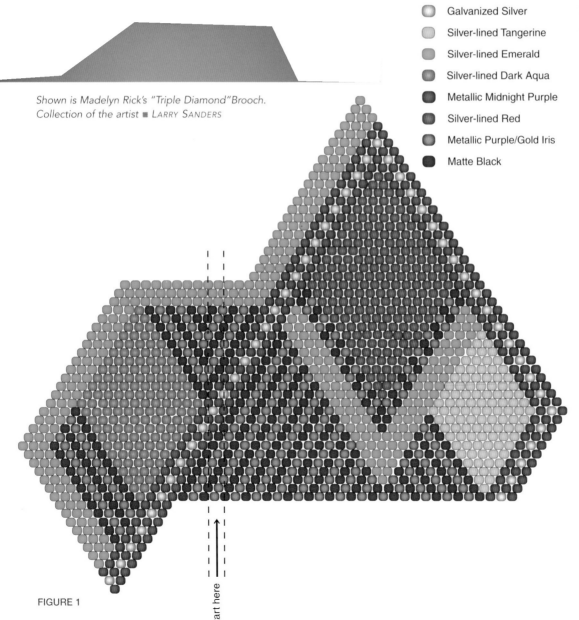

Shown is Madelyn Rick's "Triple Diamond" Brooch. Collection of the artist ■ LARRY SANDERS

○ Galvanized Silver

○ Silver-lined Tangerine

○ Silver-lined Emerald

○ Silver-lined Dark Aqua

● Metallic Midnight Purple

○ Silver-lined Red

○ Metallic Purple/Gold Iris

● Matte Black

FIGURE 1

start here

MATERIALS

Cylinder seed beads

  1 gram galvanized silver

  2 grams silver-lined tangerine

  2 grams silver-lined emerald

  3 grams silver-lined dark aqua

  1 gram metallic midnight purple

  5 grams silver-lined red

  2 grams metallic purple/gold iris

  2 grams matte black

Silamide thread

size 12 beading needles

wax

4" x 5" Ultrasuede panel

1 base metal pin stem with holes for sewing

To simplify the instructions, I have used these abbreviations.

  a = add

  gt = go through

MAKING THE PEYOTE STITCH PANEL

1 To begin, thread a needle onto a 64" length of thread, and double it to create a 32" length. Locate the vertical dotted lines in Figure 1. Following the color pattern, and pulling tightly after each bead is added, bead to the right of the dotted lines until the entire right half of the panel is complete. If you run out of thread, add a new length as shown in Figure 6 on page 19.

2 Next, bead to the left of the dotted lines until the left half of the brooch is complete. Anchor the thread by going back through 1" or more of beads, and snip.

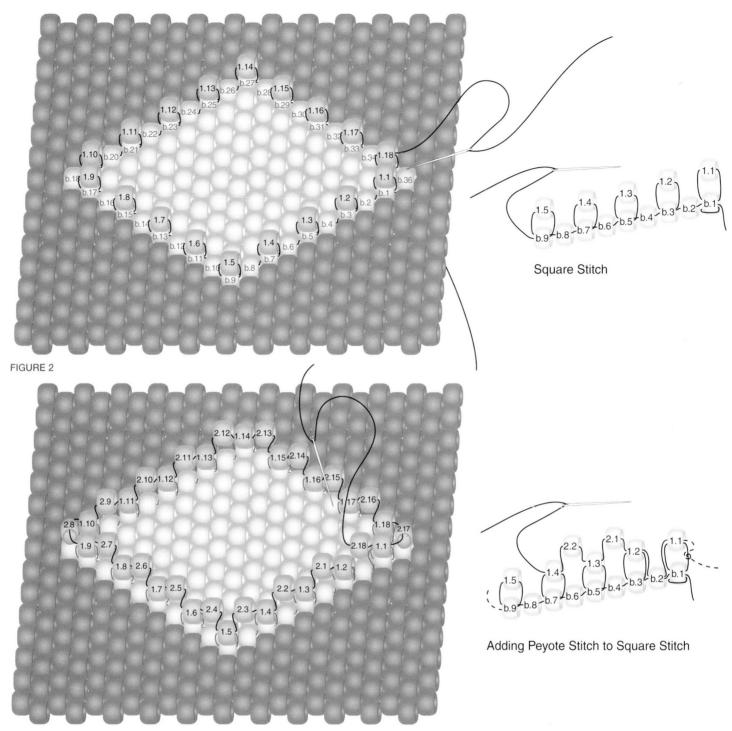

FIGURE 2

Square Stitch

FIGURE 3

Adding Peyote Stitch to Square Stitch

ROWS 1-6 OF THE FIRST PYRAMID
(the foundation rows)

Each pyramid begins with a row of beads attached to the peyote stitch panel with square stitch.

1 To begin the first pyramid, which will be worked in silver-lined tangerine, thread a needle onto a 56" length of thread, and double the thread to create a 28" length.

Following Figure 2, left and right, insert the needle up through the base to the right of bead b.1. Leave a 6" tail as you go left through bead b.1, then circle around and go back left through bead b.1 again. a bead 1.1, and go left through beads b.1, b.2, and b.3. a beads 1.2-1.17 in this same manner. After adding bead 1.18, gt beads b.35, 1.18, and 1.1. Anchor Row 1 by going

through beads b.2 and 1.2. Remember to pull tightly after every stitch.

2 The rest of the pyramid is worked in peyote stitch. To begin Row 2, a bead 2.1, and gt bead 1.3. (See Figure 3, left and right.) a bead 2.2, and gt bead 1.4. Continue working until you have added bead 2.18 and gone through beads 1.2 and 2.1.

3 Begin Row 3 by following Figure 4. a bead 3.1, and gt bead

2.2. a bead 3.2, and gt bead 2.3. a bead 3.3, and gt bead 2.4. a bead 3.4, and gt bead 2.5. a bead 3.5, and gt bead 2.6. a bead 3.6, and gt bead 2.7. Continue working until you have added bead 3.18 and gone through beads 2.1 and 3.1.

4 Add Rows 4-6 in the same manner. After adding bead 6.18, gt beads 5.1, 6.1, 5.2, and 6.2. Now all of the pyramid's foundation rows are in place.

DECREASING NORTH AND SOUTH IN ROW 7

To shape the pyramid to a point at the top, you must begin decreasing the number of beads per row starting in Row 7.

1 Following Figure 4, a bead 7.1, and gt bead 6.3. a bead 7.2, and gt bead 6.4. a bead 7.3, and gt bead 6.5. a bead 7.4, and gt bead 6.6. a bead 7.5, and gt bead 6.7. a bead 7.6, and gt bead 6.8. a bead 7.7, and gt bead 6.9.

2 a bead 7.8, and create the north decrease by going through beads 6.10 and 6.11. Pull firmly. Continue working around Row 7 until you have added bead 7.16.

3 Create the south decrease by going through beads 6.1, 6.2, and 7.1.

DECREASING EAST AND WEST IN ROW 8

1 Following Figure 5, a bead 8.1, and gt bead 7.2. a bead 8.2, and gt bead 7.3. a bead 8.3, and gt bead 7.4.

2 Now decrease at the west point by going through beads 7.4 and 7.5. Pull tightly. a bead 8.4, and gt bead 7.6. a bead 8.5, and gt bead 7.7. a bead 8.6, and gt bead 7.8. a bead 8.7, and gt bead 7.9. a bead 8.8, and gt bead 7.10. a bead 8.9, and gt bead 7.11.

3 a bead 8.10, and then decrease at the east by going through beads 7.12 and 7.13. Continue until you have added bead 8.14 and gone through beads 7.1 and 8.1.

WORKING EVEN IN ROW 9 AND DECREASING NORTH-SOUTH IN ROW 10

In Row 9 there are no decreases; you "work even," as Madelyn calls it.

1 Following Figure 6, a bead 9.1, and gt bead 8.2. a bead 9.2, and gt bead 8.3. a bead 9.3, and gt bead 8.4. a bead 9.4, and gt bead 8.5. a bead 9.5, and gt bead 8.6. a bead 9.6, and gt bead 8.7. a bead 9.7, and gt bead 8.8. a bead 9.8, and gt bead 8.9. a bead 9.9, and gt bead 8.10. a bead 9.10, and gt bead 8.11. a bead 9.11, and gt bead 8.12. a bead 9.12, and gt bead 8.13. a bead 9.13, and gt bead 8.14. a bead 9.14, and gt beads 8.1 and 9.1.

2 In Row 10, once again decrease at the north and south points of the pyramid. Follow Figure 6 to complete Row 10.

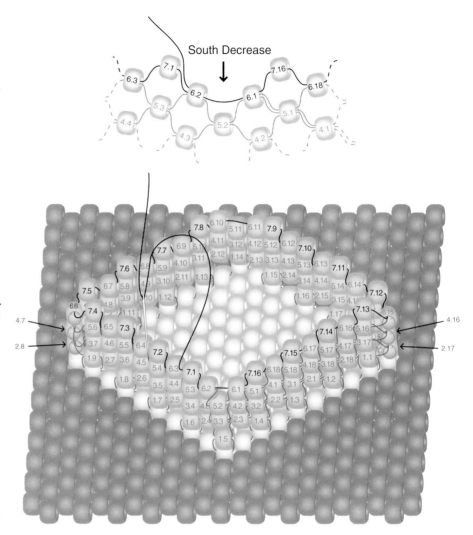

South Decrease

FIGURE 4

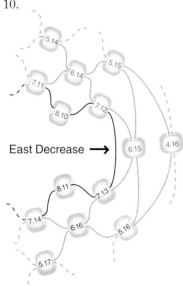

East Decrease

FIGURE 5

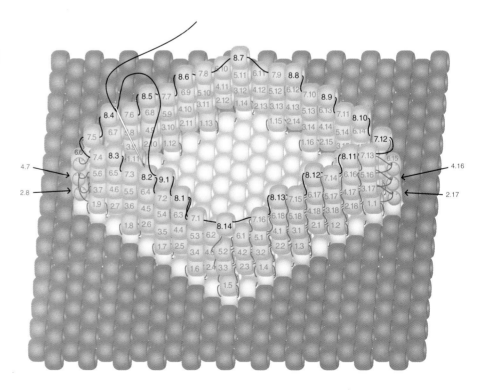

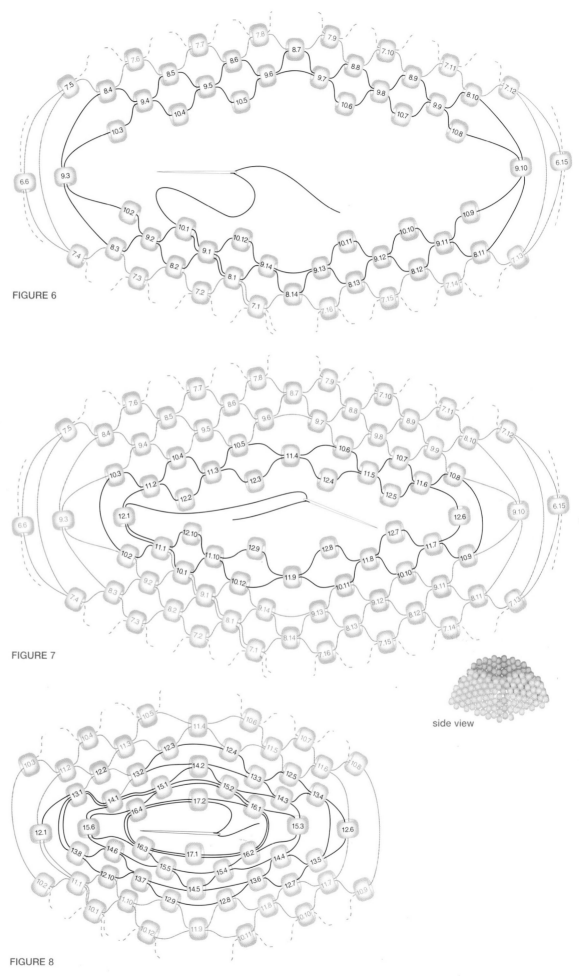

DECREASING EAST-WEST IN ROW 11 AND WORKING EVEN IN ROW 12

1 Following Figure 7, begin Row 11 by adding bead 11.1 and going through beads 10.2 and 10.3 to create the west decrease. a bead 11.2, and gt bead 10.4. Continue working until you have added bead 11.6.

2 To create the east decrease, gt beads 10.8 and 10.9. a bead 11.7, and continue until Row 11 is complete.

3 Follow Figure 7 to add Row 12, which is worked even, with no decreases.

FINISHING THE TOP OF THE PYRAMID

1 Following Figure 8, complete the top of the pyramid. The pattern of decreases is as follows:

Row 13: decrease north-south

Row 14: decrease east-west

Row 15: work even, no decrease

Row 16: decrease north-south

Row 17: decrease east-west

2 After adding bead 17.2, reinforce the pyramid by going back through beads 16.1, 16.2, 17.1, 16.3, 16.4, and 17.2 several times. Work the excess thread diagonally down through eight or nine rows of beads, and snip.

MAKING THE REMAINING TWO PYRAMIDS

The remaining pyramids are worked in the same way as the first one, with Rows 1-6 having no decreases, Row 7 having a north-south decrease, Row 8 having an east-west decrease, and Row 9 being worked even. This pattern then repeats to the top of each pyramid.

FINISHING THE BROOCH

1 Set the brooch on top of the Ultrasuede panel and cut the Ultrasuede to fit the brooch, allowing a $^1/_4$"-$^1/_3$" extra border of Ultrasuede on all sides.

2 Fold the border under one side, and begin stitching the Ultrasuede to the beadwork. Stitch around the perimeter of the beadwork first and then in the center until the Ultrasuede panel is securely attached.

3 Next, stitch the pin stem through the Ultrasuede. For extra security, stitch the pin stem into the beadwork as well.

FIGURE 6

FIGURE 7

side view

FIGURE 8

NOTES

References are to sources cited in the Selected Bibliography unless otherwise noted.

ENTERING THE DOOR TO INVENTIVENESS
p. 3 "You must enter the door to inventiveness.": Scott, p. 1; **p. 8** "Picasso-esque": See "Pin-Pricked Deities: The Art of Joyce Scott," by Keith Morrison. In Carlin, p. 61; "Natasha St. Michael": Hector 2003, p. 10 and "Force of Nature," by Pam O'Connor. In *Bead and Button* 62 (2004): 130-134; **p. 9** "Liza Lou": It should be noted that Liza Lou does not consider herself a beadworker per se and does not want her work shown in publications devoted to beadwork. Pers. comm., Jasmine Levett, Deitch Projects Gallery, June, 2003.

HIGHLIGHTS OF BEADWORK HISTORY
p. 10 "Rarely has . . . depicted.": Yang, pp. 250-251. This is the most complex of the eight reconstructed Western Zhou face masks diagrammed in "The Face of the Other World: Jade Face-Covers from Ancient Tombs," by Wang Tao and Liu Yu, in *Chinese Jades*, Rosemary E. Scott, ed., Colloquies on Art & Archaeology in Asia, No. 18, London: Percival David Foundation on Chinese Art, 1997, pp.133-146. Although not all would consider the jade platelets "beads" per se, they are certainly, at the very least, beadlike. Thus, the face masks in which they once appeared, if not examples of "beadwork" per se, were certainly beadwork-like compositions; "modest, single-strand necklace": Not everyone would classify such a structure as "beadwork." Allen, Part 1 distinguishes "work with beads," in which the primary focus is on the beads themselves, i.e., a simple necklace of strung beads, from "beadwork," in which the primary focus is on their placement relative to one another. While this distinction is valuable, it is difficult to apply; there are many examples that could fall into either category, depending upon the inclinations of the analyst. I find it more helpful to posit a continuum of beadwork technique organized by degree of structural complexity, from threadless techniques to simple threaded constructions such as single- and multiple-strand necklaces to complex categories such as sewing, netting, and weaving, which can be classified by analogy with their textile counterparts; "sewing, netting . . . weaving": For the only attempt I have seen to classify beadwork techniques as textile techniques, and a problematic attempt at that, see Seiler-Baldinger, pp. 114-121; "The first . . . leaves.": "Beads, Trade and Cultural Change," by Joyce Diamanti. In Lankton, p. 8; "most numerous of human artifacts": Liu 1995, p. 11; "'Long-range' . . . scholars": Bednarik, p. 1 *ff*.; "'Short-range' . . . scholars": www.handthoughts.com/worldsoldest beads/htm; **p. 11** "Evidence of . . . beads.": Henshilwood et al., Holden, p. 369; "Why were . . . function?": Dubin 1987, pp. 22-26; "Scholars now . . . status.": www.handthoughts.com/worldsoldest beads.htm; "twisted vegetable fiber threads": Barber 1991, pp. 39-41; "For this . . . B.C.E.": Barber 1991, Fig. 4.20; "Some of . . . Republic.": For other evidence from the European Upper Paleolithic, see Francis 1997, p. 4 and Barber 1991, p. 39; "There, about . . . ore.": Dubin 1987, pp. 24-25, and Randall White, "Representation Technology and Society Before Lascaux" (1996) at www.insticeagestudies.com/library/representation technology.html; **p. 12** "Shown here . . . faience.": see *Egyptian Jewellery*, by Milada Vilímková and Dominique Darbois. London: The Hamlyn Publishing Group Ltd., 1969, Fig. 85. "But most. . . sand.": Egyptian faience beads were made in various ways with different formulas as discussed in Andrews, pp. 57-59, Liu 2000, pp. 58-59, and Nicholson, p. 9 *ff*.; "Although they . . . here.": Pers. comm., Robert K. Liu, Ph.D., 2003. cf. Allen, Part 1; "Moreover, because . . . after-

life.": Friedman, p. 15; "Thanks in . . . traditions.": I would define "beadworking tradition" as a consistent though not necessarily unchanging use of beads in a single culture or region over a period of time no shorter than two generations. Three pre-requisites for any tradition are the availability of beads and threads (or a matrix) and the knowledge of at least one beadworking technique. See Allen, Part 2; "While there . . . period.": Dalley, pp. 12-14, Francis 1980-1982, Part 2, p. 6, Zettler and Horne, pp. 94-95; "The more . . . beads.": Andrews, Fig. 37 and Metropolitan Museum of Art, pp. 430-431; "This small face . . . stitch.": I have examined this piece. It appears to be authentic, not restrung, and definitely made of what we would call peyote stitch; "It was . . . shroud.": Bosse-Griffiths 1978, p. 105; **p. 13** "Between about . . . beadweaving.": Barber 1991, pp. 154-155, 172; "King Tutankhamun . . . beadwork.": Vogelsang-Eastwood, Figs. 1:8, 2.11, etc.; "While these . . . time.": Dalley, p. 12; "Pictorial beadwork . . . beadwork.": Dubin 1987, p. 42, and Friedman, p. 160; "During the . . . spirits.": Yang, pp. 390-393. For more on the symbolic significance of jade in the shroud of Liu Sheng, see "The Prince of Jade Revisited: The Material Symbolism of Jade as Observed in Mancheng Tombs," by Wu Hung, in *Chinese Jades* (op. cit), pp. 147-169. (As to whether this jade shroud should be considered a piece of "beadwork," see the first note for p. 10.); "How else . . . specimens?": as Peter J. Francis, Jr. pointed out long ago, we must cull information about beadwork from scholars in many disciplines. Francis 1980-1982, Part 2, p. 6; "In Egypt . . . medium.": Riefstahl, Figs. 11, 46 and Metropolitan Museum of Art, Figs. 66, 67, 69; "Far more . . . texts.": Dalley, p. 10 *ff*.; **p. 14** "Indian writers . . . horses.": Francis 1997, pp. 4-5; "By about . . . materials.": Francis 1997, pp. 4-5; "An early . . . decoration.": Unpub. Eng. Trans. of *Xunzi*: 18 *Zhenglun* by Joy Beckman (2001); "In later . . . lanterns.": These references come from English translations I commissioned in 2001-2002 from Joy Beckman and Licheng Gu, Ph.D. of entries under *zhu* ("bead" or "pearl"), *zhubian* ("beadwork"), *xiaozhu bianjie* ("fine beadwork"), *mizhu* ("seed bead"), *zhuxie* ("beaded shoes"), etc. in Chinese dictionaries, encyclopedias, and typology books such as *Hanyu Da Cidian* and *Gujun Tushu Jicheng*, which reference earlier historical and literary works such as the *Northern History*: Biographies 79.67 ("a beaded net used as a bribe"), *Mingshi Liezhuan* 331 ("woven gold beaded Buddhist cassock"), etc. Of course, I am assuming that actual pieces of beadwork inspired the references in these texts. I am grateful to Kenneth J. DeWoskin, Ph.D. for identifying the Chinese sources that would be most productive; "The Poltalloch . . . Scotland.": Sheridan and Davis, pp. 4-9; "In English . . . 1553.": "A Vocabulary of Seed Beadwork," by Peter Francis, Jr., in *The Margaretologist*: 10 (2) (1997): 9; "Glass seed . . . glass.": Small glass beads were also blown into molds. See Francis 2002, p. 11; "Other languages . . . Italian.": Francis 2002, p. 11; "The earliest . . . Egypt.": Lankton, p. 43; "In the . . . India.": Francis 2002, p. 30 and Lankton Fig. 7.7; "Everything is . . . Lord.": quoted in Francis 1980-1982, Part 4, p. 6; **p. 15** "The Kathi . . . panels.": Pers. obs.; "It is . . . time": Francis 2002, p. 76; "The third . . . France.": Dubin 1987, p. 107 *ff*.; "One of . . . stitch.": I have only seen a 4"-x-5" color transparency of this piece, to which the beadwork could conceivably be a late addition. Victoria & Albert Museum, Cat. 8588-1863, Image CT13779; "A bead . . . trading.": My thanks to Luigi Cattelan, Ellen Benson, and The Bead Museum, Washington, D.C. for allowing me to photograph this and other bead and beadwork sample cards. Other cards appear as Plate 6 in Saitowitz and as Plates IVA-VIIIB in "The

Giacomuzzi Bead Sample Book and Folders," by Karlis Karklins, in *Beads, The Journal of the Society of Bead Researchers* 14 (2002): 31-63; "Southern Song Dynasty": "Jiangxi De'an Nansong Zhoushi mu qingli jianbao" ("Brief Report on the Excavation of the Zhou Tomb of Southern Song Dynasty in De'an"), by Jiangxi Province Cultural Relics and Archaeological Institute, De'an County Museum. In *Wenwu (Cultural Relics)* 9 (1990): 10. I am grateful to Joy Beckman for telling me about this bag, part of a hair ornament from ca. 1274 C.E.

MATERIALS, TOOLS, AND TECHNIQUES
p. 16 "charlotte": According to Allan Shore, Jr., president of Elliott Greene & Co., New York, charlottes look like single-cuts but are actually cut five times, and the name originated with his company. *Bead & Button* 62 (2004): 10; "Glass types . . . satin.": "A Vocabulary of Seed Beads," op. cit., pp. 11-13; **pp. 20-21** "Nets may be . . . diagonally.": For simplicity and brevity I have grouped into one large category called "netting techniques" a number of distinct techniques, including linking, looping, knotting, and plaiting-like techniques but not weaving techniques. See Seiler-Baldinger, p. 114-121.

ASIAN INSPIRATIONS
p. 22 "The rare . . . techniques.": Liu 1998; "Many centuries . . . long.": Gong Yan and Ho and Bronson, p. 117. My thanks to Hu Jian Zhong of the Palace Museum, Beijing, for giving me a copy of Gong Yan's article and granting me the right to reproduce the image of Emperor Qianlong's beaded armor; "The enormous . . . brushstrokes.": Holmgren and Spertus, pp. 86-93; "Captain James Cook . . . century.": Kaeppler, Figs. 151-153, 211, etc.

HAN BEADWORK, MAINLAND CHINA (#1)
p. 24 "A seventeenth . . . circumstances.": Birch, pp. 49-58; "Nowhere is . . . like.": In Chinese, the word for bead, *zhu*, can mean a pearl or a bead of any other material. A knotted net jacket with glass beads is shown in Han Han, p. 88; "Worn beneath . . . perspiration.": Garrett, pp. 79-80; "Here is . . . circulation.": The technique is diagrammed in Hector 1995, Fig. 15.

HAN BEADWORK, MAINLAND CHINA (#2)
p. 32 "The Chinese . . . Dynasty (1644-1911).": Han Han, p. 101 and *Catalogue of the Exhibition of Ch'ing Dynasty Costume Accessories*, Plate 165; "mei, or 'plum blossoms'": Pers. comm., Jing Lingfei and Chen Ying, May 2000; "These plum . . . pentagon stitch.": Instructions for making *mei* using a single thread with two working ends are given in Yun Lei, pp. 44, 47, 49, but *mei* are also made with one working thread end in contemporary Beijing. Pers. obs., 1999-2001.

ANCIENT JAPANESE BEADWORK
p. 38 "Part of . . . Japan.": Blair, pp. 383-384; "Shown here . . . family.": Blair, p. 346.

KATHI BEADWORK, GUJARAT STATE, INDIA
p. 40 "A dozen or . . . interior.": My discussion of Kathi beadwork is based on M. A. Dhaky's essay in Nanavati et al., p. 59 *ff*., and pers. obs.; "single-layer scallop stitch": The technique is shown in Hector 1995, Fig. 10 (center). A variation of this technique is used by the Xhosa (see pp. 95 and 96 of this book).

SA'DAN TORAJA BEADWORK, SULAWESI, INDONESIA
p. 46 "Kandaure are . . . 1976.": *LebensMuster, Textilien in Indonesien*, by Heide Leigh-Theisen and Reinhold Mittersakschmöller. Vienna: Museum für Völkerkunde, 1995, Fig. 5; "Kandaure are . . . metal.": Taylor and Aragon, pp. 185-187; "Some kandaure . . . powers.": Nooy-Palm, pp. 255-256, cf. Taylor and Aragon, pp. 185-187; **p. 47** "In Toraja . . . task." Maxwell, p. 83.

STRAITS CHINESE BEADWORK, PENANG, MALAYSIA
p. 52 "'Straits,' or *Peranakan*": Cheah, p. 65; "A typical set...tassels.": Ho Wing Meng, p. 30 *ff*.; "demanding netting technique": Hector 1995, Fig. 9.

KENYAH BEADWORK, INDONESIAN/MALAYSIAN BORNEO

p. 56 "Only high . . . motifs.": Whittier and Whittier, p. 52; "A Kenyah . . . designs.": Tillema, Plates 152-153, 155; "Humans could . . . adulthood.": Sellato, pp. 23-24; "One such . . . body." Sellato, pp. 44-45; "Another kind . . . figure." Sellato, pp. 46-47 and Maxwell, p. 61; **p. 57** "baby carrier panel": The technique is diagrammed in Hector 1995, Fig. 9. (The Dayak also used the techniques in Hector 1995, Figs. 11a, 11b, 12b, 16, and 17.)

AMBAI ISLAND BEADWORK, PAPUA, INDONESIAN NEW GUINEA

p. 62 "For example . . . east.": Taylor and Aragon, pp. 276-277; "Traditionally, without . . . beads.": Howard, pp. 97-98; "multiple vertical-thread technique": Hector 1995, Fig. 17.

AFRICAN AND MIDDLE EASTERN INSPIRATIONS

p. 68 "Current usage . . . Emirates.)": http://au. encarta.msn.com/encyclopedia_761579298/Middle_ East.html; "aromatic cloves": *A World of Necklaces: Africa, Asia, Oceania, America*, by Anne Leurquin. Isabel Ollivier, trans. Milan: Skira Editore S.p.A., 2003: p. 32; "amuletic wall hanging": *The Jews of Kurdistan: Daily Life, Customs, Arts and Crafts*, by Ora Schwartz-Be'eri. Jerusalem: Israel Museum, 2000, Fig. 35; "cast metal beads": *Traditional Crafts of Saudi Arabia*, by John Topham (with Anthony Landreau and William E. Mulligan). London: Stacey Int'l., 1982: Figs. 154-155; "Another fascinating . . . Man.": Pickler and http://mysite.freeserve. com/beadworksnake/index.jhtml. My thanks to Carole Morris for alerting me to Pickler's research; "In fact . . . mid-1970s.": Pers. comm., Ani Afshar, 2002; "In the . . . king.": Northern, pp. 17-23 and Notue, pp. 112-115; **p. 69** "Kirdi apron": Margret Carey believes this may be a "back apron." Pers. comm., August 2004. See Carey 1991, Fig. 13; "Bakuba hat": This hat may be from the Pende region. See Carey 1991, p. 47.

ANCIENT EGYPTIAN BEADWORK (#1)

p. 70 "By about . . . spacers.": Andrews, Fig. 37; "Judging by . . . net.": Jick, p. 50; "Another masterpiece . . . band.": *Ancient Egyptian Jewellery*, by Alix Wilkinson. London: Methuen & Co. Ltd., 1971, p. 46. cf. Andrews, p. 140; "One of . . . form.": Andrews, pp. 140-141; "Many fine . . . (ca. 1897-1878 B.C.E.).": Andrews, see index under "Sithathoriunet," p. 207; "Dozens . . . of hair.": Andrews, p. 109.

ANCIENT EGYPTIAN BEADWORK (#2)

p. 76 "beadwork cobras": It is of course possible that the beads were stitched to linen but I think it far more likely, given the relative positions of the beads (not to mention the antiquity in Egypt of the production of freestanding panels of beadwork, which stretches back to at least the Fifth Dynasty of 2465-2323 B.C.E.), that they were united into peyote stitch panels that was then stitched to the linen ground. The small gold panels are inscribed with the *Aten* cartouche of the Sun, see Carter and Mace (2), p. 113; "Egypt's African . . . art.": Carter and Mace (3), p. 115; "Several pairs . . . Tutankhamun.": Carter and Mace (I): 123-124; **p. 77** "We don't . . . place.": Freestanding three-dimensional human figures have been made by other beadworkers such as the seventeenth-century English and twentieth-century Zuni and Zulu, but always with armatures and in more or less symmetrical formats; "When asked . . . man.": Carlin, p. 44.

YORÙBÁ BEADWORK, NIGERIA

p. 84 "A Yorùbá king . . . 1982.": Carey 1991 discusses the disputed beadwork of a past Èlepè, pp. 28-29; "Traditional Yorùbá . . . format.": Brinkworth, pp. 728-732 and Drewal and Mason, pp. 54-62; "Thus, for . . . substance.": Drewal and Mason, p. 26; **p. 85** "As one . . . generations.": Thompson, p. 8 and Drewal and Mason, p. 64; "When faced . . . forces.": Drewal and Mason, pp. 21-22, 26; "all-seeing abilities": Carey 1991, p. 30.

MAASAI BEADWORK, KENYA

p. 86 "King (Oba) Akenzua II": *The Royal Arts of Africa*, by Suzanne Preston Blier. New York: Harry N. Abrams, Inc., 1998, p. 47 and Fisher, p. 81; "coral beadwork": The coral came from the Mediterranean via Portuguese and other traders. Carey 1991, p. 26; **p. 87** "Crocheted beadwork . . . World War 1.": Pickler, pp. 18-19.

DINKA BEADWORK, SUDAN

p. 90 "Men and . . . structures.": Fisher, pp. 48-53; "Along with . . . conflict.": "Genocide Warning: Sudan" www.ushmm.org/conscience/sudan/sudan. php; **p. 91** "right angle weaves": I am including in a generic "right angle weaves" category any technique that inclines beads at right angles, regardless of the number of threads involved or the connections formed; "Now, late . . . inches.": For a single unit of modern Chinese cubic right angle weave, see the blue cubic *mei* on page 32 of this book; for modern Chinese examples of cubic right angle weave that are two layers in depth and made with a single thread with two working ends, see Yun Lei, pp. 50-52, 62.

XHOSA BEADWORK, SOUTH AFRICA

p. 94 "Long before . . . discrimination.": "The History of Apartheid in South Africa" http://www-cs-students.stanford.edu/~cale/cs201/apartheid.hist. html; "A hush . . . chief.": Proctor and Klopper, pp. 62-63; "As a . . . well.": Costello, p. 72. These collars are worn by married men and women. Carey 1986, Fig. 36.

NDEBELE BEADWORK, SOUTH AFRICA

p. 100 "When Poppie . . . sand.": Pers. comm., Kevin Friedman, 2001.

MSINGA (ZULU) BEADWORK, SOUTH AFRICA

p. 106 "The sample . . . whip.": Wood, No. B119 in Plate B119/124; "She suspected . . . century.": Pers. com., Marilee Wood, 1997; "Her colleague . . . District.": Jolles Plate 8(D); "Still hoping . . . fieldwork." My thanks to Frank Jolles for recommending Phumzile Dlamini and to Phumzile for undertaking this fieldwork; "These hanging . . . Natal.": Pers. com., Creina Alcock, 2003. See "The Waaymoek-Nhlawe-Mdukatshani Copper Wire Weaving Groups," by Creina Alcock. Unpub. paper, 2001 and "Decorative Wirework in African Material Culture of Southern Africa," by Walter Ortmann, in *De Arten* 56 (1997): 9-24.

EUROPEAN INSPIRATIONS

p. 112 "One of . . . 3000 B.C.E.": Barber 1991, Fig. 4.20; "Not until . . . netting.": One of the earliest published examples of European bead netting is a tablet woven stole, Cat. 8588-1863, Image No. CT13779 in the Victoria & Albert Museum, London, which is embellished with small squares of glass beads united in what looks like peyote stitch. I have not seen the piece in person, only studied it in a 4"-x-5" transparency; "Two panels . . . pearls.": Mann and Cohen, p. 235; "They shimmered . . . France.": See Ecalle (unpaginated); "Popular motifs . . . architecture.": Haertig, Plates 254 *ff.*, 385-392, 401-456, etc.; **p. 113** "Verena Sieber-Fuchs": Dubin 1987, Plates 332-333, 338; "Greek key motifs": Pers. comm., Margret Carey, April 2003. Carey believes this piece might date to the "Liberty" period; "Arte Ziio line of bracelets": Flanagan, pp. 18-21.

SEVENTEENTH-CENTURY ENGLISH BEADWORK

p. 114 "stumpwork": Baker, pp. 11-12; "Several dozen . . . collections.": Pers. obser., 1983-1992, of twenty-four baskets housed in European and American collections; "While some . . . kinds.": Baker, pp. 24-26; "Other beadworkers . . . elements.": For the two major basket styles see Simpson, pp. 194-195; "worked in peyote stitch": Pers. obs., 1983-1992; "doubled-thread or multiple-thread right angle weave": Gray identifies as "Traditional English Right Angle Weave" a technique that uses a doubled (or folded) single thread with two working ends. Later seventeenth-century English beadwork basket mak-

ers used this and a second technique that orients beads at right angles using multiple doubled threads or wires. Pers. obs., 1983-1992.

J. M. VAN SELOW BEADWORK, 1760s GERMANY

p. 120 "He would . . . gardens.": Holm, Figs. 50, 54, 56, 61-63, and Simpson, p. 193; "Only a . . . debt.": Albrecht Raag, unpub. Eng. trans. of Bilzer.

WIENER WERKSTÄTTE BEADWORK, 1920s AUSTRIA

p. 122 "Small flowers . . . Werkstätte.": Buxbaum, pp. 85, 95; "Small local . . . media.": Neuwirth, pp. 13-14; "Rejecting the . . . value.": Joseph Hoffmann and Kolo Moser, quoted in Schweiger, pp. 42-43; "By 1905 . . . textiles.": Kallir, p. 31.

FUNERARY BEADWORK, FRANCE

p. 124 "White wreathes . . . men": Zola, quoted in Wolters, p. 45; "So great . . . required.": Gumpert, p. 1. A bead sample card owned by John and Ruth Picard inscribed "*Carte A. Edition 1901, Articles Pour La Couronne Funéraire*" shows the many colors on offer that year (Pers. obs., The Bead Museum, Washington, D.C., 2002); "Around 1880 . . . manufacture": Poli, p. 70. Wolters, p. 47 states that wreaths were also made by prisoners; "In this . . . Belgium.": There may be as many as sixteen wreaths in this image. Pers. com., Karen Hendrix, 2003; "Two large . . . France.": Pers. comm., Karen Hendrix, 2003. See http://www.usgennet.org/usa/topic/preservation/dav1 /pg174.htm; **p. 125** "Family members . . . elsewhere.": A page from a wreath catalogue appears in Opper and Opper, Fig. 5; "Although beaded . . . loss.": Pers. obs., Père Lachaise Cemetery, Paris, 1994; "In a photograph . . . France.": Stefany Tomalin called this image to my attention.

AMERICAN INSPIRATIONS

p. 130 "This early . . . skull.": See Taylor et al.; "Presumably, he . . . control.": Dubin 1999, p. 199; "The arrival . . . detail.": Dubin 1987, p. 275; **p. 131** "The making . . . assistants.": Girouard, p. 359; "This flag . . . powers.": Pers. comm., Marilyn Houlberg, 2002.

PLAINS AND PLATEAU BEADWORK

p. 132 "Marcus vividly . . . broncos.": Callister and Crow, pp. 8-9; "Marcus thinks . . . painting.": For the photo of Chief Minthorn, see Rainer, Plate 22; **p. 133** "The first, . . . century.": Marcus found the photo in Fleming and Luskey, Fig. 8.30.

ACHOMAWI/ATSUGEWI BEADWORK, CALIFORNIA

p. 134 "An unknown . . . photograph.": Benson L. Lanford brought this to my attention; "three late . . . sashes": All three were rewoven in the later twentieth century. Pers. comm., Benson L. Lanford, 2003. See Lanford, pp. 62 *ff*; "Beads have . . . B.C.E.": Barber 1991, pp. 154-155, 172; "True beadweaving . . . threads.": Needle-weaving or off-loom techniques, on the other hand, involves either a single thread or a single set of threads, not two sets of threads; "loose-warp techniques," "fixed warp techniques,": Barth, p. 125 *ff* and Lessard, 58 *ff*.; "Hiawatha' Wampum Belt": Josephy, pp. 44-51; "Other wampum . . . 1620s.": Dubin 1999, pp. 170-171, Dubin 1987, pp. 266-267; **p. 135** "According to . . . Seneca.": Pers. com., Chief Irving Powless, Onandaga Nation, 2003; "quail feather motif": Richard Conn identified the quail feather motif on this bag. Pers. comm., Carol Lee, 2003; "It was . . . century.": Dubin 1999, Plate 898; "Don Pierce . . . fifties.": Scherer, p. 45.

HUICHOL BEADWORK, MEXICO

p. 144 "The same . . . holes.": Yturbide and Mozzi, pp. 54-57; "visual prayers": Lemaistre, p. 317 *ff*; "the gods will drink the prayers": Lumholtz, p. 161; "beaded gourds made a century ago": Lumholtz, pp. 161-168; "Together, they . . . ritual.": Meyerhoff, p. 56.

CHIMÚ BEADWORK, PERU

p. 150 "Tomb 1 . . . old.": Alva and Donnan, pp. 55-125; "In contrast . . . 1460s.": Rowe, Figs. 172-173; "More beaded . . . Valleys.": Rowe, Figs. 164-167; "mysterious figures . . . textiles": Dubin 1987, Fig. 266; "Iridescent mother . . . pectoral.": Levenson, Plate 469.

SELECTED BIBLIOGRAPHY

Allen, Jamey. "An Essay on Beadwork." http://www.nfobase.com/html/an_essay_on_beadwork_.html.

Alva, Walter, and Christopher B. Donnan. *Royal Tombs of Sipán.* Los Angeles: Fowler Museum of Cultural History, 1993.

Andrews, Carol. *Ancient Egyptian Jewelry.* New York: Harry N. Abrams, Inc., 1990.

Baker, Muriel. *Stumpwork, The Art of Raised Embroidery.* New York: Charles Scribner's Sons, 1978.

Barber, E. J. W. *Prehistoric Textiles: The Development of Cloth in the Neolithic and Bronze Ages with Special Reference to the Aegean.* Princeton, NJ: Princeton University Press, 1992.

Barber, Elizabeth Wayland. *Women's Work, The First 20,000 Years: Women, Cloth and Society in Early Times.* New York: W.W. Norton & Company, Ltd., 1994.

Barth, Georg J. *Native American Beadwork.* Stevens. Point, WI: R. Schneider Pubs., 1993.

Bedford, Emma (ed.). *Ezakwantu: Beadwork from the Eastern Cape.* Cape Town: South African National Gallery, 1994.

Bednarik, Robert G. "Beads and the Origins of Symbolism." http://www.semioticon.com/frontline/pdf/bednarik.pdf.

Ben-Amos, Paula. *The Art of Benin.* London: Thames and Hudson, 1980.

Berrin, Kathleen (ed.). *Art of the Huichol Indians.* New York: The Fine Arts Museums of San Francisco and Harry N. Abrams, Inc., 1978.

Bilzer, Bert. "Führer durch die Schausammlung Perlmosaiken von J.M. van Selow." Braunschweig: Städtisches Museum. *Arbeitsberichte aus dem Städtisches Museum Braunschweig* 69 (1969). Unpublished English translation by Albrecht Ragg, Ph.D. (2002).

Birch, Cyril. *Stories from a Ming Collection, Translations of Chinese Short Stories Published in the Seventeenth Century.* New York: Grove Press, Inc., 1958.

Blair, Dorothy. *A History of Glass in Japan.* New York: Kodansha International Ltd. and The Corning Museum of Glass, 1973.

Blakelock, Virginia. *Those Bad, Bad Beads.* Wilsonville, OR: Virginia L. Blakelock, 1988.

Bosse-Griffiths, Kate. "Some Egyptian Bead-Work Faces in the Wellcome Collection at University College, Swansea." *Journal of Egyptian Archaeology* 64 (1978): 99-106.

—. "The Use of Disc-Beads in Egyptian Bead-Compositions." *Journal of Egyptian Archaeology* 61 (1975): 114-124.

Brinkworth, Ian. "The Crown makers of Efon-Aliye." *West African Review* 29 (372) (1958): 728-732.

Buxbaum, Gerda. "The Opulence of the Poor Look." In *Jewels of Fantasy, Costume Jewelry of the 20th Century,* edited by Deanna Farneti Cera. New York: Harry N. Abrams, Inc. (1992): 49-110.

Callister, Lori, and Kerry Crow. "Master Beadworker Marcus Amerman." *Northwest Indian* 1 (1) (1998): 8-9.

Carey, Margret. *Beads and Beadwork of West and Central Africa.* Princes Risborough: Shire Pubs. Ltd., 1991.

—. *Beads and Beadwork of East and South Africa.* Princes Risborough: Shire Pubs. Ltd., 1986.

Carlin, Kim (ed.). *Joyce J. Scott Kickin' It With the Old Masters.* Baltimore: The Baltimore Museum of Art and Maryland Institute, College of Art, 2000.

Carter, Howard, and A. C. Mace. *The Tomb of Tut-ankh-Amen: Discovered by the Late Earl of Carnarvon and Howard Carter.* 3 vols. London: Cassell and Company, Ltd., 1927-1933.

Catalogue of the Exhibition of Ch'ing Dynasty Costume Accessories. Taipei: National Palace Museum, 1986.

Cheah, Hwei-Fe'n. "Beads in Time, Towards a Chronology of Nonya Beadwork." *Arts of Asia* 34 (4) (2004): 65-77.

Chee, Eng-Lee Seok. "The Straits Chinese Bridal Chamber." *Arts of Asia* 7 (3) (1987): 108-114.

Conn, Richard. *Native American Art in the Denver Art Museum.* Seattle: University of Washington Press, 1979.

Costello, Dawn. *Not Only for Its Beauty, Beadwork and Its Cultural Significance Among the Xhosa-Speaking Peoples.* Pretoria: University of South Africa, 1990.

Crabtree, Caroline, and Pam Stallebrass. *Beadwork, A World Guide.* New York: Rizzoli International, 2002.

Dalley, Stephanie. "Hebrew Taḥaš, Akkadian Duḥšu, Faience and Beadwork." *Journal of Semitic Studies* 45 (1) (2000): 1-19.

Deeb, Margie. *The Beader's Guide to Color.* New York: Watson-Guptill Publications, Inc., 2004.

Drewal, Henry John, and John Mason. *Beads, Body and Soul, Art and Life in the Yorùbá Universe.* Los Angeles: UCLA Fowler Museum, 1998.

Dubin, Lois Sherr. *Native North American Jewelry and Adornment.* New York: Harry N. Abrams, Inc., 1999.

—. *The History of Beads from 30,000 B.C. to the Present.* New York: Harry N. Abrams, Inc., 1987.

Ecalle, Martine. *Perles et Broderies Chez Victor Hugo.* Paris: Ville de Paris and Maison de Victor Hugo-Hauteville House, 1972 (unpaginated).

Falola, Toyin, and O. B. Lawuyi. "Not Just a Currency: The Cowrie in Nigerian Culture." In *West African Economic and Social History,* edited by David Henige and T. C. McCaskie. Madison: University of Wisconsin, 1990.

Fisher, Angela. *Africa Adorned.* New York: Harry N. Abrams Inc., 1984.

Fitzgerald, Diane. *Contemporary Beadwork III: Zulu Beaded Chain Techniques.* Minneapolis: Beautiful Beads Press, 1997.

Flanagan, Madaleine. "European Fashion Jewelry." *Bead & Button* 16 (1996): 18-21.

Fleming, Paula Richardson, and Judith Luskey. *The North American Indians In Early Photographs.* New York: Harper & Row, 1986.

Francis, Peter J., Jr. *Asia's Maritime Bead Trade: 300 B.C. to the Present.* Honolulu: University of Hawaii Press, 2002.

—. "Beadwork Beads." Parts 1-6. *The Bead Society of Los Angeles Newsletter* 6 (3-7), 7 (3-4) (1980-82).

—. "A Short History of Beadwork." *The Margaretologist* 10 (2) (1997): 4-13.

—. "Glass Beads of China." *Arts of Asia* 20 (5) (1990):118-127.

Friedman, Florence Dunn (ed.). *Gifts of the Nile, Ancient Egyptian Faience.* New York: Thames and Hudson, 1998.

Garrett, Valery M. *Chinese Clothing, An Illustrated Guide.* New York: Oxford University Press, 1994.

Girouard, Tina. "The Sequin Arts of Vodou." In *Sacred Arts of Haitian Vodou,* edited by Donald J. Cosentino. Los Angeles: UCLA Fowler Museum of Cultural History, 1995.

Glass Tapestry: Plateau Beaded Bags from the Elaine Horwitch Collection. Phoenix: The Heard Museum, 1993.

Gong Yan. "Jinyinzhu yunlongwen jiazhou" (The Cloud Dragon Design Suit of Armor Made of Gold and Silver Beads.) In *Zijin cheng (Forbidden City)* 24 (1985): p.45. Unpublished English translation by Kenneth J. DeWoskin, Ph.D. (2001).

Gray, Vera. "Traditional English Right Angle Weave." *Newsletter of the Bead Society of Great Britain* 62 (2002): 9.

Gumpert, Anita. "The World of Rocaille." *The Bead Society of Greater Washington Newsletter* 7 (1) (1990): 1-4.

Haertig, Evelyn. *More Beautiful Purses.* Carmel: Gallery Graphics Press, 1990.

Han Han. *Zhongguo gu bo li (Chinese Antique Glass).* Taibei: Yi shu jia chu ban she, 1998.

Hector, Valerie. "Master Class. Polygon Weave and its Variations." *Ornament* 21 (2) (1997): 67-70.

—. "The Maturing of a Medium, Contemporary Beadwork in Europe and North America." *Surface Design Journal* 27 (3) (Spring 2003): 6-11.

—. "Prosperity, Reverence and Protection, An Introduction to Asian Beadwork." *Beads, The Journal of the Society of Bead Researchers* 7 (1995): 3-36.

Henshilwood, Christopher, Franceeso d'Errico, Marian Vanhaeren, Karen van Niekerk, and Zenobia Jacobs. "Middle Stone Age Shell Beads from South Africa." *Science* 304 (2004): 404.

Ho, Chuimei, and Bennet Bronson. *Splendors of China's Forbidden City: The Glorious Reign of Emperor Qianlong.* London: Merrell Publishers Ltd., 2004.

Ho Wing Meng. *Straits Chinese Beadwork and Embroidery, A Collector's Guide.* Singapore: Times Books International, 1987.

Holden, Constance. "Oldest Beads Suggest Early Symbolic Behavior." *Science* 304 (2004): 369.

Holm, Edith. *Glasperlen. Mythos, Schmuck und Spielereien aus fünf Jahrtausenden.* Munich: Callwey, 1984.

Holmgren, Robert J., and Anita E. Spertus. *Early Indonesian Textiles from Three Island Cultures.* New York: Metropolitan Museum of Art, 1989.

Hong Shouzi. "Zhuxiu" ("Pearl Embroidery"). Unpublished English translation by Int'l. Lang. & Comm. Centers, Chicago, IL (2004). In *Zhongguo da bai ke quan shu* 71 (1991): p. 666-667. Shanghai: Xin hua shu dian Shanghai fa xing suo fa xing.

Houlberg, Marilyn. "Magique Marasa, The Ritual Cosmos of Twins and Other Sacred Children." In *Sacred Arts of Haitian Vodou,* edited by Donald J. Cosentino. Los Angeles: Fowler Museum of Cultural History, 1995.

Howard, Michael C. "Sireu, Beaded Skirts from Papua." *Hali* 125 (2002): 94-98.

Jick, Millicent. "Bead-Net Dress from Giza Tomb G77 40Z, Old Kingdom, Reign of Khufu." *Ornament* 14 (1) (1990): 50-53.

Jolles, Frank. "Traditional Zulu Beadwork of the Msinga Area." *African Arts* 26 (1) (1993): 42-53.

Josephy, Alvin M. Jr. *500 Nations, An Illustrated History of North American Indians.* New York: Alfred A. Knopf, 1994.

Kaeppler, Adrienne. *Artificial Curiosities, An Exposition of Native Manufactures Collected on the Three Pacific Voyages of Captain James Cook, R.N.* Honolulu: Bishop Museum Press, 1978.

Kallir, Jane. *Viennese Design and the Wiener Werkstätte.* New York: George Braziller in assoc. with Galerie St. Etienne, 1986.

Lanford, Benson L. "Great Lakes Woven Beadwork." *American Indian Art* (Summer 1986): 62-75.

Lankton, James W., M.D. *A Bead Timeline Vol. 1: Prehistory to 1200 C.E.: A Resource for Identification, Classification, and Dating.* Washington, D.C.: The Bead Museum, 2002.

Lemaistre, Denis. "The Deer that is Peyote and the Deer that is Maize." Translated by Karin Simoneau. In *People of the Peyote, Huichol Indian History, Religion, & Survival,* edited by Stacy B. Schaefer and Peter T. Furst. Albuquerque: University of New Mexico Press, 1996.

Lessard, Dennis. "Great Lakes Indian 'Loom' Beadwork." *American Indian Art* (Summer 1986): 55-69.

Levenson, Jay A., (ed.). *Circa 1492, Art in the Age of Exploration.* New Haven: Yale University Press, 1991.

Lillie, Jacqueline. "Beads at Work, An Artistic Vision." Unpublished notes for lecture presented at the College of Marin, California, May 1, 2000.

—. *Perlenschmuck, Beads at Work.* With a Personal Appreciation by David Revere McFadden. Vienna: J. I. Lillie, 1990.

Liu, Robert K. "Comparisons of Ancient Faience Ornaments." *Ornament* 23 (3) (2000): 56-61.

—. Review of "Great Cities, Small Treasures: The Ancient World of the Indus Valley, Feb. 11-May 3, 1998, the Asia Society." *Ornament* 21 (3) (1998): 19.

—. *Collectible Beads, A Universal Aesthetic.* Vista, CA: Ornament, Inc., 1995.

Lumholtz, Carl. *Symbolism of the Huichol Indians. Memoirs of the American Museum of Natural History* 3 (2). New York: Knickerbocker Press, 1900.

Mann, Vivian, and Richard I. Cohen (eds.). *From Court Jews to the Rothschilds, Art Patronage and Power 1600-1800.* New York: The Jewish Museum, 1996.

Maxwell, Robyn. *Textiles of Southeast Asia, Tradition, Trade, Transformation.* Melbourne: Oxford University Press and the Australian National Gallery, 1990.

Metropolitan Museum of Art. *Egyptian Art in the Age of the Pyramids.* New York: The Metropolitan Museum of Art, 1999.

Meyerhoff, Barbara G. "Peyote and the Mystic Vision." In *Art of the Huichol Indians,* edited by Kathleen Berrin. New York: The Fine Arts Museums of San Francisco and Harry N. Abrams, Inc., 1978.

Morris, Jean, and Eleanor Preston-White. *Speaking With Beads, Zulu Arts from Southern Africa.* New York: Thames and Hudson, 1994.

Moss, Kathlyn, and Alice Scherer. *The New Beadwork.* New York: Harry N. Abrams, Inc., 1991.

Muller, Kal. "Huichol Art and Acculturation." In *Art of the Huichol Indians,* edited by Kathleen Berrin. New York: The Fine Arts Museums of San Francisco and Harry N. Abrams, Inc., 1978.

Munan, Heidi. "Social Status Gradations Expressed in the Beadwork Patterns of Sarawak's Orang Ulu." *Beads, The Journal of the Society of Bead Researchers* 7 (1995): 55-64.

Nanavati, J. M., M. P. Vora, and M. A. Dhaky. *The Embroidery and Bead Work of Kutch and Saurashtra.* Baroda: Department of Archaeology, Gujarat State, India, 1966.

Neuwirth, Waltraud. *Wiener Werkstätte, Avantgarde, Art Deco, Industrial Design.* Vienna: Dr. Waltraud Neuwirth, 1984.

Nicholson, Paul T. *Egyptian Faience and Glass.* Shire Egyptology Series No. 19. Princes Risborough: Shire Publications Ltd., 1993.

Nooy-Palm, Hetty. *The Sa'dan Toraja, a study of their social life and religion: Vol. 1, Organizations, symbols and beliefs.* The Hague: Martinus Nijhoff, 1979.

Northern, Tamara. *The Sign of the Leopard, Beaded Art of Cameroon.* Ex. cat. University of Connecticut, 1975.

Notue, Jean Paul. "Elephant Mask." In *Africa, Arts & Culture,* edited by John Mack. New York: Oxford University Press, 2000.

Opper, Marie-José, and Howard Opper. "French Beadmaking: An Historical Perspective Emphasizing the 19th and 20th Centuries." *Beads, The Journal of the Society of Bead Researchers* 3 (1991):47-59.

Orchard, William C. *Beads and Beadwork of the American Indians.* 2d ed. New York: Museum of the American Indian, Heye Foundation, 1975.

Pickler, David. "Turkish Prisoner of War Beadwork." *Bead Society of Great Britain Newsletter* 68 (2003): 18-19.

Poli, Doretta Davanzo. "Le Conterie Nella Moda E Nell' Arredo." In *Perle e Impiraperle, Un Lavoro di Donna a Venezia tra '800 e '900.* Venezia: Arsenale Editrice (1990): 67-73.

Proctor, André, and Sandra Klopper. "Through the Barrel of a Bead: The Personal and the Political in the Beadwork of the Eastern Cape." In *Ezakwantu: Beadwork from the Eastern Cape,* edited by Emma Bedford. Cape Town: South African National Gallery, 1994.

Rainer, Howard. *A Song for Mother Earth.* Wilsonville, OR: Beautiful America Publishing Co., 1998.

Riefstahl, Elizabeth. *Patterned Textiles in Pharaonic Egypt.* New York: Brooklyn Museum, New York, 1945.

Rowe, Anne Pollard. *Costumes and Featherwork of the Lords of Chimor, Textiles from Peru's North Coast.* Washington, D.C.: The Textile Museum, 1984.

Saitowitz, Sharma. "Towards a History of Glass Beads." In *Ezakwantu: Beadwork from the Eastern Cape,* edited by Emma Bedford. Cape Town: South African National Gallery, 1994.

Scherer, Alice. "A Sensual Appreciation, Don Pierce." *Ornament* 18 (4) (1995): 44-47.

Scherer, Alice, and Valerie Hector. "Doubling Up: South African Double-Faced Stitches." *Beadwork* 1(3) (1998): 22-26.

Schweiger, Werner J. *Wiener Werkstätte, Design in Vienna 1903-1932.* New York: Abbeville Press, 1984.

Scott, Joyce J. *Fearless Beading.* Rochester, NY: Visual Studies Workshop, 1994.

Seiler-Baldinger, Annemarie. *Textiles, A Classification of Techniques.* Washington, D.C.: Smithsonian Institution Press, 1994.

Sellato, Bernard. *Hornbill and Dragon, Kalimantan, Sarawak, Sabah, Brunei.* Jakarta: Elf Aquitaine Indonésie, 1989.

Sheridan, Alison, and Mary Davis. "The Poltalloch 'Jet' Spacer Plate Necklace." *The Kist* 49 (1995): 1-9.

Simpson, Jeffrey. "Antiques: European Beadwork, The Gleaming Intricacy of an Age-Old Craft." *Architectural Digest* 51 (11) (1994): 192ff.

Stevenson, Michael, and Michael Graham-Stewart (eds.). *South East African Beadwork, 1850-1910, from Adornment to Artefact to Art.* Vlaeburg, South Africa: Fernwood Press, 2000.

Swain, Margaret. *Embroidered Stuart Pictures.* Princes Risborough: Shire Publs. Ltd., 1990.

Taylor, Dicey, Marco Biscione, and Peter G. Roe. "Epilogue: The Beaded *Zemi* in the Pigorini Museum." In *Taíno, Pre-Columbian Art and Culture from the Caribbean,* edited by Fatima Bercht, Estrellita Brodsky, John Alan Farmer, and Dicey Taylor. New York: El Museo del Barrio and The Monacelli Press, 1997.

Taylor, Paul Michael, and Lorraine V. Aragon. *Beyond the Java Sea, Art of Indonesia's Outer Islands.* New York: The National Museum of Natural History and Harry N. Abrams, Inc., 1991.

Thompson, Robert Farris. "The Sign of the Divine King, An Essay on Yoruba Bead-Embroidered Crowns with Veil and Bird Decoration." *African Arts* 3 (3) (1970): 8-17, 74-80.

Tillema, H. F. *A Journey Among the Peoples of Central Borneo in Word and Picture.* Singapore: Oxford University Press, 1989; under the auspices of the Rijksmuseum voor Volkenkunde, Leiden.

Tucker, Marcia. "Adventures in Liza Land." In *Liza Lou,* by Peter Schjeldahl and Marcia Tucker. Santa Monica: Smart Art Press, 1999.

Weber, Betty J., and Anne Duncan. *Simply Beads, an Introduction to the Art of Beading from N. and C. America, Africa, & The Middle East.* Culver City, CA: Western Trimming Corporation, 1971.

Wells, Carol Wilcox. *The Art and Elegance of Beadweaving.* Asheville: Lark Books, 2002.

Whittier, Herbert L., and Patricia L. Whittier. "Baby Carriers, A Link Between Social and Spiritual Values Among the Kenyah Dayak of Borneo." *Expedition* 30 (1) (1988): 51-58.

Winters-Meyer, Mary. *Linked Chain Stitch Basics,* Vol. 1. Champaign, IL: The Beading Banshee, 1998.

Wolters, Natacha. *Les Perles, Au Fil Du Textile.* Paris: Syros, 1996.

Wood, Marilee. "Zulu Beadwork." In *Zulu Treasures, of Kings and Commoners.* Durban: Local History Museum and KwaZulu Cultural Museum, 1995.

Yang, Xiaoneng (ed.). *The Golden Age of Chinese Archaeology, Celebrated Discoveries from the People's Republic of China.* New Haven: Yale University Press, 1999.

Yturbide, Teresa Castelló. "Mexican Beadwork." In *La Chaquira en México,* edited by Teresa Castelló Yturbide and Carlotta Mapelli Mozzi. México: Museo Franz Mayer and Artes de México, 1998.

Yun Lei (ed.). *Zhongguo Chuanzhu Shipin.* Xiandai Nuhong Congshu, San Ci. (*Chinese Bead Ornaments.* Modern Needlecraft Series, Vol. 3.) Artux, Xinjiang: Kirgiz Language Press, 2001.

Zettler, Richard L., and Lee Horne (eds.). *Treasures from the Royal Tombs of Ur.* Philadelphia: University of Pennsylvania Museum of Archaeology and Anthropology, 1998.

INDEX